T0386749

HERMANN GOERING

GOERING

BEER HALL PUTSCH TO
NAZI BLOOD PURGE 1919–34

Blaine Taylor (*b*. 1946) is the author of twelve histories with illustrations on war, politics, automotives, biography, engineering, architecture, medicine, photographs, and aviation.

The well-read historian is a former Vietnam War soldier and Military Policeman of the US Army's élite 199th Light Infantry Brigade under enemy Communist Viet Cong fire during 1966–67 in South Vietnam. He was awarded twelve medals and decorations, including the coveted Combat Infantryman's Badge/CIB. A later crime and political newspaper reporter, Taylor is also an award-winning medical journalist, international magazine writer, and the winner of four political campaigns as press secretary for county, state, and US Presidential elections, 1974–92.

During 1991–92, he served as a US Congressional aide and press secretary on Capitol Hill, Washington, DC. Blaine lives at Towson, MD/USA.

Previously Published books by Blaine Taylor

Guarding the Führer: Sepp Dietrich, Johann Rattenhuber, and the Protection of Adolf Hitler (1993)

Fascist Eagle: Italy's Air Marshal Italo Balbo (1996)

Mercedes-Benz Parade and Staff Cars of the Third Reich (1999)

Volkswagen Military Vehicles of the Third Reich (2004)

Hitler's Headquarters from Beer Hall to Bunker 1920–45 (2006)

Apex of Glory: Benz, Daimler, & Mercedes-Benz 1885–1955 (2006)

Hitler's Chariots Volume 1: Mercedes-Benz G-4 Cross-Country Touring Car (2009)

Hitler's Chariots Volume 2: Mercedes-Benz 770K Grosser Parade Car (2010)

Hitler's Engineers: Fritz Todt and Albert Speer/Master Builders of the Third Reich (2010)

Hitler's Chariots Volume 3: Volkswagen from Nazi People's Car to New Beetle (2011)

Mrs Adolf Hitler: The Eva Braun Photograph Albums 1912-45 (2013)

Dallas Fifty Years On: The Murder of John F. Kennedy—A New Look at an Old Crime, 22 November 1963–2013 (2013)

Hermann Goering in the First Wold War: The Personal Photograph Albums of Hermann Goering (2014)

HERMANN GOERING

BEER HALL PUTSCH TO NAZI BLOOD PURGE 1919–34

THE PERSONAL PHOTOGRAPH ALBUMS OF HERMANN GOERING

BLAINE TAYLOR

FONTHILL

Dedicated to ace lens man John Durand, Ellicott City, MD, USA for both his enduring friendship and wonderful photographic artistry that has vastly improved all our joint efforts during 1974–2014; from British Ambassador to the United States Sir Oliver Wright to the backhoe loaders of UK/US JCB/John Cyril Banford; from the leaders of the Maryland Democratic Party to the unequalled West Point Museum of the US Military Academy, NY/US; my books, and much more. Here's to the next forty years!

Remembering the Dearly Departed:
Dolores E. Michael Marino, 90, of Baltimore, who died 18 February 2015—
mother of my first campaign manager, the late Michael F. Marino.
Gone, but not forgotten! RIP.

Fonthill Media Language Policy

Fonthill Media publishes in the international English language market. One language edition is published worldwide. As there are minor differences in spelling and presentation, especially with regard to American English and British English, a policy is necessary to define which form of English to use. The Fonthill Policy is to use the form of English native to the author. Blaine Taylor was born in the USA and educated at Towson University, and now lives in Towson, MD; therefore American English has been adopted in this publication.

Fonthill Media Limited
Fonthill Media LLC
www.fonthillmedia.com
office@fonthillmedia.com

First published in the United Kingdom and the United States of America 2015

British Library Cataloguing in Publication Data:
A catalogue record for this book is available from the British Library

Copyright © Blaine Taylor 2015

ISBN 978-1-62545-033-3

The right of Blaine Taylor to be identified as the author of this work has been asserted by him in accordance with the Copyright, Designs and Patents Act 1988.

Typeset in Sabon 10pt on 13.5pt
Printed and bound by CPI Group (UK) Ltd, Croydon, CR0 4YY

CONTENTS

ACKNOWLEDGMENTS

I extend my thanks to photographic consultant Stan Piet of Bel Air, MD, USA, for producing the Goering Album photographs shown herein from the Library of Congress at Washington, D.C., as well as photos from other sources.

I also thank the world-famous publisher-editor-author Roger James Bender of San Jose, CA for his invaluable aid in solving various mysteries of Goering's career, and for providing selected illustrations.

I give thanks to my fellow authors Michael D. Miller, Andreas Schulz, and the late Phil Nix (1938–2012) for biographical data and photographic identification of various Reich Forestry personnel, especially Mr Miller.

I thank Mrs Erika Burke of Pearland, TX for her usual yeoman's work in translating German language material on Goering into English for both me and you.

I give thanks to Ms Margaret Gers of the Enoch Pratt Free Library Periodicals and Reference Rooms of Baltimore City; to Mrs Joan Lattanzi of the Towson main branch of the Baltimore County Public Library, and the US National Archives of College Park, MD, USA; and to Ms Susannah Horrom of Baltimore's Kelmscott Book Shop, all in Maryland. All helped me find articles and books that were invaluable in bringing the following text to you, the reader.

All illustrations are from the various collections held within the Library of Congress at Washington, D.C., unless specifically credited elsewhere at the end of the caption. The vast majority is also published here for the very first time anywhere in the world. I particularly want to thank publisher Alan Sutton and his able staff for making this book a reality.

As with all of my previously published photo histories, I have also occasionally used other views from other collections to flesh out the narrative where appropriate, and these are also credited as such.

A NOTE REGARDING THE ALBUMS

As with the first volume in this series, the vast majority of the images in this book come from the extensive collections held in the American Library of Congress—the Hermann Goering Archives—at Washington, D.C., USA.

Unlike the first volume—the photographs of which were taken by non-professional photographers, including Goering himself, using amateur cameras and films—those in the present work were taken by more professional staff with better equipment and film. I believe the results published herein reflect this.

In 1980, the Library of Congress/LC published a work entitled *Special Collections in the Library of Congress: A Selective Guide*, compiled by Annette Melville. In the work, some of Goering's photographers were mentioned by name:

> Various identified and unidentified amateur, commercial, and news photographers, including Emil Bieber, Rosemarie Clausen, Erich Engel, Heinrich Hoffmann, Robert Kropp, Helmuth Kurth, Robert Rohr, Eitel Lange, *Scheri Bilderdienst* (Picture Service), Carl Weinrother, and Weltbild/World Pictures.

Robert Kropp was Goering's personal valet or manservant during 1933–45 and sometimes performed double duties as a lens man, while Hoffmann was Adolf Hitler's own personal photographer, photographing Goering as well on occasion.

Initially, the collection had been entitled by the Germans as the *Photo-Archiv Generalfeldmarschall Goering* (*Photo Archive of General Field Marshal Goering*), but in 1940 and thereafter the nomenclature instead became *Der Reichsmarschall des Grossdeutschen Reiches-Archiv*, or *The Reich Marshal of the Greater German Reich-Photo Archive* to its end.

Paul Vanderbilt—in *Photographs of Nazi Origin*—noted of the Goering Collection, 'in all there are an estimated 18,500 photographs, not counting duplicates, in 47 albums … received in the summer of 1948…' In 1992, I selected 2,500 of these 18,500 for this now-realized series of works. This would not have been possible but for the Library of Congress allowing my photographer, Stan Piet, to photograph the original prints from the actual albums using a photo copy stand. As I turned the pages of the albums, Stan refocused and snapped away.

The results mainly lay dormant until 2014, except for some illustrated articles in various international magazines and in some of my prior published books, where all were credited. Thus, fully twenty-two years passed!

In the 19 December 1974 edition of *The Suburban Times East* weekly newspaper in Baltimore County, MD, I first wrote directly about the albums in a series devoted to all of my various research efforts regarding Nazi photo archives. It was entitled *Part Five: Goering, Vain Reich Marshal,* and inside a single photo was published for the first time worldwide.

A dozen years later I found myself working as part of a team of photo researchers preparing the later, highly successful Time-Life Books series *The Third Reich,* to which I also lent my entire library of books on Nazi Germany to help make it the great publishing venture that it became. Fortunately, I got them all back!

Mr Vanderbilt also noted:

> The Goering photograph albums are said to have been found at Berchtesgaden in the Bavarian Alps, where Goering—like Hitler—had a retreat. The materials were gathered as they were found, and those not of strategic significance were turned over to the Library of Congress Mission in Europe for transfer to the appropriate collection in this country.

I believe that process began during 1945–47, but the more interesting question arises as to exactly *where* the Goering Albums were found. Since his Alpine residence, *Haus Goering,* was bombed by the RAF on 25 April 1945, I doubt if the albums were there, although that is certainly possible. Safer bets, however, would be either in his command train, *Asia,* parked near Berchtesgaden down below, or at his nearby *Adjutantur* (Adjutancy) Luftwaffe headquarters, both also captured by the US Army. I shall endeavor to find the answer!

In the July 2002 edition of *WWII History Magazine,* my article entitled *The World of Hermann Goering* was published, in which four of the overall nine photographs presented were from the HGA.

The photographs in the first and now this volume—as well as in the succeeding installments—are as I first saw them in 1967. I had just returned home from my own lost war in South Vietnam, in what was once called Indochina. Other photographs have been added to round out the view from other public and private sources that I have discovered since. They reveal Hermann Goering not as we have come to see him, but as he saw himself.

TIMELINE

The Saga up to Now

1892	Conceived in Haiti
12 January 1893	Born at Marienbad Sanatorium, Rosenheim, Upper Bavaria
1898–1903	Furth public school
1903–05	Attended Gymnasium/High School at Ansbach
1905–09	Attended Cadet School at Karlsruhe
1909–11	Attended Cadet Academy at Gross-Lichterfelde outside Berlin
April 1911	First trip to then Savoyard Italy
13 May 1911	Passed Fahnrich/Officer Candidate examination
1913	Passed Abitur
March–December 1913	War Academy for Officers
20 January 1914	Lieutenant effective 22 June 1912
1 July–14 September 1915	Attends Flight School at Freiburg
3 October 1915	Flies first aerial mission as a fighter pilot
18 August 1916	Promoted Oberleutnant/1st Lieutenant
2 November 1916	Wounded by enemy fire in right hip and grazed on right knuckles
17 May 1917–6 July 1918	Commanding officer of Jasta 27, fighter planes
January 1918	Engaged to Marianne Mauser-Muhltaler of Mauterndorf
2 June 1918	Awarded *Pour le Mérite* (For Your Merit, also known as *Blue Max*), the highest Prussian Order, by Kaiser Wilhelm II
7 July 1918–30 July 1919	Commanding Officer of *Jagdgeschwader* (Fighter Squadron) 1
26 July–22 August 1918	On leave
22 August 1918	Hospitalized for tonsillitis
11 November 1918	Armistice between Germany and Allies ends the First World War
November 1918	Demobilizes his unit at Aschaffenburg, Germany

Events Covered in this Volume

Spring 1925–Summer 1926	Resides with Carin at Stockholm at No. 23 Odengatan, and flies again as a pilot in Sweden
6–30 August 1925	Voluntary admission for morphine addiction to Aspudden Nursing Home, Stockholm; on the 30th, breaks into medicine cabinet for eukodal (oxycodone) and injects himself twice; threatens staff with cane sword, overcome and straitjacketed for transport to Katarina Hospital
2 September–7 October 1925	Civil commitment by wife Carin to the Langbro Asylum near Stockholm
7 October 1925	Certified drug free and released by Prof. Olof Kinberg
12 November 1925	German arrest order officially rescinded
22 May 1925–'early June' 1926	Voluntary commitment at Langbro to complete another detoxification program; again released, certified completely cured by Assistant Medical Superintendent Dr C. Franke
Summer 1926–January 1927	Works as salesman for BMW aircraft engines in Sweden, then returns to Germany as a salesman on commission for the Swedish Tornblad Self-Opening Parachute Company, partners with Paul Korner in Berlin as his driver
1927	Allegedly goes to Turkey for opium, and reportedly travels to London
7–26 September 1927	Third stay at Langbro Asylum to combat continued morphine usage, and released again
Fall 1927	President von Hindenburg declares a political amnesty for all offenders, allowing Goering to return to Germany without fear of arrest and trial
January 1928	Opens a Berlin office on Geisbergstrasse for parachute sales, shared with aviation businessman Fritz Siebel
1 April 1928	Rejoins Nazi Party as member No. 23 after having been deleted from its membership rolls in 1925
20 May 1928	Elected to the German Reichstag (parliament) as a Nazi Deputy representing Election District 4 Potsdam I (from 31 July 1932); simultaneously becomes a paid consultant to BMW, Heinkel, and German Lufthansa passenger airline
November 1928	Takes a luxury apartment on Berlin's Badenstrasse
14 September 1930-January 1933	Hitler's official party representative at Berlin
October 1930	Named Reich Arbitrator of the Nazi Party
13 October 1930-4 June 1932	2nd Deputy to NSDAP Delegation Chair Dr Wilhelm Frick in Reichstag
17-18 January 1931	Visits Kaiser Wilhelm II at Doorn, Holland; other dates cited are 8-30 January 1931, and also 18-19 January 1931.
April 1931–1933	NSDAP Political Commissar Berlin
May 1931	First political mission to Rome for three weeks to court Vatican
October 1931	Named Führer of National German Air Association
10 October 1931	First joint meeting of Goering, Hitler, and von Hindenburg
17 October 1931	Death of Carin at Stockholm; Goering later attends her funeral

November 1931	NSDAP fundraising mission to Rome
December 1931	Named to Inspectorate for NSDAP Party Flight Matters, and Vice President of HDAC/National German Automobile Club
18 December 1931–13 April 1932	Named SA Führer to the SA High Command Leadership
Spring Break (!) 1932	On Isle of Capri
20–21 May 1932	Second visit to the Kaiser at Doorn
1 July 1932–26 January 1934	Named to SA Headquarters, but again, not a command post
31 July 1932	Reelected to Reichstag
30 August 1932–23 April 1945	Elected Reichstag President
November 1932	Second official party mission to Rome
14 September–January 1933	Serves as the Führer's personal and political representative at Berlin for fundraising from business, banking, and air manufacturing firms
1 January 1933	SA Obergruppenführer
22–30 January 1933	Plenipotentiary for negotiations for NSDAP to enter the German cabinet
30 January–5 May 1933	Reich Minister Without Portfolio in cabinet and also appointed Reich Commissioner for Air Transportation, the latter being renamed Reich Commissioner for Aviation two days later; heads Prussian Police under Vice Chancellor Franz von Papen
2 February 1933	Bans KPD/German Communist meetings and demonstrations in Germany
3 February 1933	Bans SPD/German Social Democratic newspaper *Vorwarts/Forward* in Germany
20 February 1933	Establishes *Hilfspolizei/Hipo*/Auxiliary Police of 50,000 NSDAP SA and SS men to serve alongside the Prussian Police, and also creates the concentration camp system for political foes
23 February–17 July 1933	Establishment of *Police Troop z. b. V. Wecke* of 414 men; becomes State Police General Goering on 22 December 1933 and then Regiment General *Goering* on 1 April 1935
27 February 1933	The Reichstag Fire
5 March 1933	Last free Reichstag election of the Weimar Republic
21 March 1933	First fully Nazi Reichstag convenes
25 March 1933	Named DLV Minister
10 April 1933–23 April 1945	Minister President of the Free State of Prussia, and also establishes the FA/Research Office for intelligence wiretapping of telephones (transferred in 1937 to the Reich Aviation Ministry)
10-20 April 1933	Mission to Italy to meet with both Mussolini three times and with the Pope once, on 12 April 1933
11 April 1933–30 April 1934	Prussian Minister of the Interior and Chief of the Prussian Police
26 April 1933	Establishes the Secret State Police/Gestapo and names as its Director Rudolf Diels
27 April 1933–28 February 1935	Empowered to build secret Luftwaffe/Air Force

29 April 1933	Named President of the Reich Air Defense Association
5 May 1933–23 April 1945	Reich Minister for Aviation
13 June 1933	Formal establishment of Secret State Police/*Gestapo* a.k.a. *Gestapa/Geheime Staats Polizei*
8 July 1933	Named President of the Prussian State Council and Guardian of the Prussian Academy of the Arts; goes on a mission to the Vatican to have a signed Concordat with the Catholic Church
17 July–22 December 1933	*State Police Group Wecke z. b. V* established formally
30 August 1933	Promoted to Army General of Infantry, effective from 10 January 1931
14 September 1933	Created General of *Landespolizei* (State Police)
26 October 1933	Dedication for *Jagdhaus* (Hunting Lodge) Carinhall
4 November 1933	Testifies at Reichstag Fire Trial at Leipzig
6–7 November 1933	Visits Mussolini to deny German plans to seize Austria
2 December 1933–26 June 1936	Officially Chief of the Prussian Secret State Police (Gestapo)
22 December 1933–1 April 1935	State Police Group General Goering designated, commanded by Wecke
27 January 1934	Named Honorary Leader of SA Standard 1, Berlin
March 1934	Hunts at Polish State Hunting Ground Bialowieza at invitation of the Polish Government
20 April 1934	Appoints Himmler as Gestapo Deputy Head under Goering, succeeding Diels; loses Gestapo altogether to Heydrich as Chief of the Security Police (Gestapo and Criminal Police/Kripo combined) on 26 June 1936, when Himmler becomes Chief of the German Police nationwide
2 May 1934	Goering named Supreme Head of Prussian State Police
15–25 May 1934	Diplomatic mission to the Balkans in SE Europe—billed as a vacation—to Budapest, Belgrade, and Athens to thwart Italian territorial desires
1934–36	Co-Chair with Gen. Werner von Blomberg of the German Olympic Committee for Equestrian Events
5 June 1934	Death of Hermann von Epenstein, Goering's godfather
10 June 1934	Dedication of Reich Hunting *Hof* Carinhall
20 June 1934	Transfer of body of Carin Fock Goering from Sweden to reburial at Carinhall
30 June–1 July 1934	Conducts Nazi Blood Purge of SA and others from his Berlin palace
3 July 1934–23 April 1945	Reich Minister of Forests and Prussian State Master of Forests; also named Reich Master of the Hunt simultaneously
October 1934	Represents Germany officially at the State Funeral at Belgrade of the assassinated King of Yugoslavia Alexander I
7 December 1934–23 April 1945	Appointed Deputy to the Reich Chancellor in All Matters of Government Leadership, in essence, as the second man in the German State after and under Hitler

INTRODUCTION:
HERMANN GOERING AND I

Hermann Goering

Hermann Wilhelm Goering's mother was reported as saying, 'Hermann will either be a great man or a great criminal.' As it turned out, he became both.

The Allied criminal indictment against Goering at Nuremberg, Germany, and as issued by the then-unique International Military Tribunal on 11 November 1945, reads as follows:

> The defendant Goering between 1932-45 was: a member of the Nazi Party, Supreme Leader of the SA [Brownshirts], General in the SS, a member and President of the Reichstag/Parliament, Minister of the Interior of Prussia, Chief of the Prussian Police and Prussian Secret Police, Chief of the Prussian State Council, Trustee of the Four Year Plan; Reich Minister for Air, Commander-in-Chief of the Air Force, President of the Council of Ministers for the Defense of the Reich, member of the Secret Cabinet Council, head of the Hermann Goering Industrial Combine, and Successor Designate to Hitler.
>
> The defendant Goering used the foregoing positions, his personal influence, and his intimate connection with the Führer/Leader in such a manner that: he promoted the accession to power of the Nazi conspirators and the consolidation of their control over Germany set forth in Count One;
>
> He promoted the military and economic preparation for war set forth in Count One, he participated in the planning and preparations of the Nazi conspirators for wars of aggression and wars in violation of international treaties, agreements, and assurances set forth in Counts One and Two; and he authorized, directed, and participated in the war crimes set forth in Count Three;
>
> And the crimes against humanity set forth in Count Four—including a wide variety of crimes against persons and property.

Goering was universally acknowledged as both a Nazi and as defendant No. 1 on trial. On 30 September 1946 the Tribunal's Chief Justice—the eminent British jurist Lord Geoffrey Lawrence—said of Goering, in his judgement against him:

There is nothing to be said in mitigation.

For Goering was often—indeed almost always—the moving force, second only to his Leader. He was the leading war aggressor, both as political and as military leader; he was the director of the slave labor program, and the creator of the oppressive program against the Jews and other races, at home and abroad.

All these crimes he frankly admitted. On some specific cases, there may be conflict in testimony, but in terms of the broad outline, his own admissions are more than sufficiently wide to be conclusive of his guilt.

His guilt is unique in its enormity. The record discloses no excuses for this man.

Thus, Hermann Wilhelm Goering was pronounced guilty on all four counts of the indictment and sentenced to death by hanging. Ironically (with a few exceptions) the Allied guilty verdict placed Goering exactly where he wanted to be in history—second only to Hitler.

Like his fellow defendants, he viewed the entire eight-month-long trial by their enemies as no more than 'victors' justice'—as, indeed, it was. The moral of the trial was, he said bluntly, 'Don't lose a war.'

On the evening of 15 October 1946, he was scheduled to be hanged first of the eleven condemned men on the 16th, but he took poison that killed him within minutes—but not until after a most painful death. He died at 10.50 p.m., a little over two hours before he was scheduled to be hanged.

The Allied indictment failed to mention that he was also a German Field Marshal and the ranking officer of all the armed forces of both world wars to date, as the Reich/Imperial Marshal appointed by Führer Adolf Hitler more than six years before. This last was as a sort of six-star general, a title that still stands in military history.

It also failed to mention that he was addicted to morphine (and other drugs) for many years of his adult life—indeed, maybe for the last twenty-two years—and that he had even once been confined to a straitjacket and legally committed to an asylum for the insane in Sweden by his first wife.

And yet, just a few short years later, this same Hermann Wilhelm Goering was both one of the mightiest men on earth and also one of the richest—a rise up from poverty virtually unheard of in modern times.

He also helped create one of the globe's greatest air forces, but did all that he felt he could to prevent the outbreak of the Second World War. Truly, his life and career have no like in modern history, and one has to hark back to the Napoleonic Wars to find anyone similar. Indeed, only one other commander in military history held a title remotely like his own: Prince Eugene of Savoy in the eighteenth century.

The Author

As a boy, I first read about Goering in the early biographies by Willi Frischauer and the team of Roger Manvell and Heinrich Fraenkel, the latter published in 1962, when I was a sophomore in high school. I still have that original copy, too, and reread it in preparation for the current work.

Like Goering, I, too, always wanted to be a soldier, and succeeded in becoming one in a controversial war. Both of us attended infantry officer candidate schools; he made it, I did not. He served as both an aerial observer and pilot, and later created the German Parachute Corps, while I attended Ground Week of Airborne School at Ft. Benning, GA/USA. He flew all or many of the major German aircraft of his era, while I flew in some of the famous military aircraft of my own time—the Bell Huey and smaller bubbletop two-seater helicopters, and the larger Chinook transport chopper of the Vietnam War.

Like my subject, I, too, returned home from my soon-to-be-lost war to a country that disavowed my service to it in the main. Both of us began our non-military careers in a time of social ferment that lasted for decades, and both left the military for domestic politics.

In this study—as far as possible—I have let the principal characters speak in their own voices, in their own words, from their letters, diaries, autobiographies, memoirs, speeches, official reports, and personal statements at the time. Thus, this is a pictorial biography based in the main on primary sources, rather than on that of secondary authors.

For me, researching biographies has been an exciting and fascinating adventure. It is probably fair to assert that all authors have at least some preview of their subject as they enter into the bulk of their research. This has been true of myself, but I have made it a point to follow the elusive trail wherever it may lead. Often, pre-conceived notions thus fell by the wayside, while newer, different ones emerged; 'new' material emerged that challenged old assumptions, those both of myself and of previous biographers.

The late Harry Truman opined, 'The only history that is new is that which you do not know.' I concur, and that is why I find the biographical format so rich and rewarding. I hope that you will as well.

Blaine Taylor
Berkshires at Town Center
Towson, MD, USA
1 September 2015
Centennial of the First World War 1914–18

1

CARIN, 1919–22

Arminius (or 'Hermann the German') and the Battle of the Teutoburg Forest, AD 21

The ancient Germanic historic figure was the warrior whom our Hermann always believed he was named for, the man whose Germanic Cherusci had destroyed an army of two entire Roman Legions of 18,000 soldiers of Emperor Augustus Caesar.

In effect, it was one of the most decisive victories in all of recorded military history in that it halted the advance of the Roman Empire into the Germanies for good. The Rhine River thus become the eastern boundary for the successors of Emperor Augustus as well.

Arminius (18/17 BC–AD 21) was his Latin name, with Hermann being the Germanic version. Arminius is said to mean 'great', while Hermann has been defined as 'soldier, army man, or warrior'—and our subject was all of these. The great religious reformer Martin Luther is credited with being the first person to equate the two names as one. A nickname for Arminius was alleged to be 'Blue Eyes', and these our subject had as well.

In 1808 playwright Heinrich von Kleist penned his play *Hermann's Battle,* which was published in 1821 and staged in 1860; it was especially popular during the Third Reich of Hermann Goering.

During 1839–71, a massive stone statue of Arminius—sword held bravely aloft—was constructed as the Hermann Memorial on a hill near Detmold, in the Teutoburg Forest. In 1897, a similar second statue was built in New York, the United States, and known as *The Hermann Heights Monument.*

In more recent years, Arminius-Hermann has even been the subject of songs by numerous rock bands, and is also a character in the videogame *Total War: Rome 2.*

Unlike our Hermann, however, Arminius was assassinated. In a revealing self-characterization, Goering once boasted, 'I am the inheritor of all of the chivalry of German knighthood!' Combining that with what had been said of him at school—'This boy always likes to have his own way'—there was a powerful duality that remained with him throughout his entire life.

Dejected Veteran, 1918

The end of the First World War in Europe found Hermann Goering, aged twenty-five, both officially defeated and out of work in a country seething with upheaval and revolution, and with no real employment prospects to speak of. Indeed, reportedly he was even once set upon by an angry mob that attempted to rip off the medals he won in the war.

In his 1934 book *Germany Reborn*, Goering recalled:

> One ... will be amazed to see what a high percentage of the Social Democratic leaders and agitators were Jews! But now—in the days of the postwar rising—these Jewish leaders sprouted from the ground like poisonous fungi.
>
> Wherever Soldiers' Councils were formed, Jews were the leaders, those very same Jews who had not been seen out at the front, but had been employed in the supply departments at the base, or had filled indispensable official and military posts at home.
>
> In the streets, the mob raged. Soldiers had their badges and shoulder straps torn off. The flag ... was trampled in the mud. On all buildings fluttered the Red flag of rebellion. Everywhere there was disorder and dissolution.

The Clan Goering

Despite Goering's difficult situation in 1918, he had survived the greatest war in history, and all of his family was alive and well—with the exception of his late father, who had died in 1913. This included his widowed mother, Fanny, who lived in Munich, where he resided as well. Hermann had two sisters—Paula Rosa Elizabeth Goering Huber (13 May 1890–30 November 1960) and Olga Sophie Therese Goring Rigele (16 January 1889–7 October 1970)—and two brothers—lawyer Karl-Ernst Goring (3 August 1885–4 October 1932) and businessman Albert Gunter Goering (9 March 1895–20 December 1966).

After having his family tree investigated when he was in office during the 1930s, Goering claimed to be related to Jacob Burckhardt (1818–97) of the Eberle-Eberlin family, a famed Swiss art and cultural scholar. Ironically, the latter predicted those who practiced rabid nationalism and militarism in the twentieth century would be themselves central to great occurring cataclysms—exactly as Goering was.

He was reportedly also related to German aviation pioneer Count Ferdinand von Zeppelin, romantic nationalist Hermann Grimm (1828–1901), the industrialist Merck family (owners of the Merck pharmaceutical company), anti-Nazi Catholic writer and poetess *Baronin* (Baroness) Gertrud von Le Fort, and President of the International Red Cross, Swiss diplomat Carl J. Burckhardt.

Presumably, Goering had saved at least some of his Army pay during the war, and he lived for a time immediately after the conflict with fellow ace Ernst Udet at Berlin; he then lived with his widowed mother in Munich as he thought about what to do next. Another account has it that both he and Udet spent some weeks living in Munich in the rooms of their former Royal Flying Corps opponent, Captain Beaumont, who was then attached to the Allied Control Commission (which was sent to dismantle the German Air Force).

Setting the Stage 1918–19

The first six months of Goering's postwar odyssey occurred during the period of December 1918–28 June 1919, when he was at Copenhagen (according to eyewitnesses who knew him there). Before we follow his trajectory to Denmark, however, it is instructive to consider first the world in which he now lived and what was going on around him.

On 6 December 1918, an Allied force occupied Cologne in the Rhineland, opposite France, while on the 27th the Poles seized Posen in the east. On 5 January 1919, there was the communist Spartakist uprising in Berlin that was brutally suppressed by German Army troops loyal to the new, leftist Social Democratic government. Five days later, a communist Soviet Republic was proclaimed at the port city of Bremen, while on 21 February the Jewish communist Premier of Bavaria Kurt Eisner was assassinated.

From February into mid-March 1919, there were more communist uprisings at both Berlin and Munich, and another Soviet Republic was proclaimed on 4 April. Lasting less than a month, it was crushed on 1 May 1919 by right-wing Free Corps and Army troops led by German Army Gen. Franz Ritter ('Knight') von Epp, a man with whom Goering's own career would be linked all during 1928–45.

On the 1 June a French-sponsored Rhineland Republic was announced, a move by France to tear away the Reich's western border for good; however, it later collapsed via lack of domestic support. On 28 June 1919, Germany signed the Versailles Treaty that later almost all Germans would come to hate, particularly Goering—but where was he during these six months of turmoil and upheaval?

Incredibly—and despite his allegedly impassioned Berlin speech of December 1918—the surprising answer is that he was simply not involved with any of it. Rather, he turned his back on Germany and went abroad, to neighboring Scandinavia, to seek his fortune elsewhere.

Thus, unlike German Army Corporal Adolf Hitler—who sought to join the political left during this same period, but was rejected—and fellow pilot Rudolf Hess—who joined an anti-communist Free Corps unit—Hermann Goering simply left his country behind, perhaps for good. For all his later talk of 'fighting for Germany', he took no part during what was, perhaps, one of the land's most dramatic and fateful periods in its history to that point. Instead, like Udet, he sought to earn a living elsewhere, both as an aerial acrobat and a flying chauffeur for hire (by passengers who could afford his fee).

One of the great mysteries of Goering's controversial life now arises: why did he give up the only real job he had been trained for, that of a professional military officer? He may have been unwanted by those who were even then building Germany's new, but much-reduced, officer corps.

Goering gave a different answer to this question, however, before the Allied tribunal at Nuremberg in March 1946:

> I rejected the invitation to enter the *Reichswehr* ['Republican Army'] because from the very beginning, I was opposed in every way to the Republc that had come to power through the Revolution. I could not bring it into harmony with my convictions.

This, to me, sounds both convincing and true.

Reportedly, he was also the only Richtofen Flying Circus veteran not invited to any of its postwar reunions. One reason for the above was probably the fallout from his December speech at Berlin, attacking Gen. Reinhardt for cozying up too quickly with the new communist masters, while another may be the still-touchy subject (even today) of exactly how he earned his wartime aerial kill tally. It seems that Goering was shunned by the Army just when he might have needed its pay the very most. So, then; how did he come to be a civilian pilot-for-hire in two foreign lands?

Denmark, 1919

At Copenhagen, all reports seem to agree that Goering was 'given' the Fokker F7 aircraft in which he performed his daring aerial acrobatics for enthusiastic crowds at Kastorp. He was known as 'The Mad Flyer', and received the Fokker F7 as payment for his work there.

He also provided brief flights for passengers on Sundays at 50 Crowns per trip, thus allowing him to live rather well in Danish hotels for most of 1919. Once, a seagull shattered his propeller, causing him to spiral down from 7,500 feet—to a safe landing, nonetheless.

Reportedly, he was also the life of the various dinner parties to which he was invited as the still-famous last commander of the celebrated Richthofen Flying Circus. On 28 June 1919, however—upon the announcement of the terms of the anti-German Versailles Peace Treaty in the Danish press—Goering shouted out, 'One day we will come back, to write another treaty!' This both startled and antagonized his fellow diners.

He was convinced by his then-married lover—with whom, he crowed, he took champagne baths—that, a year on, it was time for him to leave Denmark for other climes and opportunities. This he did sometime in December 1919.

Sweden, 1920–22

However, Goering was involved in his first wreck upon landing in southern Sweden. On coming into Ljungbyhed Airfield, he smashed his plane's wheels; he went on to Stockholm by rail. He was not immediately accepted for employment as a pilot by *Aktiebolaget Svensk-Luftratrafik* (Swedish Air Service), but was finally hired (initially as a mail courier pilot) in spring 1920.

Until then, his practical advice was listened to by the Swedish air authorities, and he was even interviewed in the Stockholm daily press about his previous stunt flying. Regarding fatalities, Goering was quoted thus: 'The art of flying must always have its victims.' This demonstrated once more his lifelong devil-may-care attitude toward violent death in either war or peace.

Meanwhile, his damaged other Fokker aircraft had been repaired, and on 11 April 1920 Goering morphed into a dangerous stunt pilot from Danish skies, replicating his feats in Sweden and creating a sensation, as it was some of the first stunt flying ever witnessed there.

The Stockholm paper *Swedish Daily News* asserted:

The German fighter pilot—Captain Goering—has now obtained his long awaited fighter—a veteran of the Western Front. It is a Fokker with with a 185 hp BMW engine, with which he made a trial flight over Gardet today, executing a series of loops and other aerobatics at heights of between 3,000 and 4,800 feet. Next Sunday, Stockholm's popular 'air chauffeur' will continue his passenger carrying flights.

He had also sold—as the designated company agent for the Swedish air market—the German-made, spring-loaded, self-opening Heinicken parachute, which served to save its pilots by billowing out aloft as soon as they baled out of their aircraft.

To facilitate sales, newly minted salesman Hermann Goering wrote and designed his own brochure, a copy of which was preserved in the Royal Library at Stockholm. Referring to himself as 'Formerly Commodore of Baron von Richthofen's Flying *Geschwader* [Fighter Squadron] No.1', Goering wrote the ad copy himself:

The purpose of the parachute is to save the airman from disaster … One can always obtain a new aircraft, but it is a matter of far greater difficulty to replace the airman, since—to get a man fit for military service transferred to the air force—is a matter of considerable difficulty in any case, because his training … takes a long time.

Thus, the parachute—quite apart from its essential purpose of saving a valuable human life—has become a very important factor in air defense.

These were words that would come back to haunt Luftwaffe commander Hermann Goering during the Battle of Britain in 1940, when irreplaceable pilots were shot down in great numbers by the RAF in the skies over England.

The brochure copy continued:

In order that the 'non-automatic' parachute may function [a Goering swipe at Heinicken's chief competitor, the American-manufactured Irvin, activated by a pilot-pulled ripcord] the aviator must be able himself to release the parachute.

He must, therefore, have perfect control of mind, nerves, and body … but of one thing one can never be quite certain—the workings of the human mind and soul…. I make bold to state that I have shown—in the many aerial acrobatics in which I have taken part—that fear and slackness are not numbered among my qualities, yet I should never be so pretentious as to guarantee that, in making a jump in the circumstances that I have mentioned, my own nerves would be under control.

In later years, Goering was described by one wag as 'the only man whose career *rose* by parachute!' He continued selling them right up to 30 January 1933, when he became a member of the German cabinet.

When not airborne, Goering soon became the lion of the Stockholm nightlife and social scene (as he had been in Copenhagen), both at dinner parties and dances. In the winter of 1921, however, his life took a sudden turn that would dominate it for the next decade.

Enter Count Eric von Rosen (2 June 1879–25 April 1948)

Swedish Count Carl Gustav Bloomfeld Eric von Rosen was already a well-known explorer, ethnographer, and honorary doctor in 1920. In the 1930s, he would also become a main figure in his country's own upper-class, Nazi-type movement—well before Goering did in Germany.

He was also the husband of Stockholm's prominent Countess Mary von Fock von Rosen (1886–1967), and the couple had six children. The Count was a Swedish Nazi, having been a co-founder of Sweden's National Socialist Bloc.

Nazi hagiography later had it that Count Eric von Rosen knew Goering, and hired him on 20 February 1920 to fly in a bad snowstorm from Stockholm to his ancestral home of Rockelstad Castle, on Sweden's Lake Baven, in Sörmland. Despite the weather, the Count opted for a chancy flight instead of a dull, two-hour train ride to Sparreholm, followed by a dreary car trip to his snow-bound castle.

Upon landing safely—and due to the bad weather—the Count graciously asked his pilot to stay the night at the castle. That was not all, however; there was also a beautiful woman, the likes of whom Hermann Goering had never encountered before.

Goering legend has it that the young pilot met and fell in love with the Count's then-houseguest and sister-in-law, the still-married but separated from her husband Countess Carin von Kantzow, at first sight. I believe, however, that this alleged 'accidental' meeting in which the four people—the trio of Swedes and Hermann Goering—spent the evening dining, drinking, and singing Swedish folks songs before a roaring fire was more than just happenstance. It strikes me as an all-too-convenient occurrence, and was more likely an arranged 'blind date' by the Count for the handsome pilot and Countess Carin. Most likely, both the Count and his dreamy, romantic relation had read the press accounts of the younger expatriate aviator's derring-do in the skies over the nation's capital.

The setting itself also had a powerful effect on the young, romantic Hermann Goering, reminding him of his experiences during boyhood at Hermann von Epenstein's castles, Veldenstein and Mauterndorf. Here he was, back in a similar setting once more; weaponry hung from the walls of the von Rosens' Great Hall, next to hunting trophies of heads and antlers of both deer and elk, highlighted by the figure of a stuffed bear at the foot of the main staircase—killed with spear alone by the Count.

And now—as if all that had not been enough to turn the impressionable aviator's head—came this lovely vision of Swedish womanhood. Even more potent than this, however, was the fact that the history-minded Carin had been pro-German during the First World War, during which her own country had stayed neutral. Here—on her very doorstep, so it seemed—was an actual example of that land's bemedaled heroism at her feet, and he was available. It was a heady mix for both of them.

As fate would have it, the Count was even then using the ancient runic swastika symbol as his own, personal icon; he first encountered it while at school in Gotland, Sweden. Reportedly, Count von Rosen used this alleged Viking twisted cross to emblazon his personal luggage taken for a 1901 trip to North America.

Sweden had a tradition of culture, political alignment, and goodwill with neighboring Finland, stretching back several centuries. When Finland secured her independence from Bolshevik Russia in 1918, the Count donated an aircraft that became the first such in the new Finnish Air Force—a Morane-Saulnier MS Parasol/Thulin D. This premiere aircraft had a blue swastika as its icon, set against a white background. Indeed, the FAF in time even took this compelling roundel as its own national air force identification marking.

The saga of Hermann and Carin further has it that Goering saw a swastika embedded into a metal form on the Count's fireplace, and may even have known that at the same time a small, new political party in Germany had adopted it as its trademark. Indeed, on 14 March 1935—while Goering back in Nazi Germany, proclaimed everywhere as the number-two man in German Nazism—the Count was the main speaker at a Stockholm rally on the subject of Swedish National Socialism; the handbill announcing him bore a curved swastika at the top center.

Enter Carin von Fock von Kantzow (1888–1931)

Count von Rosen's beautiful, tall, buxom, raven-haired, dreamy, and somewhat-exotic sister-in-law would play one of the most dominant and influential roles in Goering's life and career—one perhaps even greater than that of Hitler, a later player. She was the love of his life, his first wife, and someone whom he never forgot.

Born Carin Axelina Hulda von Fock in Stockholm on 21 October 1888, she was thus five years older than her future lover and second husband. She was the daughter of Swedish Army Col. Baron Carl von Fock of the capital, Stockholm, whose family originally hailed from Germany's Westphalia. Her mother was Huldine Beamish von Fock (1860–1931), from the Anglo-Irish Cork family—who brewed *Beamish & Crawford* stout, a firm co-founded by her great-great grandfather William Beamish. Huldine Beamish's Irish father reportedly served in Great Britain's famed Coldstream Guards; his daughter left Queenstown, South Africa, to marry her future husband in 1880.

Huldine's mother (and thus Carin's maternal grandmother), Mrs Beamish, had been twice widowed before she settled in Sweden, where in 1894 she founded the later-renowned private religious sisterhood known as the Edelweiss Association; this society had a profound effect on both Carin and her second husband, Goering. The chapel was located in a smallish structure in a walled garden to the rear of the von Fock family home in Greve-Ture-Gatan, Stockholm, and still stood in 1962. When Goering first visited in 1920, the Countess von Rosen served as its Sister Superior.

The fourth of five daughters, Carin's sisters were her later biographer, Fanny von Fock von Wilamowitz-Mollendorff (1882–1956), Mary von Fock von Rosen (b. 1886), Elsa von Fock, and Lily von Fock. Initially, all of her relatives were taken with the colorful figure of Hermann Goering, though not as much as Carin. To her, young Hermann seemed to be the very personification of the hero she had longed to meet all her life.

Soulmates

After dinner, circling a piano, the Swedish songs were also joined by some German tunes, further convincing the star-struck pair that they had found a perfect match. Carin's elder sister, Fanny, later described this idyllic first meeting in her autobiography:

> Her deep blue eyes met Hermann Goering's searching glance. This splendid woman … a feeling of exultation began to beat in his breast! He stood there, tongue-tied and in awe. It was as if he had always known her. The love that sprang up instantly between them cannot be explained … It, too, lives in blood and in the soul!

Thus the dreamy lovers had their romance chronicled in a best-selling book in Germany, fifteen years later, by a third party who was no less affected than they. At the time, Carin was thirty-two years old and Hermann was twenty-seven.

Carin's Jilted First Husband: Count Nils Gustaf von Kantzow (1885–1967)

The son of Gustaf Ludvig and Emma Hilda Julia von Kantzow, Count Nils was a captain in the Royal Swedish Army. The Count, twenty-four, married Carin Axelina Hulda von Fock, twenty-one, on 7 July 1910, and in 1913 they had their only child, Thomas von Kantzow. The highlight of the Count's military career was his pre-First World War stint in Paris as military attaché to the Swedish Embassy to Republican France; his pretty young wife accompanied him. Most of the rest the Count's career took place in a succession of usual garrison towns; as a young wife and mother, Carin found these locations boring after growing up in her nation's capital city—not to mention Paris.

The von Kantzow family was reportedly related to the Portuguese Bosanquet clan, as well as to the Portuguese royal family. Count Nils is also said to have taken part in the 1908 London Olympics, on the Swedish men's gymnastics team.

Formally, the Nils-Carin marriage endured from July 1910 until December 1922, and over that twelve-year timeframe they simply grew apart—with Carin only commenting later that the Count was not as quick-witted as she in understanding jokes.

Meanwhile, Carin's sister Mary had married Count von Rosen, while her elder sister Fanny wed a German officer, Richard von Wilamowitz-Mollendorf, who was killed in the First World War. Thus Carin was surrounded by nobility from two countries—Germany and Sweden. All had been pro-German during the First World War, even in the face of Sweden's official neutrality—which would occur again in the twentieth century's second global conflict.

The von Kantzow Son: Count Thomas von Kantzow (1 March 1913–27 May 1973)

Thomas was born in Overlulea, and was to know Goering personally, on and off, from 1920 to 1934. At the time of her initial tryst with Hermann in 1920–22, Carin was still a married (but separated) woman with a son aged eight-to-ten years old, and their open affair scandalized polite Stockholm society.

Later, Thomas recalled his own first impressions of Goering and his mother: 'I noticed that she hardly ever took her eyes off him ... I sensed that she was in love with him.' Carin told Fanny, 'We are like Tristan and Isolde! We have swallowed the love potion and are helpless—oh, so ecstatically helpless!—under its effect!'

Thus two drama queens met and became as one. The affair began in earnest back at Stockholm, with a meeting at her parent's home that was followed by praying together in the clan's nearby Edelweiss Chapel; this was Hermann's first experience with religion. Next came their joint presence at a masked ball in the winter of 1921, followed by Goering sending her his own written poetry—another first for him.

At length, Hermann persuaded Carin to ask Nils for a divorce, but the Count begged off, playing for time as the hot romance cooled in the light of practicality; after all, Carin was a Countess and mother, and her new lover was little more than a sometimes-employed passenger pilot.

Over time, Count Nils reconciled himself with Carin's divorce and remarriage, but her austere father, Col. von Fock, never did. Indeed, he was completely estranged from his wayward daughter until her death eleven years later.

Thomas was sent to live with the von Rosens, where he learned that his mother had left his father to live openly—and thus, in the eyes of society, in sin—with her lover, Capt. Goering, in a Stockholm apartment. In later years, Thomas recalled, 'I liked him at first sight.' Originally, his father had felt the same way.

Adulterous Lovers, 1920–22

Goering was not only infatuated with Carin's beauty and sexual passion, but also seduced by both her maternal caring for him and his own newfound religious piety. Hermann later sent a letter to Carin's mother on the subject:

> The beautiful moment I was allowed to spend in the Edelweiss Chapel. You have no idea how I felt in this wonderful atmosphere ... so quiet ... lovely, that I forgot all the earthly noise, all my worries, and felt as though in another world ... like a swimmer resting on a lonely

island to gather new strength before he throws himself anew in the raging torrent of life.

In 1945 the joint love letters of Carin and Hermann were stolen by US Army soldiers from the then-German Reich Marshal's special train, *Asia*, which was parked in a rail siding at Berchtesgaden Station, near the Obersalzberg, in Bavaria, South Germany. They have still not been found and published. Perhaps someday they will be, revealing yet another dimension to this unknown portion of Goering's tumultuous life.

Before they began living openly together as unmarried lovers at Stockholm, Carin continued to live with Nils under the same roof, with him tacitly accepting what, for him, was a sad and embarrassing situation. Carin wrote to Hermann: 'He took it all very calmly, and even said that he was glad to know that I was happy, and had not been all by myself.' That 'understanding' had its legal limits, however, as Count Nils refused Countess Carin's desire for custody of young Thomas, fighting her in the Swedish court system as well for both common property and their joint finances. Prior to actually leaving Nils for Hermann, Carin wrote the following to Goering:

> More and more I realize how much you mean to me. I love you so much! To me, you are really my ideal in everything. You do everything so sweetly … You remember me with so many little things, and that makes my life so happy. Now—for the first time—I realize how accustomed I have become to you. It is difficult for me to say it … I want you to feel it in your dear, beloved heart!
>
> If I could only say that with kisses and embraces, darling! I would like to kiss you from one end to the other without stopping for an hour! Do you really love me as much as you say? Is that possible?

In 1962, a pair of Goering biographers asserted that in 1920 he returned to Munich to live with his mother, Mrs Fanny Goering, and that—in time—Carin followed. Thus Carin met the 'other woman' in Hermann's life, his widowed mother, who was then almost a decade removed from her own adulterous love affair with her Jewish lover, von Epenstein, in 1913. Carin lived with her future mother in law—a Bavarian former barmaid and adulterous mistress—for a month in 1923.

They reportedly got along, but Fanny lost her temper one evening at a family dinner, exclaiming of her son, 'Look how he has compromised Carin! In Germany, it is a scandal for a woman to live the way she did and do the things she did! He was placing her in an impossible position in German eyes, and—as a German officer—he must have known it.' Nils was refusing to grant her a divorce, and the fact that Hermann and Carin were living together openly was controversial in the caste-conscious Reich.

Leaving Mrs Goering's house, the couple set up home in a small hunting lodge at Hockreuth, near Bayrischell, 6 miles from the Bavarian capital city of Munich—where Goering had first learned to ski in 1917.

Hermann became a freshman college student at a Munich University, studying politics, history, and economics. There are no accounts of him attending class, though, nor taking exams, and thus Goering never graduated. One of his fellow students was a former German Army pilot named Rudolf Hess.

The couple was essentially penniless, with Carin selling her paintings and handicrafts to pay the bills; she had left Thomas, her son, behind in Sweden. When she became sick, Carin sold her fur coat to pay her medical bills; however, her faithful, dutiful husband, Nils, bought it back for her and sent her a one-way railroad ticket for Stockholm.

Meanwhile, Carin's mother, Huldine, was opposed to her daughter's illicit liaison with Goering (like Carin's father), and relations with Fanny Goering had also deteriorated; Carin called her 'a conceited, idiotic old monkey'. It would seem that Hermann had his hands full with all of this as he tried to find a living to support them; however, Fanny Goering died in 1923, thus removing any mother-in-law problems forever for both the first and second Mrs Hermann Goering.

On 11 May 1922, Carin wrote the following to her mother:

> Bavaria is a lovely countryside, so rich, so warm, and so intellectual and strong—so unlike the rest of Germany! I am very happy here, and feel very much at home. When I feel homesick for Sweden, it is really only a longing for mama. Nils [!], the little boy, and those I love, but just that painful, insane longing means that I am nearly always melancholy [as nearly all her images from that period attest]. Oh, my own, dear mama! If only one did not have such powerful love within one.

In November 1922, the happy but still-adulterous couple moved into a villa at No. 30 Dobereinerstrasse, near Reginwaldstrasse, in the Munich suburb of Obermenzing. This put Goering closer to his work with the NSDAP, as at first he took the streetcar back and forth every day. They wcre eventually able to make a mortgage downpayment on their new home as well.

Carin furnished the new house in the Biedermeir style with funds provided by her long-suffering and presumably still-lovelorn husband—the truly tragic figure in the triangle. Carin and Hermann lived there until 9 November 1923, when they fled Bavaria for Austria. Carin's own paintings graced the walls. Her other visual contribution to their new domicile was a bowl of red roses next to her favored white harmonium, near a pink curtain and a marital bed with a blue brocade canopy, veiled with white lace. Hermann's study boasted the traditional, heavy, German carved-oak furnishings, and a window painting of armored knights, while Carin had tinted pink windows. Their basement featured an open fireplace with oaken cupboards on the surrounding walls—in effect, a dry run for his later and far more elaborate home on the Schorfheide, outside Berlin, in 1933.

The Swedish Divorce (December 1922) and Hermann's Disputed Remarriage Date

Carin's long-awaited divorce from Nils was made official on 13 December 1922, followed by a pair of Hermann-Carin weddings—one in Sweden, and the other in Germany. In 1962, Manvell and Fraenkel asserted that the correct year of the Goerings' marriages was 1922, whereas the most-often-presented date for the marriages by other

English-language biographers was 1923. At any rate, they were married twice—once at Stockholm, Carin's home town, reportedly in a civil ceremony on 25 January 1922/3, and then again at Hermann's home town, at the Munich City Hall, on 23 February 1922/3, with the bride wearing white. The Munich Park Hotel reception was attended by just two von Fock family members—Carin's elder sister Fanny, and her daughter, Dagmar. Most of the bride's Swedish family remained adamantly opposed to their marital union. The von Fock family had not yet come to terms with their daughter's darling Hermann, especially as they felt that he had shamed their Carin.

Goering's old air pal, Maj. Karl Bodenschatz, reportedly brought greetings from their former Flying Circus airmen: 'That's what we always said: "*Unser Goering*" will always do better than anyone!' Allegedly, a Richthofen Squadron Guard of Honor for the new bride and groom was made up of what veteran friends in attendance Goering had retained from the war.

The couple's brief honeymoon took place at the Hockreuth hunting lodge, near Bayrischell, in the mountains near the Austrian-German frontier.

Meanwhile, Nils still pined away for his 'lost treasure'. Carin asserted, 'God! How wonderful it is to have a husband who does not take two days to see the point of a joke!' As for her deserted son, Thomas, Carin wrote to him:

> You see, sweetheart, he has made your mama very happy, and you must not be upset about it. It will not interfere with our love for each other, dearest Thomas. You see, I love you best of all!

By all accounts—though he still denied Carin custody of their son—Nils provided a generous alimony settlement for his lost wife, and it was this money that mainly supported the newly married Goerings from 1922 to 1928. In effect, therefore, Carin's second husband lived off the support of her first. With their finances buttressed in this way, Hermann bought a new, 25-horsepower Mercedes-Benz 16 automobile. Their social standing, meanwhile, had also ramped up, with Hermann leaving behind his non-existent career as a student for his heady new life in politics—where he would even have an actual troop command!

Left: Swedish Countess Carin Hulda von Fock von Kantzow Goering (1888–1931), flashing the smile that won Hermann Goering's heart at their very first meeting. She married Goering in Munich, Bavaria, on 3 February 1922 or 1923 (accounts differ); she had left behind her husband of ten years and her only son. Note her contemporary 'bob' hairstyle. (*Wilamowitz-Mollendorff, Library of Congress (W-MLC)*)

Right: Carin's mother, the Anglo-Irish Swedish Baroness Huldine Beamish von Fock, sent money and food to the Goerings during their exile from Germany. To Carin, Hermann was 'the hero she had always dreamed about'; Hitler called Carin 'the mascot of the movement'. (*W-MLC)Above:* Carin's father, Swedish Army Colonel Baron

Above: Carin (right) with her younger sister, Lily von Fock Martin (her favorite). Like their parents, Carin's sisters opposed her scandalous divorce and remarriage. (*W-MLC*)

Right Carl von Fock, disapproved of daughter's marriage to Goering. The von Fock family home was located at No. 68 Grev Turegaton. (*W-MLC*)

Above left: Thomas von Kantzow (1913–73, left) was Carin's son from her first marriage, whom she left behind in Stockholm when she ran off to Germany to marry her adulterous lover. In time, all three were reconciled; Thomas called Hermann 'Uncle Goering'. Towards the end of Carin's life, Thomas said that Hermann looked like 'a cuddly bear fondling its cub'. (*W-MLC*)

Above right: Hermann and Carin in the Bavarian Alps during the early part of their marriage. He uses a cane due to his rheumatism from the First World War. The Swedish Press called Carin 'the most beautiful woman in Sweden'; Hermann was also handsome, with blue eyes and wavy hair. (*W-MLC*)

Left: Hermann wearing hiking socks and boots near Bayrischell, in the Bavarian Alps, in this 1922 photograph of the happy couple. Note also his white shirt and tie, and Carin's apron. Like his mother before him, Hermann found himself in a love triangle with a married woman and her doting husband. (*W-MLC*)

Right: Another idyllic view of the happy couple—prior to the onset of their troubles from 1923–31. Hermann is again brandishing a cane. He was fluent in German, English, and Swedish, and later (while broke and living in Stockholm) undertook translation work for other expatriates like himself. From 1924–28 he was poor and unemployed; since he was a fugitive from justice in Weimar Germany, he was legally unable to return home and run in the Reichstag elections in May 1924. (*W-MLC*)

Below left: The Goerings at the famous St Mark's Square, Venice, during their Italian exile. Two pigeons perch on Carin's right arm as Hermann carries a trusty *Baedeker Guide Book* in his left and, cane in right, on 5 September 1924. While in Rome, Hermann reportedly grew fat by eating pasta; one biographer asserted that 'he was marked for obesity by his heavy bone structure'. (*W-MLC*)

Above right: The couple is still smiling here despite their dire financial straits, with both of them unemployed. Hermann vowed to never be in such poverty again. Carin wrote that she and Hermann could not live with her parents or sisters in Stockholm due to lack of room, but the truth was that they were not wanted there during their exile from Germany. Later, Hermann would be committed to an insane asylum and Carin would die from tuberculosis. (*W-MLC*)

Left: Carin is very ill here, as seen in her face; this is a detail taken from a portrait of her that was taken during the last stage of her short, sickly life. Fighting for custody of her son at court in Stockholm, all her sisters testified against Hermann and caused her to lose the case. (*HGA*)

Below left: A somber Carin, perhaps pondering her cruel fate; she had given up everything for her lover only to die young and lose him anyway. Her first husband, Nils, reportedly later suffered from dementia. As Carin lay dying in fall 1931, she urged Hermann to return to Germany, exclaiming, 'As long as Hermann is here, I cannot go. I cannot bear to leave him.' (*W-MLC*)

Below right: According to her older sister and biographer, Baronin Fanny von Fock, Countess von Wilamowitz-Mollendorff, this was 'the last picture of Carin Goering'. From 1921–23, the couple lived partly on investments inherited from Hermann's father after his death in 1913. (*W-MLC*)

The famous Edelweiss Chapel in the garden of the Stockholm house of the von Fock family; in a letter to Carin's mother, Hermann claimed to have found great spiritual peace here. It was also here that Countess von Fock presided over the Order of Edelweiss Sisters, of which Elizabeth, Princess zu Weid, was a member.

Left: A memorial altar to Carin, featuring a somber portrait of her at top centre, in Hermann's 1933 Berlin palace. This was the first of many shrines to his late wife that were scattered across his multiple German residences. (*HGA*)

Right: A somber portrait of Carin that was commissioned by her widower after her death in October 1931. After her death, Carin's body was placed in the Edelweiss Chapel, behind her parents' home in Stockholm. Her sister Lily told Hermann of his wife's death; wild with despair, he reportedly threw himself across her coffin, screaming and weeping. (*HGA*)

2

HITLER, 1922–23

On 10 October 1922, Goering, twenty-nine, first saw Nazi Party leader Adolf Hitler, thirty-three, at a political meeting on Munich's famous *Konigsplatz* (King's Plaza). Later, after hearing Hitler speak, Hermann told Carin, 'I am *for* that man, body and soul!'

The Goering literature asserts that he made taking over the offered command of the Führer's unruly political soldiers—the SA (Storm Troopers)—contingent upon his first joining the small political party as an ordinary member. Hitler agreed. 'I wanted a small party,' Goering explained to Captain Gilbert in 1946, 'so that I could become a big man in it.'

SA commander Captain Goering recruited 11,000 men, organized into a trio of *Standarten* (Regiments). When Carin's estranged parents briefly visited their daughter in Bavaria, their son-in-law was off tending to his new political and martial duties.

His new vocation prompted Hermann and Carin to move from Bayrischell into Munich proper, so that now SA leader Captain Goering would be closer to his new command. His new car meant that Goering's brief career as a Munich tram commuter ended as well.

It is my conclusion that Hitler—a conservative regarding the outward appearance of family matters—made Goering's SA command posting contingent upon both Carin's legal divorce and her subsequent remarriage. This is arguably a more plausible reason for the delay in officially announcing Goering's ascension to SA Führer. Indeed, this situation seems to have replicated itself again during 1934–35, regarding Hermann's second wife—as we will see.

Carin first met Hitler at the Nazi Marsfeld rally outside Munich on 28 January 1923. Ironically, she emerged as even more of a Nazi racist than her husband, already being virtually a Swedish Nazi who hated both Jews and communists—stating they were, in fact, one and the same. While Hermann might tend to look the other way regarding Jews, Carin's strident stance bucked him up all through the remaining years of their marriage.

The SA was now under impressive martial management for the first time in its existence. Hitler was delighted to review the troops from a standing position in his SA

Commander's personal car, the Mercedes-Benz 16—a stance that the Führer employed as much as possible from 1922–39 in his own vehicles. In 1942, Hitler recalled the following of Goering:

> I liked him. I made him the head of my SA. He is the only one of its heads who ran the SA properly. I gave hwim a disheveled rabble. In a very short time, he had organized a division of 11,000 men!

On trial after the end of the Second World War, Goering remembered:

> At first, it was important to weld the SA into a stable organization, to discipline it, and to make of it a thoroughly reliable unit to carry out the orders that I or Adolf Hitler should give it.
>   I strove from the beginning to bring into the SA those members of the party who were young and idealistic enough to devote their free time and their entire energies to it … In the second place, I tried to find recruits among laborers.

On 13 March 1946, Goering gave more testimony to the IMT:

> One side or the other still had weapons from the war, and sometimes critical situations arose … and we had to send the SA as reinforcements to other localities.

Similarly to Hitler's father, Goering's father had been much older than Goering's mother, and he had also been born of his father's second wife. Both were incurable romantics, physically brave, hardy, impulsive, and each vain after their own style.

However, one of the cardinal aspects of Hitler and Goering's relationship has never been discussed; how was it that a much-decorated officer came to subordinate himself, body and soul, to a lowly, enlisted soldier? Like his fellow officer and pilot Rudolf Hess—and almost every other Nazi who ever heard Hitler speak—Goering was impressed by Hitler's oratorical skills. Perhaps the answer to the question is found in Hitler's political leadership skills; after the Second World War, Goering told Gustave (a.k.a. Mark) Mahler Gilbert MD:

> I had tried to found a revolutionary party myself among the officer veterans. I remember a meeting at which they were discussing getting meals and beds for veteran officers.
>   'You damned fools!' I told them. 'Do you think an officer who is worth his salt cannot find a bed to sleep in, even if it happens to be the bed of a pretty blonde? Damn it, there are more important things at stake!'
>   Somebody got fresh, and I banged him over the head. Well, of course the meeting broke up in an uproar. I never did get anywhere in trying to get a following for my revolutionary party.

As if on cue, Adolf Hitler arrived to rescue him from his political dilemma. He told Dr Gilbert:

The first time that I saw Hitler was in 1922. There was a protest meeting in Munich against the demand to extradite some of our generals. Some little nationalistic parties were represented, and Hitler was just one of the audience. I was there, too, because I considered it outrageous that Germany should be so humiliated as to have to hand over its generals to foreigners.

They were making ... bourgeois nationalistic speeches. Every once in a while, somebody would run up to Hitler and ask him if he wanted to speak, but he said he didn't want to. I asked who he was, and somebody told me that was Hitler, leader of the National Socialist Party, who was against Versailles, etc.

That interested me immediately, and I asked where I could hear him speak. They told me I could hear him ... at the Café Neumann ... I just sat unobtrusively in the background ... Hitler ... said he did not want to disturb the unity of the other meeting, but he did not approve of such weak protests.

'No Frenchman is going to lose sleep over that kind of harmless talk,' he said. 'You have got to have bayonets to back up your threats.' Well, that was what I wanted to hear. He wanted to build up a party that would make Germany strong and smash the Treaty of Versailles ... I said to myself, 'That's the party for me! Down with the Treaty of Versailles, Goddamn it! That's my meat!'

So a few days later, I go down to party headquarters—quite modestly—and fill out a membership application. Well, of course, there is something of a sensation when they see who I am, because—I can say without vanity that, among the young officers—I was still something of a leader.

You know, I succeeded Baron von Richthofen, we were classmates at Lichterfelde. Anyway, somebody tells me that Hitler would like to see me immediately. He tells me that it was a stroke of fate that I should come to him just as he was looking for somebody to take charge of the SA.

In fact, Hitler was delighted to have the famous Captain Goering among his chief lieutenants. In Kurt Ludecke's 1937 memoir *I Knew Hitler*, he recalls that the Führer chortled, 'Imagine it, a war hero with the *Pour le Mérite*, and he does not cost me a cent! Excellent propaganda!' Thus was established Hermann's essential value to the party from the start—an officer with a major reputation among so many dull, enlisted men.

Former First World War veteran and fellow officer Gregor Strasser (1892–1934) took a different view, asserting that Goering was 'a brutal egoist who did not give a damn about Germany, as long as he could amount to something'.

Goering's First Nazi Command: Militarizing the SA, 1923

Hitler had established the SA on 3 August 1921, both to protect him while speaking and also to disrupt the meetings of the Nazi Party's opponents—mainly the KPD communists and SPD socialists. From the start, Hitler viewed them as political shock troops only, while their Staff Chief, Capt. Ernst Röhm (1887–1934), instead longingly saw them as Germany's future national Army.

Goering took over his new command from former naval officer Hans Ulrich Klintsch, then also a member of the independent Ehrhardt Brigade. Knowing what Hitler wanted and what he did not, Goering was nonetheless allowed to instill what the Brownshirts lacked most of all—martial discipline and a unit core cohesion, to which both the present and larger future squads would need to adhere. Goering later wrote:

> He wanted an energetic young officer, and I was just the man he was looking for. We agreed to postpone the announcement for a month, but I started right in to train the SA as a military organization—military!—I'll tell the world it was military!

Actually, the embryonic SA had already had a regular military command structure as of May 1922, but it had not been put into practice as both Hitler and Goering desired. Accordingly, Goering immediately established an SA Headquarters command that he modeled on the typical German Army General Staff organization:

> For men like me, it was a chance to wipe out the disgrace of Versailles—the shame of the defeat, the [Polish] Corridor right through the heart of Prussia—it was pure patriotic idealism. I joined the party precisely because it was revolutionary, not because of the ideological stuff! Other parties had made revolutions, so I figured I could get in one, too!

According to his press chief, Dr Gritzbach, in 1938, Goering soon had his SA trainees 'practicing with rifles, machineguns, and truck driving', thus making of the Storm Troops Germany's first motorized force. Gritzbach wrote:

> The captain was on the move day and night. The right man was in the right place, and the first leader of the SA did his duty with iron tenacity … On 28 January 1923, Hermann Goering reported to the Führer that the 'Storm Divisions' had been formed. They were paraded … Their standard was consecrated, and … it would be unfurled in the storm.

Ironically, it now emerged that the Nazi Party had also acquired a more fervently anti-Semitic Goering family member—Carin. Her husband later practiced anti-Semitism on and off as it suited his personal and political purposes, while the first Mrs Goering was a true believer; this was a carryover from being influenced in Sweden by her brother-in-law, the Count von Rosen, a man who was much admired by her new husband.

Soon, Carin's letters home referred to Hermann as 'The Beloved One'. She informed Thomas, now ten years old, that 'the Führer embraced the Beloved One and told [Carin] that if he said what he really thought of his achievement, the Beloved One would get a swollen head'. Hitler had clearly already taken his own measure of Goering's major character trait—personal vanity. Carin continued, 'I said that my own head was already swollen with pride, and he kissed my hand and said, "No head so pretty as yours could ever be swollen!"' Thus two drama queens had been joined by a third; Hitler was a shrewd judge of character and had already sized up the Goerings, winning them over to his cause.

Putzi's Recollection, 1923

Munich piano impresario Ernst '*Putzi*' ('Little Fellow') Hanfstangl remembered the Goering couple in 1923:

> Goering was a complete condottiere, a pure soldier of fortune, who saw in the Nazi Party a possible outlet for his vitality and vanity. Nevertheless, he had a jovial, extrovert manner, and I found myself very much at home with him. Before long, we were on 'thou' terms, and that was probably as much due to our wives as anything.
>
> Carin Goering … was at least a lady, a woman of charm and education, and she and my wife Helene saw a lot of each other. Goering had a certain humorous contempt for the little squad of Bavarians around Hitler, whom he regarded as a bunch of beer-swillers and rucksack-carriers with a limited, provincial horizon.
>
> In his overloud way, he at least brought a whiff of the great outside world with him, and his war record with his *Pour le Mérite* had given him a much wider set of contacts.
>
> He and Carin lived extremely well, although most of the money was hers … My wife and I used to go out there sometimes, but not very often, for we had no car, and had to rely on the Goerings to get us there and back … I remember rebuking Goering once at one of the Munich cafes for screwing a monocle into his eye and then looking round with a stupid air of superiority that the wearers of such objects usually affect.
>
> 'My dear Hermann,' I told him, 'this is supposed to be a working class party, and if you go around looking like a *Junker* [landowner], we shall never attract their support!' Whereupon he looked rather deflated and sheepish, and stuffed the glass in his pocket.

I found no photographs of Goering wearing a monocle in any of his personal photograph albums, either. Putzi continued:

> Hitler found Goering useful, but was a little cynical about his *ménage*. He called on us late one evening after he had been out at Obermenzing and mimicked the pair of them for my wife. 'It is a real love nest! It is "darling Hermann" this and "darling Hermann" that,' imitating Carin's slightly too affectionate voice. 'I have never had such a home, and will never have one!' in a sort of mock sentimentality, 'I have only one love, and that is Germany.'
>
> The Goerings also had an unpleasant looking gardener named Greinz, to whom I took an immediate dislike, and who was to play a highly dubious role before the year was out. He was always outwardly full of the true party spirit, barking slogans and flashing his eyes, but I never trusted him.
>
> 'Hermann,' I said one day, ''I will bet any money that fellow Greinz is a police spy.'
> 'Now really, Putzi,' Carin broke in, 'he is such a nice fellow, and he is a wonderful gardener!'
> 'He is doing exactly what a spy ought to do! He has made himself indispensable.'

Later, Putzi asserted heatedly that he believed Greinz had also betrayed Hitler to the police after the Beer Hall *Putsch*, while the latter was hiding at Hanfstaengl's country home.

Following her husband's lead, Carin also joined the embryonic Nazi Party as a member. Despite making fun of her in private, Hitler was very glad indeed to have a titled Swedish Countess among his members. In sum, the Goerings proved to be a major national draw for the then-struggling, largely provincial NSDAP.

The NSDAP May Day Oberwiesenfeld Fiasco of 1 May 1923

By spring 1923, all of the various component contingents and units under Hitler and Goering were getting anxious to actually do something. On 1 May, a mass Nazi anti-Left rally was called for the Oberwiessenfeld outside Munich, and this time with many members bearing arms supplied by the Army.

Earlier, Goering had failed in his efforts to procure arms—including some artillery pieces—from the *Landespolizei* (or, as they were popularly called due to the colour of their uniforms, the Green Police).

Former German Army First World War Lieutenant Otto Strasser recalled seeing Goering in command of the SA on the Oberwiesenfeld, where they were joined by Dr Weber's *Bund Oberland Korps* and also Capt. Heiss's *Reichsbanner* (Imperial Flag) formation. He also remembered that 'Goering's uniform was much too tight for him'—an image of things to come. In his 1940 memoirs, Strasser recollected:

> Goering was an Air Force officer and an accomplished soldier who would certainly not have chosen adventurism if he could have remained in his chosen profession … He was a man of barely average intelligence and of pronounced physical brutality. He liked food, drink, and conviviality.

Reportedly, both Hitler and Goering now wore steel helmets, but no photo has yet emerged depicting Hitler so attired. Furious, Munich local Army 7th Infantry Division commander Gen. Otto von Lossow (1868–1938) demanded that his still-serving Captain Ernst Röhm ensured the arms were returned immediately. It did not help when Goering later recklessly threatened the General's life, but he was not arrested. On another occasion, Goering bombastically swore to fire on the SPD if its men paraded in the Munich streets—but he failed to when they did.

With the arms from the May Day demonstration duly returned, all three sheepish NSDAP leaders lost face with their men; it was a most public humiliation for them all. The insult rankled until six months later, when the trio again tried to foment an armed insurrection against the Socialist Berlin Weimar Republic—via its fractious, subordinate, provincial Munich government.

In October 1923, Lt Wilhelm Bruckner—Goering's subordinate as commanding officer of SA Storm Troop Munich—warned Hitler that his men were champing at the bit to do something—anything:

> We have so many unemployed in the ranks—men who have spent their last on uniforms—that the day is not far off when I will not be able to keep a hold on them unless you act. If nothing happens, we will lose control.

Hitler believed him. So did Otto Strasser, who recalled, seventeen years later, 'Despite discussions week after week, no serious steps had been taken by Goering.' Hitler wanted action. By the time that something did happen, Goering reportedly commanded fully 15,000 SA from across Bavaria.

Hermann Takes Center Stage: The Beer Hall Putsch, 8–9 November 1923

On 8–9 November 1923—two days before the fifth anniversary of Imperial Germany signing the Armistice that ended the First World War—Hitler called for his Nazis to invade an already announced Munich rally by the city's governmental office elite. In the event, it turned out to be both an ill-conceived and ill-executed attempt to take over the Weimar Republic by force, via co-opting the Bavarian government's own pre-set plans to defy the Reich capital.

Hitler's hidden motive was to prevent the local government and military from possibly having Bavaria secede from the national Reich, and also, maybe, joining Catholic Austria to form a state totally separate from Berlin. This was the very last thing that Hitler wanted, so he acted to forestall it.

The local, anti-Berlin power triumvirate was actually onstage—Army commander Gen. Hermann von Lossow, government chief Gustav Ritter von Kahr (1862–1934), and Green Police Chief Col. Hans von Seisser, (1874–1973).

At 8.30 p.m. a convoy of heavy trucks converged at the gated archway front of the *Burgerbraukellar* beer hall. In its van, an open car, was a steel-helmeted man with a drawn saber, standing on its running board.

True to form, Hermann Goering was at last making his grand entrance to Nazi lore. The trucks blocked off both ends of the street on Goering's orders, thus keeping away any government reinforcements. Dozens of his men, wielding rifles with fixed bayonets and submachine guns, rushed the entrance, shouting, 'Police out of the way! Clear the entrance! Get inside that building! All "Blue Police" inside!' Machineguns were also deployed on tripods. Still carrying his unsheathed sword, Captain Goering leaped from the running board, ran up the steps and through the archway, and then announced to his SA men, 'The Berlin government—the Reich government—is deposed. We recognize only the dictatorship of Ludendorff-Kahr-Hitler!'

Appearing to one eyewitness 'like Wallenstein on the march', Goering spun on his heel and entered the beer hall smartly. The Führer's burly bodyguard, Ulrich Graf (1898–1945), ran ahead to tell Hitler that the chronically late Goering was on time for once. These were the very men whom Hitler had been waiting for inside, before he could make his own dramatic move. Goering moved towards the hall's closed doors. 'There will be no shooting,' Goering told a local police officer. 'Keep your men under control, and there will be no trouble from mine, but do not attempt to leave the building—it is surrounded.'

Kahr was then still addressing the crowded hall of 3,000. Still brandishing the naked steel blade of his sword, Goering, his men, and Hitler's own entourage threw open the doors and boldly strode into the hall; in total, twenty men pushed their way forward toward the stage ahead. Due to the crush and tumult of the surprised crowd, it took the Nazis five minutes to reach the stage.

Hitler fired a single shot into the ceiling in order to gain everyone's attention, mounted the platform, shouted that the National Revolution against Berlin had begun, and claimed that the famous general of the First World War—Erich von Ludendorff (1865–1937)—was *en route* to lead the revolt. Holding the stunned Bavarian triumvirs at gunpoint, he prodded them into a side room, off-stage, to gain their enlistment in his announced crusade to seize power in Republican Germany.

Goering was left behind onstage with his SA men, well-armed with rifles and even some machine guns from the local Army depot. As time dragged on and the overheated crowd became surly and restive, Goering discharged a single pistol round into the ceiling to get them to calm down. 'After all,' he said, 'you have your beer! What are you worrying about?' This boorish and arrogant behaviour was an accurate representation of how both he and the Nazis in toto would conduct themselves a decade later, when they were in office.

The arrival of Ludendorff—even in civilian clothes, instead of his famous uniform— gave heart to all, convincing the triumvirate (at least outwardly) to sign on with the trio of revolutionaries. Hitler left to see how his Nazi compatriot Captain Röhm was doing at the occupied Bavarian War Ministry, leaving Goering in command at the beer hall, with all three captive officials still conferring. Without anything more to do, Goering set out a reconnaissance officer to gauge the mood of the city and the local military. His report was that the mass of the people seemed to be with them, but that the soldiery outside their control area appeared to be getting ready for battle.

Some of Goering's men were mustered outside, and he joined them there—'like a field marshal surveying his legions', as one recalled.

'I want to congratulate you on what you did tonight,' said Goering. 'It was a good job!' He then ordered that Hitler's bodyguard unit was to seize the local socialist newspaper—*The Munich Post*—but not to smash its presses. He also ordered the arrest of the city's communist mayor and the entire seven-member city council; they were to be held as hostages and future bargaining chips. These orders were duly fulfilled.

Acting under Goering's command that night was his aide, Sgt Julius Schaub (1898– 1967), who would later become the Führer's top personal adjutant from 1941–45. When Schaub confronted the startled mayor and councilmen at a meeting at the *Rathaus* (City Hall), he blurted out, 'I bring you orders from my Commander, Captain Goering, to raise the black-white-red [old Imperial] banner immediately!'

Undaunted, Mayor Eduard Schmid, sixty-two, retorted, 'Who is this Captain Goering? I have never heard of him!' Schaub briefly retreated, waiting for NSDAP reinforcements. When he returned, the mayor was pulled from his chair by his jacket collar and slammed against a wall, while Socialist Councilman Albert Nussbaum was clubbed in the head with a rifle butt. The Mayor and seven councilmen were brought back to the Nazi-occupied beer hall as hostages.

Goering's mixed bag of captured and detained political prisoners eventually num- bered fifty-eight, including senior citizens and even some wives and daughters who had insisted on accompanying the captives. Feeling their oats, some of Goering's men beat them, while others threatened executions that he ordered halted: 'We do not have the right or authority to execute—yet.'

Reportedly, it was Ludendorff who allowed the Bavarian trio to leave for the night, as they had given their word as officers to reunite with the conspirators at daylight. Instead, they revoked the oath of fealty extracted from them at gunpoint, and instead organized their own counter-coup against the Nazis and their other political allies.

Upon Hitler's return to the beer hall, he was upset to find that the trio had been let go, and was uncertain what to do next. Goering asserted, 'Those fellows did not come over to our side after all. They broke their word to the Führer, but the people are with us.' That last statement was true, both inside the beer hall and, later, in the mass gatherings in downtown Munich when daylight came. 'We are going to try the whole thing over again,' Goering concluded. To this end, he dispatched his subordinate, Lt Bruckner, to see if he could find a band to cheer up the now somewhat dispirited, listless NSDAP and other would-be revolutionaries.

Meanwhile, Gen. Ludendorff ordered that the entire force would march in the daylight to relieve Röhm at the War Ministry. Earlier, the general had soundly rejected Goering's suggestion that they should retreat to his Rosenheim birthplace instead, to await the arrival of more men; reinforcements were, indeed, on the way. Hitler agreed with the general in overruling Goering, for both believed that an open civil war might break out if they followed Hermann's way. Knowing that Captain Röhm was already surrounded at the Bavarian War Ministry, they feared they might also be closed in if they delayed any longer at the beer hall.

'We march!' barked Ludendorff, and so they did. Their die had been cast; about 2,000 men set forth, with Ludendorff, Hitler, and Goering in the van of the column. The marchers were cheered and encouraged by the population of Munich all along their route. The line of the march was organized thus: a trio of men side-by-side in columns of four, with fully a dozen such columns filling the streets. They looked impressive, but not flexible in deployment for action in a martial sense. The Führer's protection unit—the *Stosstrupp Hitler*—was on the left, the Munich SA regiment was in the center, and the partner *Bund Oberland* was on the right (the most honored post). The revolt's leadership corps marched in front, in two ranks, behind deployed skirmishers and standard bearers. Munich Infantry School students took the rearmost position, along with the SA Cavalry Corps.

Meanwhile, pro-Hitler nationalist leader Julius Streicher (1885–1946) was addressing a huge crowd in the city's downtown center.

No one—it was later asserted—thought that there would be any sort of fighting, and had they believed there would be, the formations would have been organized for combat instead. Conversely, they hoped that the other side would be marginalized by their apparent resolve, and either fade away or possibly join them. None of the marchers as yet knew the full scope of the Bavarian triumvirs' about-face.

During the initial phase of the march downtown, Hitler saw first-hand a sample of Goering's ruthlessness in action. Lt Bruckner's recruited band had simply gone home, and thus there was no music; neither could any photographs be taken of this historic

event, as Hitler had neglected to bring along his personal lensman, Heinrich Hoffmann. At the first Green Police roadblock at the Cornelius Bridge, SA Führer Goering strutted back and forth on the Rosenheimerstrasse, playing for time, and barked out, 'Get the prisoners—Schmid, Nussbaum, and the other councilmen. I want them at the rear of the column, and if there is any trouble, shoot them!'

Horrified, Hitler told Goering that he wanted no Socialist Party martyrs, and ordered Goering to send the elected hostages back to the beer hall. Goering's threat worked, however, as the marching columns were duly allowed to cross the contested span and continue on.

At a second crossing, the police formed a line and ordered the marchers to stop. Goering snarled, 'Keep going. Move ahead slowly.' As he heard the policemen being ordered to load their rifles with live ammunition, Goering yelled out, 'Do not shoot at your comrades!' Before either side realized it, a trumpet blast caused the marchers to rush the police line with fixed bayonets, clearing the roadway. Thus Goering's pluck, resolve, and luck kept the march going.

Goering was not one of those who ran when the firing broke out at the third and final roadblock—at the *Feldherrnhalle* (Field Marshals' Hall) near the Odeonsplatz—and he received his own critical wounding in Hitler's service. Either the Bavarian State (Green) Police or the Nazis opened fire, and in the resultant melee, fourteen NSDAP and three Green Police were killed outright, with Goering himself being hit in the groin and right thigh. Bender claims that Goering's groin wound missed an artery by mere millimeters; he fell to the pavement in pain. His NSDAP Party rival Alfred Rosenberg (1893–1946) saw him lying there from behind in the also-fallen second rank. One (possibly exaggerated) eyewitness account alleged a pile of fallen SA bodies in mounds 'a yard high'.

Bleeding profusely from 'reactionary bullets', Goering later claimed that at first he crawled to safety at the base of one of a pair of stone lions, which graced the square adjacent to the street where he had been shot. Reportedly, Goering was helped to safety by Lt Bruckner and two SA men. The sheltering stone lions remain even today.

The Storm Troopers carried him to the nearby home of Jewish furniture dealer Robert Ballin, where his wife—First World War nurse Bella Ballin, and her sister Ilse Ballin—began Goering's 'first responder' medical care. Despite knowing that their patient was a prominent Nazi, Ballin and her sister removed his boots and trousers and, to the best of their ability, cleaned and dressed his wounds with a towel. They cared for him until darkness, never calling the police either.

On the eve of his imminent arrest, Hitler named a custodian executive committee to run the Nazi Party in the meantime, with Rosenberg as interim leader and NSDAP publisher Max Amann as deputy, plus two to three other serving members—Julius Streicher, Hermann Esser, and designated fundraiser Putzi Hanfstaengl. Goering's name was left out, and it is possible that Hitler thought his SA Führer had died in the hail of police bullets.

The Goerings after the *Putsch*

Carin had herself driven to her husband's side, having been told of the collapse of the coup and his severe wounds by her elder sister, Fanny, who was an eyewitness. Early on 10 November 1923, they had Hermann carried to the clinic of a Nazi sympathizer, Professor Alwin Ritter von Asch, with the wound still bleeding.

SA man Franz Thanner drove the fugitive Goering couple to Bavaria's famous winter skiing resort of Garmisch-Partenkirchen—70 miles south of Munich—and to the home of Dutch Nazi sympathizer Maj. Schuler van Krieken (Ret.), where the Goerings reportedly hid for two days before making a run for the border by car.

At the Mittenwald frontier post, State Police Lt Nikolaus Maier—later a major general in the Luftwaffe—was notified to arrest Goering if he came there. This he did, and Goering's car was taken under police guard back to Garmisch-Partenkirchen, with the wounded man going either to the Wiggers Sanitarium or the Jeschke Hospital. Along the way, his car was greeted by enthusiastic Munich, pro-*Putsch* civilian crowds chanting, '*Heil Goering!*'—a heady first for him.

Oddly, Goering was not yet named in an arrest warrant as even von Kahr had not decided what to do with him. Since Lt Maier had no policemen to spare to guard Goering's door, he was permitted to deploy appointed auxiliary police. However, upon their arrival at 11 p.m. on 12 November, the Goerings had already fled.

Pledging his word of honor as a German officer not to escape, the wounded Goering was carried out, clad in a nightshirt and wrapped in a rug for warmth, and, again, driven by SA Man Thanner to the Mittenwald post. Noted German artifacts dealer, publisher-editor, and author Roger James Bender claims that this time they broke 'through the barrier into Austria'.

Manvell and Fraenkel asserted in 1962 that it was the local police themselves who took him to Austria on a stretcher, helping him cross the frontier with a fake passport. With or without police help in his escape, Goering was over the border and into neighboring Austria before an official pursuit was organized. Not for the first or the last time in his life, luck and daring had been on Goering's side. However, he had broken his word, and now he was a man without a country—a wanted fugitive from justice. Thus began Goering's political exile, which lasted for four of the very worst years of his life.

With Goering gone, his SA Führer command was vacant. His immediate successor was fellow First World War veteran officer Lt Col. Hermann Kriebel (1876–1941), according to one account. Another has it that interim Führer-by-Committee Alfred Rosenberg appointed former Army Maj. Walter Buch to take over the SA. In future, he would become father-in-law to one of Goering's mortal enemies—Martin Bormann.

Austrian Exile, 1923–24

Equipped with his false passport, Goering was taken to the Golden Lamb Inn at Seefeld, Austria, and later moved to the Tirolerhof Hotel at Innsbruck on 12 November 1923. The hotel was owned by a local Nazi sympathizer. For mail from Germany, Goering

took the alias of 'Dr Sopelsa', No. 9 *Bahnhofsplatz* (Train Hotel Plaza), Innsbruck.

From 13 November to 24 December 1923 Goering was an inpatient at Innsbruck Hospital. Bender asserts:

> His severe blood loss and pain from infection led to his being treated heavily with opiates. As a result, Goering became severely addicted to morphine.

Although this suggests Goering's addiction was something new, some accounts report Goering taking morphine as a fighter pilot in the First World War. Regardless, his wounds had turned septic and there was a danger of blood poisoning setting in. Carin wrote to her mother on 30 November 1923:

> Hermann is in a terrible state! His leg hurts so much he can hardly bear it. Four days ago, almost all the wounds that had healed broke out again, and there is a terrible amount of pus in the leg still. He was X-rayed, and they discovered a mass of fragments of shot as well as dirt from the street buried in his thigh muscles.
>
> They operated on him with an anesthetic, and for the past three days, he has been very feverish. His mind seems to wander; sometimes, he even cries, and sometimes he dreams of street fighting. All the time he is suffering indescribable pain. His whole leg is fitted with little rubber tubes to draw out the pus...

Carin wrote to her mother again on 8 December 1923:

> I'm sitting here by my beloved Hermann's sickbed. I have got to watch him suffer in body and soul—and there is hardly anything I can do to help him ... His wound is just all pus, all over his thigh. He bites the pillow because it hurts him so much, and he moans all the time ... It is exactly a month since they shot at him, and in spite of being dosed with morphine every day, his pain stays just as bad as ever.

The rubber drainage tubes were removed on 22 December 1923, and on Christmas Eve Goering was discharged from the hospital on crutches; he returned to reside at the Tirolerhof Hotel. The Innsbruck local Nazi SA gave them a Christmas tree.

By 27 December, Hermann was able to walk without crutches. As his health improved, the semi-invalid Goering attempted to take part in Austrian Nazi politics, even taking a night train to Vienna to visit its headquarters.

On New Year's Eve 1923–24, Hitler's lawyer reportedly visited the Goerings; Hermann did not return to Munich to stand trial with Hitler, as Hess did. The hotel management threw them a party as well, with exultant cries of, 'Heil to our hero!' More than 200 telegrams of support arrived, but not what they needed most—money.

Since Hermann was a wanted man, the Austrian government told the Goerings to leave the country, and thus he received an Austrian passport on 5 March 1924 at Innsbruck. Another German warrant for his arrest was issued on 24 May 1924.

Putzi Hanfstangl also fled to neighboring Austria, along with Rossbach and Rosenberg. He later recalled:

I went back with Carin to her hotel, and found to my surprise that she was living in opulent fashion. The rest of us exiles were going around like tramps, but this was never the Goerings' way, and their ostentation caused a lot of bad blood in the party…

Indeed, this was also the first break between the Goerings and Hitler. As for Goering himself, Putzi averred:

He simply had no sense of the value of money, and when he finally left Austria via Venice for Sweden, I helped to finance the trip. I received little thanks, and never saw my money back, yet somehow this did not cause offense. He was a very attractive, rollicking fellow, the type that can get away with this sort of thing.

Another astute observer of the Goering couple during their enforced Austrian sojourn was memoirist Kurt G. W. Ludecke, who recalled in 1937:

Mrs Goering … was a charming woman, quiet and sympathetic, who walked with a particularly handsome and free carriage.

Goering showed without reserve that he adored her. I imagine he felt in his heart that she was far superior to himself. So did I! On this first meeting—and always thereafter—I was impressed by the way that she, a foreigner, stood at his side through every trial of the party, spending her fortune on it and him.

During the Innsbruck visit, she was still somewhat overwrought from having personally engineered her husband's escape into Austria. Her health—always delicate—never recovered from that strain…

Ludecke also recalled another side of Goering:

The day of my departure, we lunched together. His mind was focused on the food … he ordered in enormous portions and stowed away methodically, easing it down with long draughts of wine.

At one moment during this stuffing performance, Frau Goering was called from the table, leaving us alone. The captain's jaws still moved up and down, but I saw an expression of pleasant anticipation come into his eyes.

Then he shifted his bulk in the chair, lifted one buttock, and gave vent to a thundering explosion. 'You will pardon me, won't you?' he asked, seeing my startled frown—and a second volley echoed the first.

On reflection, I decided to credit him with some delicacy. Who would have expected him to wait until his wife was out of range?

The first months of the Goering's lives as political exiles and legal fugitives were not all that bad, as even Carin herself admitted on 23 February 1924—their first wedding anniversary—in a letter to her mother:

We are living here so well in this hotel, the most first class one in Innsbruck.

The owner is a Hitler man, and lets us live here at cost price. We have a big bedroom with a bathroom, and even a big, comfortable sitting room. The food is very good, we eat *à la carte*, and we get a 30% reduction on everything we order!

The waiters are nearly all Storm Troop men, and idolize Hermann! The whole time that we could not pay, they were so sweet to us. They said we must not think of paying before we had got everything in order, and they would look on it as an insult. If we were never able to pay, it would not matter in the slightest, it would only be a small sacrifice they would be only too glad to make for Hermann., and—in any event—the hotel will give the whole amount that Hermann has to pay here to the Movement! [This was in early 1924, fully fourteen years before the later Nazi union with Austria.] You must admit that a thing like that is magnificent, and we meet with similar things every day, the poorest people come with everything they can, and offer it to Hitler.

Aside from Putzi, another visitor was Hitler's sister, Paula Wolf.

Goering was unsuccessful in recuperating completely from his wounds, and Carin also became ill—duty nurse Anna Beran tended to both of them. Carin wrote to her mother about Hermann's patience: 'He is so loving, patient, and kind, but at heart he is in deep despair … He was wounded—not only physically—but perhaps even more mentally.' Hermann had never thought that Hitler's revolution would be betrayed by German officers, who were honor-bound to support it. For his part, Corporal Adolf Hitler never again trusted their word.

Frischauer believed that the groin wound affected Hermann sexually, and that he and Carin were not able to have sex from then on. Factually, it is known that the two never had children of their own; Carin was unable to have any more after the birth of her son Thomas. He asserted that the couple shared a marital bed until the end of their marriage.

Hermann's potency or not is still an open question, but he was apparently able to have normal relations with his second wife later on, and also to father his daughter, Edda, in 1938. Whatever the case may be with regards to Goering's sexual dysfunction (or lack thereof), he reportedly felt the pain from his 1923 wounding until the day he died.

Above: An aerial view of Munich's famed *Konigplatz/King's Plaza* during the era of the Third Reich. This is where Hermann Goering first saw Adolf Hitler, in the fall of 1922. Goering joined the Nazi Party on 12 October 1922. (*HHA*)

Left: Captain Hermann Goering wearing a 1916-style 'coal scuttle' German Army steel helmet, emblazoned with a painted white swastika on its front, and an early-1920s Nazi armband. He is wearing a Blue Max medal and a British Sam Browne belt over a trench coat, capturing the very image he wanted to project the most—that of a daring swashbuckler, ready for anything. It was this kit that he wore during the aborted Beer Hall Putsch of 8–9 November 1923, which became a turning point in his tumultuous life. According to noted authority Roger Bender, the three white stripes on Goering's armband indicate 'an Office Leader in the rank of *Reichsleiter*'. Heinrich Hoffmann recalled this photo as his 'first portrait of Goering—dripping wet and arrayed for war'. He sold 40,000 copies of this picture in 1923 in Munich alone. (*HHA*)

Goering's SA Stormtroopers dip their colors in salute during a ceremony in snow-covered Munich in 1923. The theme of both Hitler and Goering was simple—'Red Europe: Swastika versus Red Star'. Goering's opponents mocked him as '*Der gestiefelter Kater*' ('Puss in Boots'). He called them 'the God-denying reds and the black (Catholic) rats!' (*HHA*)

German Army rifles are returned by the SA and others during the fiasco of 1 May 1923 that so embarrassed both Hitler and Goering; they vowed that they would do better next time. In 1945, speaking to interrogator George Shuster, Goering recalled, 'Boy how those beer mugs flew! One nearly laid me out!' Meanwhile, the Richthofen Association allegedly blackballed him over the unresolved questions regarding his aerial kills record during the First World War. (*HHA*)

A nervous Capt. Goering (fifth from right) bites his lip during a September 1923 inspection of the *Oberland Bund* (Highland League) Free Corps. The photograph features a First World War hero, former German Army Quartermaster Gen. Erich Ludendorff (center, wearing spiked helmet), seen here talking with what appears to be an Austrian officer; this was prior to the dramatic Nazi attempt to seize power later that fall. (*HHA*)

The arched stone gateway of the Munich *Burgerbraukellar* beer hall as it appeared during the attempted Nazi coup of 'black Friday', 8–9 November 1923. During later battles with the KPD, fists, blackjacks, table legs, brass knuckles, and even pistols were used by both sides. (*HHA*)

Following page, above: The inside of a crowded Munich beer hall in 1923, perhaps the *Burgerbraukellar* itself. It was just this kind of noisy crowd of 5,000 that Hitler and Goering faced during the night of 8–9 November. The Nazi leaders and their armed entourage entered the hall from the rear that night, facing the stage opposite. Some claim that Goering took the oaths of the top three hostages to return as valid, letting them go; when they caused the revolt to fail, Goering earned Hitler's enmity. (*HHA*)

From 1933–39 the events of 8–9 November 1923 were reenacted annually at the original location, as seen here in 1937. From left to right are Franz Ritter von Epp (standing), Deputy Führer Rudolf Hess, Adolf Hitler, his 1923 bodyguard Ulrich Graf, Goering (wearing his brown SA uniform), party photographer Prof. Heinrich Hoffmann (with his trusty Leica camera), party publisher Max Amann, Hitler's aide Julius Schaub (obscured by Amann), and Dr Wilhem Frick. The white speaker's lectern can be seen at the upper left of the frame. A group of SA men are behind Prof. Hoffmann, wearing the 1923-style Stormtrooper uniform. Hitler's bodyguard, Ulrich Graf, survived the Second World War and died in 1950, aged seventy-eight. (*HGA*)

A smiling, saluting Goering (left) strides in front of his 1923 SA battalion commander, Lt Wilhelm Bruckner (center), who was now under Goering's command. This photograph was taken at the 9 November 1937 commemoration. Bruckner was an SA lieutenant general and top personal adjutant to Hitler until 1940. Note also the smiling SA 'Old Fighters' on the right. (*HGA*)

During the putsch, Goering ordered the successful arrest of the Mayor of Munich and his entire city council by armed SA men. Mayor Eduard Schmid (left, wearing dark hat and overcoat) had never heard of the Captain who ordered his arrest. (*HHA*)

Above: Goering also saw to it that truckloads of his armed and helmeted SA men appeared in downtown Munich to add visible weight to the ongoing Nazi uprising. The man seen standing above the crowd on the Marienplatz (on the right) was Hitler's political ally Julius Streicher, addressing the very interested crowds on the morning after the *Burgerbraukellar* was seized. Up until the aborted march later that morning, the rising seemed to be a success. (*HHA*)

Right: Before the march has started on 9 November 1937, Julius Streicher (1885–1946) makes a point to Hermann Goering, again seen wearing his 1923 armband. To the left, over Streicher's shoulder, the man carrying the famed Nazi 'blood banner' is Jakob Grimminger. (*HGA*)

Another image of the 1937 commemoration of the Beer Hall Putsch. From left to right, striding, are Adolf Huhnlein, unknown man, and Dr Friedrich Weber (of the *Oberland Bund*), Goering, Hitler, Ulrich Graf, and, in the front rank, Lt Col. Hermann Kriebel. The tall, flame-topped pylons flanking the men symbolized the presence of a dead Nazi martyr killed in the original march's finale at the Odeonsplatz. According to one account, Goering himself gave the order for the marchers to fire on the *Landespolizei*. (*HGA*)

Above: Two of the stone lions on the Odeonsplatz are seen here on the left, in front of the famed Field Marshals' Hall in downtown Munich. After having been wounded in the groin by bullets fired from Bavarian Landespolizei rifles at the far left, Goering said that he crawled to safety behind these lions, from where he was then carried by SA men to a nearby flat occupied by Jews. Here, he received his initial medical treatment from two Jewish sisters, the Ballins, whom he helped escape to South America in 1939 as thanks. (*HHA*)

Right: Another view of the commemoration; Goering (left) stands at the foot of the stairs of Hitler's speaking platform at the Propylaen, an Ionian, Greek-style archway built in 1862 on the western side of the Konigsplatz. As Hitler speaks, Grimminger holds the Blood Flag behind him—so-called because it held some of the blood of the slain sixteen martyrs of 1923. At the center stands German Army Field Marshal and War Minister Werner von Blomberg, Goering's rival for command of the Army. Graf stands to von Blomberg's left, and behind the marshal is Nazi Justice Minister Dr Hans Frank. (*HGA*)

3

DRUGS, 1923–27

The Nazi Bonnie & Clyde: Life on the Run

The Goerings had not been forgotten about in Germany. In a letter to her mother, Carin stated: 'Our Munich villa is watched, our mail is being confiscated, bank accounts have been blocked, the car impounded…' Rumor has it that the Goerings were living at least partially off of Austrian NSDAP collection boxes during this period.

Overnight, it seemed, their insulated and comfortable world had been turned upside down. Their maid, Marie, stayed in their Obermenzing home to protect their possessions, selling off her own things in order to help keep their establishment financially afloat. Additionally, the gardener whom Hanfstangl had distrusted before the Nazi revolt actually now came to their aid; he fulfilled the role of secret courier, crossing the frontier to provide the Goerings with food and news, until he was caught and jailed for two weeks.

Alarmed, Carin wrote home about her stricken husband:

> I can scarcely recognize him … hollow-faced and white as snow. His whole being is different. He hardly speaks a word, depressed by this act of treachery to a degree that I would never have thought possible in this case, but I hope that his inner balance and his old energy will return when he has regained his strength.

Indeed, his energy did return, but he never regained the inner balance that had been destroyed by the Green Police bullets fired against the Nazis—a scenario he had thought impossible.

The year 1924 turned out bleakly for the Goerings; there was no political amnesty from Germany, nor did Hitler submit Goering's name as a Nazi Deputy candidate for the Reichstag elections that April. In Bavaria, Hermann was becoming an 'unperson', but this contrasted with his rising celebrity in Austria. The couple was lionized at the hotel by both management and the other patrons, Nazi sympathizers all. It was there that the couple celebrated their first (or second) wedding anniversary on 3 February 1924, with Hermann giving his wife a portable typewriter—allegedly paid for by the Austrian Nazi Party. Carin sent a letter home:

I must tell you what a lovely time we had yesterday … It began in the morning with a wonderful bunch of red roses and carnations—about a hundred of them—just as though Hermann had come into millions!

There was a lovely white silk blouse, hand-embroidered … We had a lovely day, all alone, by ourselves … This happens so rarely now—he is always surrounded by people. We had a bottle of champagne for supper, and remembered all that has happened in the past, all the difficulties that are now overcome, and all that we have gone through together, that has certainly brought us closer to one another and deepened our love and understanding of each other.

The distress of the couple served to soften the feelings of some of their estranged Swedish relatives. While Hermann remained in Austria to continue his treatments, Carin returned to Munich to raise money to finance their stay abroad—since as a political exile, Hermann could not come home himself without being arrested and jailed.

Hermann wrote to his mother-in-law as well, hoping that they might be invited to live in Sweden; however, they instead found themselves living abroad for a year in Fascist Italy. They were not wanted at Stockholm.

In Munich, the Hitler-Ludendorff trial lasted from 24 March until 1 April 1924, with Hitler refusing to have Goering join them among the accused. Hitler was possibly not taking any chances that the flamboyant Goering would become the main attraction, as he twice would later on—during the Reichstag Fire Trial a decade later, and at Nuremberg during 1945–46. Paula Hitler-Wolf visited the Goerings again, perhaps as her brother's emissary.

Following the conviction and jailing of the conspirators, the Goerings left Austria in the spring of 1924. It is believed that the reason was political, as explained by Gritzbach in 1938; he states that 'the Tyrolese government was "black"', meaning Catholic, and thus wanted to extradite the Goerings to Catholic Bavaria, where Hermann would be charged with treason.

Italian Exile: Venice–Florence–Rome–Sienna, May 1924–Spring 1925

Following several days of sightseeing in Venice and Florence, the fugitive pair next went to Rome, checking in at the elegant Hotel Eden on 11 May 1924. Safe from extradition, Goering and his wife were nonetheless chagrined to discover that *Il Duce*, Benito Mussolini, refused to recognize Hermann's claim to represent the now-jailed Hitler. Nor would Mussolini even grant Goering a personal audience, resulting in a lifelong grudge. Indeed, despite what numerous English-language authors have alleged, *Il Duce* never met with Goering until the latter was an official member of the legal government and cabinet of the sovereign state of Germany in April 1933—almost nine years later.

The reason was simple, and should have been obvious to Goering as a practical politician—as the legal ruler of Italy, Mussolini was ill-advised to meet with a fugitive following an illegal revolt in a neighboring country—a country with which his own land maintained proper diplomatic relations. On the other hand, it is to Goering's credit that he would receive the rescued Mussolini in Germany in September 1943, after the latter's overthrow in Rome the previous July—quite a reversal of fortune!

On 5 May 1924 the Goerings arrived in Venice, staying at the Hotel Britannia on the famous Grand Canal. Since the owner was again a German Nazi, Rudolfo Walther, they both lived and ate at cut-rate prices, as Carin wrote to her mother: 'The food is marvelous—lobster, soup, omelet, chicken with salad, lamb cutlets and spaghetti, and fruit for lunch yesterday!' In many ways, this enforced political exile was a long-delayed honeymoon for the expatriate couple. Carin's letter continued:

> One day we bathed in the sea off Lido. It is just like a dream.... Yesterday ended with an absolutely heavenly evening; we went out at about 10 p.m. in a gondola, from which dangled a green lamp … The Grand Canal swarmed with gondolas … and everyone sang.... How romantic it was!

However, Hermann was all too aware of their precarious financial state, and later told Thomas von Kantzow:

> I remember once standing before the Trevi Fountain at 3 a.m., and wondering what everyone would say if they found me lying at the bottom of it instead of those coins that people throw in for luck. Then I decided that the water was too shallow to drown in, and I did not want to throw myself in.

With Carin herself now unwell and Goering growing pale and fat, they lived in Italy as they had in Austria and Germany, on her alimony payments and money sent to them from their Swedish friends. They resided in Fascist Italy like this for almost a year, until the spring of 1925. It would be another time that Hermann tried to forget about in later years, a continuing embarrassment from those days of near-poverty. Carin even went to Munich to ask both Ludendorff and Hitler, released by then, for money on 15 April 1925. However, she received nothing from the latter but an autographed self-portrait: 'To the honored wife of my SA commander'. Carin was, however, able to return to Italy with enough money from other sources to take them on to Sweden via Austria, Czechoslovakia, the free city of Danzig, and Poland. Still, the Kantzow alimony money remained their main means of financial support.

Goering continued to use morphine during the entirety of their Italian exile, but none of his former biographers can identify the source from which his drugs flowed. He had displayed a limp in Austria that necessitated his use of a cane, which continued on into his time in Fascist Italy—harking back to his rheumatism of the First World War years. The couple's Austrian bills were reportedly paid for (at least partially) by the father of Friedelin Wagner, as arrangements were made for them to be received at Venice.

The Goering pair left Austria at the behest of its government—not by invitation of any kind from Mussolini or his government. In her 1935 biography of Carin, her sister, Fanny, makes the incorrect claim that Hermann met Mussolini during 1924–25—an assertion incorrectly repeated by many of his later, English-language biographers. However, Goering did meet with two other Italian Fascists while he was in the country—Italian diplomat Giuseppe Bastianini, *Il Duce*'s personal representative to Germany (via an introduction by journalist and Fascist staff member Dr Leo Negrelli), and also one Giuseppe Renzetti. The topic of debate was the thorny issue of Italy's retention of the German-speaking South Tyrol area, which had formerly belonged to Imperial Austria but was made an Italian domain after the First World War, in return for Italy fighting on the side of the Western Allies.

Goering sought to reassure Mussolini that the South Tyrol area would remain Italian after the Nazis took office in Berlin, and this was indeed the case until Mussolini's removal from power in July 1943, nineteen years later. Goering's meddling in German-Italian relations—with no brief whatsoever from his own country's foreign office—came at a very bad political moment for *Il Duce*, as he was doing all he could to remain in office himself following the murder of his main political opponent by Fascists. Undaunted, would-be Nazi diplomat Hermann Goering nevertheless began a long correspondence with Dr Negrelli on behalf of his Venetian hotel benefactor, Walther, whose Britannia Hotel had been seized because it was German-owned. Goering sent ten letters on his persistent behalf, angering both the Italians and Hitler, back in Munich.

Goering's argument was that the Jewish-owned, Italian *Banca Commerciale* wanted Walther's property to cement a hotel monopoly in Venice. In return for being his lobbyist, Walther allowed the Goerings to live at his hotel rent-free for a year, and was never repaid financially by Hermann.

As anti-Semitism did not become the official policy of the Fascist government until 1938—fourteen years later—and as Mussolini himself had a long-term Jewish mistress, Goering's efforts flopped completely. He also made new enemies by asserting that the Vatican and the Catholic Church were the outright enemies of Italian Fascism, at a time when *Il Duce* was working to complete a political reconciliation with St Peter's that would end the strife that had existed since 1871. That was duly concluded in 1929, despite Hermann's interference.

Goering's efforts angered German Catholics in Bavaria as well, where Hitler was currently desperately trying to reestablish the party as a legal entity following the Beer Hall Putsch and his release from prison. Here again, bumbling NSDAP amateur diplomat Goering was creating more domestic problems for Hitler that the Führer did not need. However, aware of Mussolini's problems with the Italian left, Goering even volunteered to fight to defend *Il Duce* and Italian Fascism against the Socialists, should that prove helpful, as he had so recently done in Germany.

Ever-watchful when money was needed, Goering asked for a loan of 2,000,000 lire from Mussolini to help rebuild the shattered NSDAP in Bavaria, but never got any money from *Il Duce* or his agents. As yet another means of acquiring money, he also volunteered to become Mussolini's Nazi biographer.

Meanwhile, in the Reich the unpopular Italian rule of the Austrian-German South Tyrol was a hot-button issue that unified Germany against what was, after all, yet another hated provision of the 1919 Treaty of Versailles. Hitler's support for Mussolini's rule of the Tyrol—via Goering or not—led the Nazi Führer to renounce his Austrian citizenship on 7 April 1925. As he did not become a German citizen (even though he had fought in the German Army all through the First World War) until 1932, Hitler was stateless—literally a man without a country—for seven years. Like the Führer, Goering also promoted a triple alliance of Germany, Italy, and Great Britain as the goal for the future.

In addition to the bogus meeting with Mussolini, some of Goering's previous biographers alleged that Hermann maintained a political correspondence with his Führer; this was also inaccurate. An apparently equally untrue claim was that Goering served as the Führer's agent to secure a Hitler-Mussolini meeting; this meeting did not occur until June 1934, when both he and Hitler had been in the German government for eighteen months. All through the eleven years of 1922–33, Mussolini refused to see Hitler—much less Goering. However, in 1924 *Il Duce* sent a general to meet with German Army leader Gen. Hans von Seeckt, who was secretly building the Black Luftwaffe at that time.

Italy saw the Nazis as anti-Semitic, anti-Catholic, and even pagan; as a result, Goering solidified his requests into only two cardinal points. Firstly, he wanted to interview *Il Duce* as a freelance NSDAP journalist, and secondly, he wanted to have the Walther problem solved to the benefit of his Venetian German hotel benefactor; however, he failed in both appeals.

In Rome, the Goerings left the more expensive Hotel Eden for the cheaper Hotel de Russie due to their chronic lack of money, and Signor Bastianini asked Hermann to leave Rome altogether. On 11 August 1924 the couple returned to Venice, where Walther asked them to vacate the Grand Hotel Britannia; again, they complied. Goering yet again wrote to the Fascists on 19 September, asking for help: 'Italy must seek to find strong allies. One such ally would be a Nationalist Socialist Germany under Hitler's leadership.' Thus a loser in the First World War addresses a victor in the same conflict, representing a party that had been banned in 1923 and the leader of which was still in prison! If nothing else, Hermann Goering was a man of persistence and panache.

Return to Sweden, 1925–27

By 22 April 1925 Carin had successfully sold their Munich home at last, and more money was being sent to the couple from Sweden; they therefore established themselves anew in Stockholm. This was in a small apartment, rented for them by Carin's family, at No. 23 Odengarten, a dismal street away from the more fashionable Ostermalm— where most of Carin's relatives lived. The Fock family helped to furnish it for them, with the rest of their furniture from Munich removed from pawnshops and returned. It was the end of the Goerings' nomadic hotel lifestyle of November 1923–Spring 1925.

The fugitives had traveled to Sweden via Austria, Czechoslovakia, and Poland overland, and by steamer across the Baltic Sea from Danzig—places where Goering was not wanted by the law. From 1938–39, under Goering's leadership, Nazi forces would invade and occupy all four locations.

Carin contracted tuberculosis, while Hermann periodically pawned his wristwatch (possibly for drugs) and resumed his prior freelancing career at Swedish newspapers, but was unable to find permanent employment. Goering's in-laws were shocked at his physical appearance; he was no longer the dashing war hero of five years ago. As for

Carin, their daughter and sister, she had developed the lung problem and heart disease that would kill here a mere seven years later, aged forty-two. As Hermann sought more permanent work, Carin visited her friends or was sick at home; it was the start of her long, fatal decline. The Stockholm lawyer Carl Ossbahr remembered that 'her wish was [Goering's] command. He was not her slave, but almost'. Out of work and with little money left, Hermann resumed piloting passengers from Stockholm to Danzig for the *Nordiska Flygrederiet* airline for many weeks, but reportedly was fired when his ongoing drug addiction was discovered.

Carin apparently helped pay for his addiction, fulfilling the role of enabler, but it the identity of his supplier remains unknown. Thomas von Kantzow, thirteen, became alarmed by his step-father's growing violence, and when Hermann threatened to leap out of an open window, to his death, Thomas yelled, 'Let him do it, Mama!'

At thirty-two, Hermann was described by one local physician as having the body 'of an elderly woman, with much fat, and a pale, white skin'. The length of his morphine addiction was now approaching two years, and he self-injected eukodal two to three times per day. He was also becoming more violently dangerous, throwing glasses and crockery at friends and occasionally even threatening Carin in his delirium.

On 6 August 1925, Goering voluntarily entered a drug rehabilitation clinic at the Aspuddens Nursing Home in Stockholm for his morphine addiction. In a letter to one of Carin's friends in Norway, he wrote: 'I want to regain my former health'; however, he suffered a violent relapse. On 30 August 1925 Goering, still a patient, broke into a medicine cabinet and injected himself with eukodal twice. He reportedly threw a knife at a nurse, and when she again refused to give him drugs, he threatened to strangle her. Bender describes another example of his erratic behaviour:

> [Goering] leaped from his bed, demanding more medication. When this was refused, he dressed himself and attempted to leave the building, but found the doors locked.
>
> He ran to his room, retrieving a sword cane that he brandished at nursing staff until they gave him the requested injections. When police and firemen came… that evening, he vainly attempted to resist, but was placed in a straitjacket and transported to the Katarina Hospital [on 1 September 1925].

Langbro Asylum for the Insane, 2 September–7 October 1925

Frightened for her own safety, Carin at last signed civil commitment papers, sending Hermann to the Langbro Asylum for lunatics, near Stockholm, for an enforced detox-ification cure. He was detained in a straitjacket and placed on the ward for violent patients. A physician who had seen Goering prior to his civil commitment recalled that 'Goering was very violent … but was not insane'. A 1925 psychiatric report asserted that although he was outwardly brave, he lacked an inner, moral courage. In Leonard Mosley's *The Reich Marshal* (1974), Mosley stated his belief that the overall effect of Goering's wounds and drug addiction had somehow destabilized his glands, leading to his weight gain.

Diagnosed as suffering from severe withdrawal symptoms, Goering again threatened suicide. He was placed in solitary confinement, where the unruly patient shouted, 'I am not insane, I am not insane! I have no business being here!' The debate continues over his sanity at that time.

Goering stayed at Langbro for three months the first time, reaching what must have been the low point of his life so far. His doctors thought him 'an evil person, a bad character', and 'a sentimental person lacking in fundamental moral courage'. His withdrawal was at its worst at the start of his confinement, and he was given sodium bromide to help him sleep; however, he was taken off the medication because it seemed to make him delusional. He would again be given sodium bromide during 1945–46, at Nuremberg Prison. One psychiatric report read:

> I saw Goering in an unvarnished condition, and it was not a pleasant sight … His character was what psychiatrists call 'hysterical' … His personality did not keep together coherently. At one moment, he displayed one personality, and a few minutes later, quite a different one.
>
> He was sentimental about his own people, and utterly callous about everybody else … One was always … afraid of him. I always knew that if I made a false step, he might do terrible things … Having been a German officer, he was not difficult to discipline … I think that explained his attitude to Hitler, too.

An iron bar was found in his room when it was searched; he was intending to use it as a weapon to prevent being recommitted to the violent ward.

Goering was medically discharged on 7 October 1925, but on 16 April 1926 Carin was diagnosed with epilepsy, and she lost a civil suit to get custody of her son from her former husband. Hermann suffered a relapse, and re-entered the Langbro Asylum on 22 May 1926 to resume detoxification. He was discharged a second time, finally cured (as some of his biographers assert), and allegedly never again returned to full morphine addiction.

Swedish anti-Nazis reportedly Photostatted Goering's medical records, and these were duly published worldwide in the 1933 publication *The Brown Book of the Reichstag Fire and Hitler Terror*. From 1928 to 1933, Goering's political opponents in Germany used his medical records to argue that he was not fit to help Hitler rule the Reich, but he managed to overcome the stigma—both with the Führer and the German people.

Nils von Kantzow had defeated Carin's suit for custody of their son by citing this certified report, signed by Dr Karl A. R. Lundberg:

> Captain Goering suffers from morphinism, and his wife Carin Goering—née Baroness von Fock—suffers from epilepsy. Their home must, therefore, be regarded as unfit for the son Thomas von Kantzow.

A Swedish court concurred. Meanwhile, Nils von Kantzow had his own problems; he was removed from a teaching post after becoming involved in a fight over Goering on a train.

From Straitjacket to Politics

Thus 'cured', Goering was able finally to secure gainful employment as a salesman, selling German-made parachutes in Sweden. He also allegedly received a salesman's post from the Bavarian Motor Works, as its representative in Sweden. Both were boons to his self-worth and overall mental state.

According to Butler and Young's *Marshal Without Glory* (1951), Goering made a trip to the United Kingdom prior to entering Hitler's cabinet in 1933. It is stated that he visited the German Embassy, stayed with his wartime friend, Captain Beaumont, for three days, and lunched at *The Savoy*. This same account asserts that he even laid a funeral wreath at the RAF memorial, in his capacity as the last wartime commander of the Richthofen Squadron; he was wearing a civilian suit, with a miniature Blue Max in his jacket lapel. Goering was supposedly later found drunk, fully dressed, lying on the floor of Beaumont's dressing room. This claim seems too fanciful, but it nevertheless makes for an engaging anecdote.

In October 1927 the first-term German Reich President and Field Marshal, Paul von Hindenburg, issued a general political amnesty for refugees like Goering; this at last allowed him to return home to Germany without fear of arrest or charges being filed against him. The Goerings had been in exile for a little over three years. With Carin ill, and no fixed address back home as yet, Hermann returned to Germany alone to seek his fortune anew in the hated Weimar Republic. He was not entirely empty-handed, however—he was granted permission to sell Swedish-made Turnblad automatic-opening parachutes in the country.

4

KAMPFZEIT, 1928-32

A Cool Reception

At Munich, Röhm arranged for Ludendorff's adjutant, Maj. Hans Streck, to allow Goering to sleep on his home's living-room couch overnight, as Hermann had very little money. In the morning, he simply dressed and left when a servant arrived to clean.

Goering found that Hitler was decidedly cool towards him, with the animosity springing from Goering's failure with Mussolini and also because of critical statements that Goering allegedly made in Austria, with regards to how the Führer had 'bungled' the Beer Hall Putsch. Additionally, some accounts have asserted that it was Capt. Goering (and not Gen. Ludendorff) who had let the trio of detained Bavarians free from the beer hall. If so, then it was really Goering who had made the coup's fatal blunder after all. It reportedly took three tension-filled meetings with Hitler for Goering to gain his desired electoral slot on the Nazi ballot for 1928.

During his absence, his party rival Alfred Rosenberg had cancelled Goering's membership. This was restored on 1 April 1928—but his command over the SA was not. Hitler might have been annoyed that Goering had not returned to stand trial with him; in fact, Goering would never regain the full command of the SA that he had enjoyed in 1923. Perhaps Goering's conduct at the Beer Hall Putsch had convinced Hitler that the Captain could prove to be a powerful threat to his own security, particularly as the number of SA recruits swelled. Hitler instead reportedly told Goering to go to the Reich capital, Berlin, and establish himself there as the Führer's personal ambassador. After that, Hitler hinted, they could reassess Goering's future in the Nazi Party.

Several early biographies claim that late in 1927, Goering secured an appointment as a Berlin salesman for BMW aircraft engines, in addition to his work for the Tornblad parachute firm. However, in 2014 a BMW spokesperson assured me that no records were found in the company's archives that substantiated this claim.

The Nazi *Kampfzeit* (Time of Struggle)

The *Kampfzeit* represented the early period of the Nazi Party, prior to the Beer Hall Putsch, but also referred especially to the ten years afterwards, until Hitler and Goering were appointed to national office on 30 January 1933. In general, these were lean years for the Nazis at the polls, with pitched street battles against the KPD (German Communist Party) and the less-radical Socialists (from the German Socialist Party); the latter had bedeviled the German right since 1848. In addition to these external struggles, Hitler and Goering faced challenges from within the party, from both its left and right wings. These continued for the first eighteen months of the Nazi's time in office, from 1933 to 1934, during which time they also faced conflict with Reich President and Field Marshal Paul von Hindenburg, the German Army, the remaining monarchists from 1918, and the Nazi SA Storm Troopers themselves.

As he explained to Dr Gilbert after the Second World War, Goering was anti-democratic by his very nature, in both theory and practice:

> The idea of a democracy was absolutely repulsive to me! Whoever heard of a new Head of State every few years, and elected representatives to tell the President what he could and could not do? … It was only the election of Hindenburg [in 1925] that made the Republic even half-way tolerable.

When asked about the program of the NSDAP at Nuremberg, Goering responded in his own, unique way:

> How often I have been asked, 'Well, what actually is your program?' I have been able to point full of pride to our simple and good SA men and say, 'There stand the bearers of our program! They bear it upon their clear, free brows, and the program is called: Germany! All the principles that can serve the rise and preservation of Germany are acknowledged as the only points in our program. All others—that may damage the Fatherland—are rejected, and are to be destroyed.

By this point Carin was very ill with tuberculosis, and was told by her Swedish doctors in January 1927 that she had a few years to live at most. In a letter to Hermann, his stricken wife stated:

> You have a right to know the truth, because you love me, and have always done everything for me … I have no fear of death … I only want His will be done, because I know that what He wills is for the best for everyone. And darling, if there is no God, then death is only rest, like an eternal sleep. One knows no more of anything, but I firmly believe that there is a God, and then we shall see each other once more up there. I want so terribly to stay with both of you [including Thomas].

Thus Carin remained behind in Sweden, in hospital, for most of a year, but in the spring of 1928 she was at last physically able to rejoin her husband in a small apartment at No. 16 Berchtesgadenerstrasse, in Wilmersdorf-Berlin, behind the famed Kurfurstdendamm.

Goering Blackmails Hitler

Reportedly, Goering wanted Hitler to put him on the Nazi Party's candidate list for the upcoming spring 1928 Reichstag Parliament elections, but at first the cagey Führer balked. A furious shouting match ensued, with Goering raging at Hitler, 'This is no way to treat a man who got two bullets in his stomach at the *Feldherrnhalle*! Either you put me up for the Reichstag, or we shall part forever as enemies!' He also threatened to sue the party for what he felt was his own investment, as well as for back-pay that he thought he was due for his period of exile from 1923–27.

Otto Strasser heard the story from his older brother Gregor, and left this account in 1940, twelve years after the events: 'Either I become a deputy, or I bring an action against the party for damages and interest for the wound I received in 9 November!' In 1928, Gregor explained to Otto, 'Koch has been thrown out! Goering is to have the seat. The swine has blackmailed Hitler!'

Hitler had backed down, and Goering ran as number seven on the NSDAP list of twelve candidates who had won Deputies' seats at the National Assembly in Berlin. Putzi noted:

> He had grown enormously fat during his years of exile, and the old hands considered that this was no advertisement for a working class party, either. Even Hitler expressed doubts about his capacity: 'I do not know if Goering is going to make it,' he used to say to me, but Goering fooled them all, developing as a speaker, although all he did was to ape Hitler's style and phrases.

He thus entered the national political consciousness of the Reich, in his own right, for the first time since the botched 1923 revolt in which he had played such a brazen role. He was an elected member of the Reichstag, comparable to the United States Congress, representing a Prussian district that included Potsdam, outside Berlin.

Nazi left-wing socialist Otto Strasser correctly saw Goering as Hitler's direct link to right-wing industrialist moneybags Fritz Thyssen and Emil Kirdorf. He wrote that 'life in the grand manner was opening out before Hitler', and especially before his acolyte, Hermann Wilhelm Goering.

Reichstag Deputy, 1928–32

Carin attended her husband's first legislative session on 14 June 1928, describing it in a letter to her mother:

> Hermann got a splendid place [Seat no. 547], next to Gen. von Epp from Bavaria. They sit alone together at a table right at the front … What a lot of Jews there are in all parties, except Hitler's!

A decade later, Gritzbach had it differently; seat no. 547 was 'in a corner in the back row', and this was far more likely as Deputy Goering was nothing but a newly arrived freshman legislator at best. Carin continued:

Hermann has a frightful lot to do, and I see him only occasionally, but he gives all his free
time to me, and we generally manage to eat together … It is difficult always having to eat
in restaurants. Things are so expensive in Berlin!

Dr Wilhelm Frick (1877–1946) was the leader of the NSDAP Deputy delegation in
the Reichstag, where Goering found himself assigned as the party expert on canals,
aviation, and communications overall. In this capacity, Goering spoke in the chamber
on 22 February 1929 concerning the State Railway Service (the *Reichsbahn*) being
controlled as a pawn by the international bondholding community. Goering thundered:

The real and only cause of this intolerable state of affairs is the exploitation of the German
Reich Railway by the [American] Dawes Plan and by Reparations … That is the core of
the evil! The Reich Railway—formerly the pride of Germany, probably the best railway
in the world … is regarded today just as something to be plundered … by our enemies …
When we come to power, we will put an end to this … and restore the free German Reich
Railway to the free German people!

As an elected Deputy, one of Goering's perks was free railway travel anywhere in
Germany as long as he held office—a tremendous asset when campaigning. To his
deputy's salary of 800 RM (about $125 in US currency at the time), Goering added a
substantial bribe from the German national passenger airline *Lufthansa*. This came via
Director Erhard Milch, and was provided so that Goering would promote German civil
aviation legislatively. He was also allegedly still selling Tornblad parachutes and BMW
aircraft engines; of the latter, twelve were bought by Goering's second country, Sweden.

After reviewing the government's June 1929 aviation budget, Deputy Goering
famously demanded, 'Why is there no Aviation Minister? Save the air arm, if you do
not, you will live to regret it!'

Goering reportedly also sought a permanent position under Milch as a sales agent,
helping cities establish airfields for Lufthansa; however, Milch would end up working
for Goering, rather than the other way around. Thus the two men had a rather dis-
jointed personal relationship from the start of their long service together and well into
mid-1944. In 1962 Manvell and Fraenkel asserted that Goering acted as BMW's Berlin
business agent, selling their aircraft engines to the government, and also for Heinkel,
from a small office shared with Victor Siebel on the Giasstrasse.

When an Italian Jew from Trieste, Camillo Castiglioni, bought BMW outright, he
continued to pay Goering as his Berlin agent; however, Goering gained him little business. Miffed, Castiglioni archly suggested that the charming Hermann should 'stop
kissing hands, and start signing contracts'.

These financial arrangements reportedly continued up to the day Goering joined
Hitler's cabinet on 30 January 1933. Fraenkel cited as his sources for the above as
Dr Justus Koch, Putzi Hanfstangl, and Milch. Both of the latter two were sometimes
friends or foes of Goering, so their testimony in these instances may be viewed as
somewhat biased at least. Despite BMW's current denials the Goering ever worked
for the company, however, one is inclined to believe that he did, and that the records

were expunged by top management in the wake of the lost war in 1945. Indeed, this would be a rather incriminating instance of outright bribery of a legislative official. Meanwhile, German steel magnates like Fritz Thyssen gave Goering sizable 'loans' that were never repaid; Thyssen established Deputy Goering in another larger and swankier apartment, which he also furnished.

Carin had come to Berlin in April 1928, and after Hermann won his election, the couple was at last able to get the remainder of their former Munich-era furniture and belongings out of pawn shops. Goering privately vowed that he would never be poor again—and he never was. On 1 December 1928 he and Carin moved into their fashionable new apartment at No. 7 Badenschestrasse, in West Berlin—a flat in one of the city's most modern areas, with a view from the fourth floor of a green lawn square, and balconies all around their unit. Centrally heated (a major medical plus for the now always ill Carin), the building's elevator was located in an underground parking garage, and opened into four large rooms and a smaller one for their maid, Cilly Wachowiak.

As a recuperating Carin lay on the living room sofa, stitching her own table linen, she was surrounded by a near-constant stream of party visitors, dignitaries, politicians, and even royals—it reminded her of their lost Obermenzing club basement, which had fulfilled the same function in what seemed like a lifetime ago. Hitler himself made their new home his headquarters whenever he was in Berlin. Carin wrote back to Stockholm, claiming that their house was 'so full of politicians that one would be driven crazy if it was not so interesting!' Indeed, the Goerings now began to move in former imperial and royal circles—ones the young Lt Goering had been part of during his days as a First World War German hero. This included the German Hohenzollern Crown Prince, Wilhelm—his former Army commander—and his younger brother, the Nazi Prince August Wilhelm—nicknamed 'Auwi' for short. There was also the Prince and Princess zu Wied and Prince Philip of Hesse, the latter the husband of Italian Princess Mafalda of Savoy, daughter of the King of Italy, Victor Emmanuel III.

The Goerings had now arrived, both socially and financially, with only Carin's ill health to mar their marital happiness and outwardly visible success. Carin enjoyed entertaining in the apartment as much as she was able to—although she sometimes had to be carried into bed from her sofa. After her death, Magda Goebbels, the wife of the *Gauleiter* (Regional Leader) Dr Josef Goebbels, assumed Carin's former role as the salon lady of the party.

Now Carin's husband was known as the 'Salon Nazi' and 'Adolf Hitler's Ambassador', he frequented all the major haunts of the Berlin upper class—the Adlon Hotel, Horcher's Restaurant, and the exclusive, Junker-populated Herrenklub. He had not changed his attitude to money over the last decade, continuing to live beyond his means, never pay his debts, and avoid paying for anything at all when he could. In a letter, Carin noted:

> Tomorrow evening, we have visitors. They include Thyssen and other industrialists, Schacht, and Hitler. I shall give them Arter och flask [a Swedish peasant dish of pork and pease pudding] and Swedish apple cakes with vanilla sauce; Cilly will serve. Princess Wied's cook will give a hand in the kitchen … It is such fun to have everything simple, and I arrange everything as nicely and as elegantly as I can.

In this way, Deputy Goering's charming and beautiful countess wife became a distinct political asset to him, Hitler, and the Nazi Party in the German nation's capital. The bad old days of 1923–27 seemed far away at last.

Ill much of the time, Carin was forced to stay at home in bed while Hermann was travelling the country for political gains, making a respectable name for himself—as he had done during the First World War. In spring 1930, Carin wrote to her mother:

> It is so empty when Hermann is away, and I have a constant yearning for him. I am so alone here, and—unlike other women—I cannot talk about my state of health to my friends and acquaintances. It is only when I think of how I can help him or the Hitler movement in some way or other that strength seems to come to me from above.

Goering was joined on the political campaign trail by Hohenzollern SA Col. Prince August Wilhelm ('Auwi') of Prussia, and soon afterwards by his portly brother, Prince Eitel-Frederick (nicknamed Eitel-Fritz). The duo lent the workers' party a patina of royalist veneer, which appealed to German conservatives. Their audiences now reached 20–30,000 people each, with stump-speaker Goering employing a demagogic style that appealed to Germany's millions of unemployed people. With Prince Auwi wearing SA brown, Hermann appeared in a darker Party Leadership Corps Uniform, his famed Blue Max gleaming on his throat. His electoral efforts paid off; the party won a land-slide victory at the polls on 4 September 1930.

After attending a Nurnberg Nazi Party Congress, Carin suffered a relapse and had to be rushed to a sanitarium at Kreuth, in Bavaria. On 14 September 1930 the Nazis won 107 seats in the Reichstag—up from the paltry dozen they had previously—as Hermann took the visiting Thomas von Kantzow campaigning with him. Thomas later recalled:

> [Goering said,] 'Wait, watch this!' and he goes chasing after a tall, blonde actress from Munich, whom he takes over to Hitler. She is tickled pink, and Hitler gets a delightful moment of relaxation … They chat … after which Hermann finds it easier to approach Hitler about the important questions he has.

Rather than restoring Goering to the SA command after firing Capt. Franz Pfeffer von Salomon, Hitler elected to become overall SA Führer himself. Even worse, he also neglected to make Goering his SA Staff Chief, instead recalling Ernst Röhm from Bolivia, where he had been advising the national Army. From September 1930 until June 1934, Röhm therefore became Goering's greatest rival in the party. One English biography suggests that Goering even sent 'anonymous letters' to German newspapers that accused Röhm of being a homosexual. In addition, Goering found himself relegated to the position of Dr Frick's Deputy NSDAP Delegation Leader on the chamber floor.

Carin was allowed to return home that fall, but she fainted on Christmas Eve while wrapping presents, falling off her sofa and onto the living-room floor. After staying in bed with a fever, she roused herself to host a dinner party on 5 January 1931.

That same month, Hitler had Goering accept the invitation of the exiled Kaiser Wilhelm II to visit his home at Doorn, Holland, for a few days. The Kaiser's second wife—Princess Hermine of Reuss—was sympathetic to the Nazis at that time, mistakenly believing that once in national office they would restore her husband to his lost Royal and Imperial thrones. Although Goering had been an ardent monarchist into the days of his early manhood, he had since come to believe that the Hohenzollerns would soon turn the Nazis out of office if they regained their old power. Deep down, Goering also believed (like many German veterans from the First World War) that in 1918 the Kaiser had simply run away to personal safety in Holland, thus leaving all the people to their fates. Indeed, there was some justification for this feeling.

Goering visited the Kaiser and Kaiserin a second time in the fall of 1932, this time for a full week. However, for the next several years Goering and Hitler only told the gullible Kaiserin Hermine what she wanted to hear. In the meantime, the Hohenzollern Commissioner-General, Leopold von Kleist, gave Goering pricey Imperial furniture and artworks from His Majesty's personal collection, and also invited Hermann to stalk and shoot on the clan's retained German forest estates.

Goering and Wagener

The memoirs of Hitler's interim SA Staff Chief, Otto Wagener (1888–1971), are often overlooked, but they are an important source for understanding the Time of Struggle. Wagener had been one of Hitler's party economic advisors prior to the Führer becoming Reich Chancellor in 1933. At some point in mid-1931, Wagener paid a courtesy call to Reichstag Deputy Goering at his apartment in Berlin's swanky *Schoneberg* (Beautiful Mountain) district. As always, and perhaps intentionally, Wagener's host was late:

> Goering came toward me, wearing a red dressing gown, his feet in red slippers with turned up toes, such as were worn in the harems of old Turkey. His corpulence actually did give him the semblance of a sultan—or a eunuch.

Goering then said, 'I enjoy wearing this toga,' and it was only then that his guest noticed 'gold-brocaded buckles that looked almost like pom-poms'. They sat themselves in Goering's den, which was 'done in a rich scarlet … a huge sword hung on the scarlet cloth'. There were signed photographs of the Kaiser, the Crown Prince, Hindenburg, and Ludendorff, and photos of other notables including Mussolini, the King of Italy, and Crown Prince Umberto. Wagener continues:

> The desk and the space behind it were slightly raised on a dais, so that—if one sat on the other side of the desk—one had to look upward while Goering, as if from a throne, looked down from a little way above … On this throne—softly illuminated by candlelight—Goering sat in overpowering corpulence, clad in his red wrapper and Turkish slippers …. I felt as if I were in the cell of a mental patient. [Wagener lit a cigar and sat down, but on the arm of the chair] … so that I was raised slightly higher than Goering … The blood rushed to his head—turning his face beet red—and his eyes shot poisonous darts up at me.

After listening to Hermann spout off on nationalism and why he was more welcomed in Italy than Hitler would be, Wagener thought to himself: 'He is nothing but a criminal! ... Is he ready for the lunatic asylum?' They discussed Italy's past and possible future as an ally of Germany; Wagener did not think very much of this, but Goering did. Goering excused himself and went to the door, and Wagener states: 'I almost felt as if he were staggering. In any case, his hands lightly felt along the edge of the table before he reached for the doorknob'. He returned after five minutes:

> His expression had changed again. His eyes looked large and shining ... I noticed that his pupils were very small—tiny ... Only later ... was I reminded that Goering was a morphine addict. I therefore assume that he left the room to give himself another injection. That would also explain his overblown behavior, that I only understood after the second part of our conversation was ended.

The second part of the conversation concerned the large donations that the party received from wealthy mining and heavy industrial magnates from the Ruhr, who used Goering personally as their financial funnel to Hitler. 'All the large amounts come to me,' said Goering, and then expressed his anger at Wagener for receiving 50,000RM from them, intending to finance a party newspaper in the Ruhr. Goering explained:

> '[That money] had been earmarked for me ... Now it will not be sent. Can you imagine the position you have put me in? I am renovating a house here on Bismarckstrasse—two floors—as a suitable residence for myself, where I can hold receptions and parties.
>   'The architects are waiting for their money, for the 50,000 Marks! ... But I also use the money I receive from the Ruhr to finance Hitler—him, personally—and occasionally the party as well.'
>   And then it flashed through my mind: 'So there is the root of Goering's power ... and that is the basis for Goering's influence over Adolf Hitler!

Goering extracted from Wagener the pledge that he would never again invade Goering's financial sources in the Ruhr. Wagener further recalled: 'As I left the room and the building, I felt as if someone had hit me over the head with a wooden mallet.' What he did not realize, however, was that the meeting had ensured that Goering viewed Wagener as his arch-enemy within the party, and Wagener only narrowly escaped being among the murder victims in the 1934 purge. However, Wagener correctly understood that Goering was nothing more than the bribed (and thus owned) agent of the rich captains of German industry, and through him Hitler would be too, if he was not already.

Two others who agreed entirely with Wagener's assessment were the Strasser brothers, Gregor and Otto. Wagener went to Hitler with his convictions about Goering, but was put off:

> Goering had long since recognized that Hitler was so naïve that he saw only what was good in others ... He did not see through any scheming—not Goering's and not others' ... He remained naïve about people, but at the same time, he was wary and distrustful ... What a brilliant fraud Goering must be!

Wagener also concluded that Goering was a nationalist, but never a socialist—and he was right. He told Hitler that he had seen Cadet Goering at Karlsruhe during 1908–10, but that he would not call that 'knowing' him then. Hitler answered, 'That I have got that man is surely a piece of good fortune!' Hitler was also had an inflated sense of Mrs Goering's wealth:

> [She is] a millionairess. I have seen pictures of the family castle. She is a countess ... That is the reason that I asked Goering to show himself in Berlin as much as possible.... Without his wife's money, that would not be possible at all ... Besides, she has relatives and friends in the circles that set the political tone, here and abroad. The woman is of special value to us.

Earlier, Hitler had refused to accept Wagener's more simple (and accurate) explanation: 'she was divorced and simply receiving child support payments for her son Thomas, who also lives with Goering'. The next day, Hitler's adjutant, Schaub (Goering's man during the Beer Hall Putsch) confronted Wagener, stating, 'I do not like Goering, either, but he does have money!'

Wagener even accurately foresaw the party's shift from socialist left to *Reaktion* right, represented by Goering:

> If Hitler is given money by Goering and it originated with the Ruhr industrialists, then in time there will be an end to our National Socialist goals, because he who pays the piper calls the tune.

Later, Wagener and Hitler discussed Goering's alleged May 1931 trip to Italy; Wagener believed that Goering's supposed meeting with Mussolini had been engineered by Hermann, and was not an invitation from Rome. Wagener described the visit's coverage in the press:

> At one blow, Goering has become the best known man in the NSDAP at home and abroad. Until now, no one has heard of him ... Goering is by no means the man in a position to represent the NSDAP ... The German people and people abroad will ... consider him at least the second man in the party, a position he has never held and must never hold...'

Wagener proved to be right on all counts, but Hitler saw it as personal jealousy, asking, 'What is it that you have against Goering? ... I am not mistaken in Goering ... He is one of the most suitable men we could promote.' The Führer stated that Goering would become the second man in the party because he had the esteem of the people. 'So, let us drop the question of Goering. I will not allow personal animosities to deflect me from my line.' Wagener moved to Berlin in spring 1932 to be better-located to oppose Goering, but to no avail. He did, however, establish a good rapport with Army Gen. Kurt von Schleicher, drawing this praise from the Führer: 'Over a period of years, Goering could not manage what you accomplished in hours.' This remained Wagner's high point in Hitler's esteem, but nothing more. He later wrote:

I saw that I could not prevail against Goering … He had already secured his position too well … There was no mistake on my part concerning his character—I was quite certain of that.

Carin's Death

Back in Berlin, Carin was deteriorating; she overheard her doctor saying that there was no hope, and she had not very much longer to live. Kneeling in desperation beside her, Hermann watched as the physician injected his doomed wife with stimulants. Carin would later write to her older sister, Fanny, stating that she already saw herself as dead: 'My soul was free for this one short instant of time.' However, her heart took a beat and her eyes opened once more to see Hermann's sorrowful gaze; she had survived, but barely. Her son, Thomas, now eighteen years old, wrote in his diary:

> If mama had died, Hermann would have broken down completely. He says himself he does not know how he would have coped … I think it could have been dangerous, given his smoldering temperament. He says I was the stronger … and that we must take this to heart and start leading a healthier, more regular life.

Her renewed but short-lived recovery of May 1931 allowed the Goerings to travel back to Rome, the scene of their 1924–25 humiliation. This time, Hermann was the rising Führer's personal representative—but he was still denied a meeting with Mussolini. Carin's health worsened, and this may have caused Hitler to replace their government-seized Mercedes of 1923 with a new one; in this vehicle, they departed in August 1931 for a carefree motor tour of rural Germany and Austria. It was the first time they had been back in Austria since late 1923. Seeing the end approaching, Thomas stayed with Carin for ten days that summer. In *The Reich Marshal*, Mosely quotes Thomas thus: 'I was very emotional when I left her. I loved my mother very much, but, oh, what a mix up she had made of my life.'

On 17 September 1931 the first of a trio of stunning blows struck both Hitler and Goering. Geli Raubal, the Führer's niece and reputed lover, reportedly shot herself with his pistol; others allege that he murdered her in a jealous rage. Hitler was disconsolate, and (for the second time in his career) attempted to shoot himself only to have his pistol knocked from his hand. In Hanfstangl's 1957 memoir *Unheard Witness*, he claimed that Gregor Strasser told him how Hitler was comforted by 'Iron' Hermann, weeping on the latter's shoulder and crying out in agony, 'Now I know who my real friend is!' As a cynical Hanfstangl termed it, this was 'pure opportunism on Goering's part'. Whether or not either side was playacting, death helped to seal an emotional bond between the two men.

On 25 September Carin's mother died in Stockholm, and Mrs Goering returned home for the funeral—against the advice of her doctors. In 1937 Goering's aide, Dr Erich Gritzbach, noted that Carin 'collapsed completely when she heard the news. She was very ill at the time herself, and immediately took to her bed'. Carin was not expected to survive the night, but she nevertheless rallied and took the trip to Stockholm; she would not return to her second home, Germany, alive. Goering himself left for Sweden when Carin took a sudden turn for the worse, and remained by her sickbed for four days. Thomas later recalled:

> He would only steal away to shave or bathe, or snatch a bite to eat when he was absolutely sure that my mother was unconscious. Otherwise, he spent all his time on his knees at the bedside, holding her hand, stroking her hair, wiping the perspiration from her face, or the moisture from her lips.
>
> I would sit in a corner of the room and watch him. Sometimes he would suddenly turn and look at me, and he would be weeping silently. We were both weeping. We both loved her very much, and our hearts were breaking.

Goering's vigil was broken by a telegram from Hitler on 4 October 1931. It read: 'Return at once. You are needed here'. The Nazi leadership had been invited to meet with President von Hindenburg, an event that they all thought would result in Hitler being named Reich Chancellor. What was Hermann to do?

By now, Carin wanted to die—'To follow mama,' as she lamented—but felt she could not die as long as Hermann was there. Thomas believed that Carin urged Hermann to go to Hitler, where he was needed to secure their ultimate goal—Nazi office. Thomas recalled: 'He began to sob. She took his head and lay it on her breast, as if he, too, were her son, and it was he who was in need of comfort.'

Her husband left, saying, 'Until I come back.'

'Yes, until you come back,' Carin assented.

The meeting at Berlin occurred on 10 October 1931, but it was a failure for the NS. Oddly, Goering did not return to Carin's deathbed over the next seven days, but allowed her to die alone. One reason may be that the Reichstag was in session until 16 October, the day before she expired.

Carin died of a heart attack at 4 a.m. on 17 October 1931, her forty-third birthday—and exactly one month after Geli's death in Munich. Her body was placed in the Edelweiss Chapel behind her parent's house. Her favorite sister, Lili, told Goering of the loss. At the funeral, he was reported to be wild in despair; he wept and screamed, and threw himself over Carin's coffin. Thus, Nazism's 'Iron Man' showed himself in human grief as 'The Widower'. The congregation sang *A Mighty Fortress is our God* and Carin's favorite song, the American tune *Home, Sweet Home*. Hermann never got over the fact that he had deserted her, in her last hours, for politics. No one was more aware than he that in marrying him, his beloved Swedish countess had lost everything else she valued—her first husband, her son, and all her wealth to boot. He was inconsolable and guilt-ridden.

After the funeral, Carin was buried in her native land, at the family plot at Lovo Kyrka Cemetery, Lovon, Sweden. Back in Berlin, Goering never returned to what had been the couple's last home together; he vacated the apartment, briefly moving instead to Berlin's Hotel Kaiserhof (Imperial Hotel), which was by that time the party's national headquarters. From there, Goering rented a bachelor's apartment at no. 34 Kurfurstindamm, in Charlottenburg-Berlin.

Hitler had already dated the young Eva Braun while he was involved with Geli, but Goering was completely bereft of women as he had been totally loyal and faithful to Carin—as far as is known—throughout their brief, tempestuous marriage. Still, the Nazi Party's two top men had lost the women they loved within thirty days of each other, in the prime of their lives; they were shattered. It is arguable that this double tragedy was a lasting bond between the two men until they took leave of each other on 20 April 1945—Hitler's fifty-sixth (and last) birthday.

Of his late wife, Goering later told her niece, Birgitta von Rosen (daughter of the Count and Carin's sister Mary), that by marrying him, Carin had lost everything—even seeing her most cherished possessions auctioned off to support him and his morphine habit. 'Something inside me snapped,' Goering recalled. 'From that moment on, I determined to do all that I could so that my Carin should live as well as she had before, and better.' Now, all that was gone forever.

In death, Carin's life was turned into a Nazi legend—first with her reburial in Germany, and later via her sister Fanny's 1935 memoir-biography *Carin Goering*. By 1943 the book had become a best-seller, with 900,000 copies sold.

In his grief, Goering (like Hitler) sought peace in the home of their mutual friend Putzi and his wife, Helene Hanfstangl—the woman who had prevented Hitler's first suicide attempt in 1923. Putzi later remembered: 'Goering sought solace for his personal isolation with us. He was still not entirely accepted in the party, and our house continued to offer him a useful retreat.'

Goering v. Gen. Wilhelm Groner

On 18 March 1932, Gen. Wilhelm Groner had his police force raid NSDAP offices across the Reich, with 170 locations in Prussia alone, charging that he was forestalling a Goering-inspired *putsch* to take over the government by force. Goering himself would repeat this act on the night of the Reichstag Fire, targeting the communists. Responding to Groner's actions, Goering called a special press conference at the NSDAP's headquarters to deny the allegations. Waving a walking stick, Goering bellowed, 'The whole idea is absurd!' He declared that the Führer had concentrated 350,000 SA men in the capital on election day to prevent bloodshed, 'to take [their] own measures for the evacuation from the city of [their] women and children so as to protect them from injury by communist mobs…'

The second Hitler/Goering meeting with President von Hindenburg occurred at the President's Palace at 4 p.m. on 30 May 1932, and lasted only eight minutes. He again refused to appoint the NSDAP Führer as his Reich Chancellor, after twice personally defeating him for the Presidency earlier that spring.

On Election Day 17 July 1932, the Nazis won 230 Reichstag seats out of a total available of 609, making the party the largest entity in the national legislative chamber.

As Goering was left behind, cooling his heels, at Dr Goebbels' Berlin apartment, Hitler saw the Reich President a third time—this time alone—with Hindenburg. Despite 14 million NSDAP votes, Hitler was yet again denied the Chancellorship of the Reich.

Emmy Sonnemann (24 March 1893–8 June 1973)

Officially, Goering remained a single bachelor for three and a half years, from 17 October 1931 until 10 April 1935—however, he reentered the dating world long before that. At some point within the first year after Carin's tragic death, Hermann went to a café to meet a woman who was to become his lover and second bride. She was the well-known German stage actress Emma Johanna Henny 'Emmy' Sonnemann—then a beefy, Brunhilde-type operetta star. She was born in Hamburg, the daughter of a wealthy, 'conservative merchant' (as she remembered him), chocolate factory owner Heinrich Sonnemann and his wife, Emmy Sagell Sonnemann. The younger Emmy became an actress at seventeen; she rejected the new, post-First World War, 'expressionist' drama in favor of the German classics, as well as the works of Shakespeare, Ibsen, and Shaw.

She was already a famous actress at Weimar's National Theater well before she met Goering, and had also played in both Hamburg and Vienna. Little did she know that one day her most famous role would be as Hitler's First Lady of the Third Reich. Her rivals for the coveted post were Magda Goebbels and Eva Braun—she never the met the latter, however. As with Hitler, who had dated Eva while still living with his niece, so too did Hermann two-time Emmy—he was seeing both Kathe Dorsch and opera singer Margarete von Schirach, the sister of the Führer's Hitler Youth Leader, Baldur.

One view of their alleged first meeting came in 1951. Goering and Pilli Korner had just finished attending a weekend Nazi rally in Weimar when Hermann decided to see the play Minna von Barnhelm at the local theater, starring Emmy Sonnemann. During the performance, Goering noticed Emmy and said to Pilli, 'A very attractive woman. I'd like to meet her.' Pilli apparently served as the would-be matchmaker, but the shy actress begged off. The two allegedly met later, at a Bad Kochberg party. In 1951, Emmy recalled, 'When I eventually met him, I was not sure whether his name was Goebbels or Goering.'

Like Carin, Emmy also had an unhappy first marriage; in her case it was to an older actor, Kurt Kostlin, of Stuttgart, whom she had married on 13 January 1916. According to Emmy, they divorced in 1924, while several other accounts insist that it was not until early 1935, just prior to her marriage to Hermann—and only after he had proposed to her. She and her first husband also remained good friends (according to Emmy), and her mother had recently died in 1932. The two women in Goering's life therefore had much in common.

Emmy and Goering himself also had numerous similarities—both were lonely, were in the prime of their lives, and loved the theatre. However, unlike Carin, Emmy had no interest at all in politics, and never would, either. When she read newspapers, she turned at once to the theatre pages. One of her friends was the former Irish Ambassador to Berlin, Charles Bewley, who later became a Goering biographer and memoirist:

> Emmy was no Carin ... In place of Carin's vivid charm and restless romanticism, she possessed the qualities of reposefulness and placidity combined with the statuesque appearance of a blonde Germania.
>
> She was not—and never could have become—an actress of the first rank, but her friends claimed that she gave an adequate stage presentation of maternal and reposeful characters of the Germania type.

She saw Hermann as 'a lame duck to be helped along', and felt sorry for him in his grief, at least at first. He found in her a respite from the pressures of daily political infighting, both before and after the Nazis took office on 30 January 1933. However, he faced a very painful, personal dilemma. He found himself torn between two women—one was alive and there for him, and the other dead and gone, a memory from the past. He spent Christmas 1932 with Emmy, and then New Year's 1933 with Carin's relatives in Sweden, at Rockelstad Castle, with Emmy being left behind in Germany to fend for herself. That New Year's Eve, however, Hermann wrote to her thus:

> My darling! I am listening to songs on the Swedish radio … What pleasure the radio set you gave is giving me! I had a concert all the way from Berlin to the Sassnitz Ferry despite the rattling of the train [the Sassnitz Ferry traveled from Germany to Sweden, and was how Carin's body would be brought to Germany on 20 June 1934]. I can pick up 30 or 40 stations from here. Yesterday, I was able to get Stuttgart for a while.
>
> For hours every day, I go for long walks by myself in the most beautiful forest you have ever seen. I am sleeping eight or 10 hours a day. I just hope that I can stay on a bit longer. They all speak so charmingly of you here, they are all very nice to me.
>
> My dear, I want to thank you from my heart for everything you have done for me. Let us hope the New Year is just as kind to us.

After their meeting, the pair started seeing each other socially, mainly talking about the theater. Goering enjoyed the life of a swinging Nazi womanizer, and seemed very unlikely to ever remarry—right up to his engagement to Emmy on 9 March 1935, a bare month and a day before their state wedding. As with Carin, Hitler had again stepped in and suggested that having a live-in lover was socially unseemly for the deputy head of state. Hermann took the hint to heart.

Transition from Carin to Emmy: Dr Kelley's Analysis, 1947

Capt. Douglas McGlashan Kelley M. D. (1912–58) was Goering's major United States Army psychiatrist at Nuremberg in 1945. In his superior memoirs of 1947, he introduced an entirely new aspect to the Carin-Hermann-Emmy romantic triangle that has been overlooked in all English-language Goering biographies until now:

> While his first wife lay dying in Sweden in 1931, Goering remained in Germany working with Hitler. Other observers have decided that Goering was unemotional because he did not hurry off to his wife's deathbed…
>
> Even more important than his future in this instance was the fact that he had been in Germany for some time, separated from his wife. When her final illness came, he was under the sway of newer enthusiasms…

Was this 'separation' legal, or did Kelley just mean that circumstances had him in one place and she in another? It is still not entirely clear.

He must always have had some deep guilt feelings about his treatment of his first wife …
and he had … become too embroiled in politics even to be at her side in death. The story of
his inattention to his wife has spread through all of Germany…. In addition, ugly rumors
of homosexual attachments had grown up, based partly on his apparent lack of need for
his wife and partly on his lack of desire for mistresses … It was to silence German gossips
… that he established her in her shrine at Carinhall… Goering was not impotent, nor was
he—as persistent rumors implied—a homosexual … His home life was a happy one, and
the devotion between Goering and his second wife seemed satisfying to both.

Transition from Carin to Emmy: Emmy's Version, 1972

Fourteen years after Dr Kelley's death, twenty-six years after Hermann's demise, and
forty-one years after Carin succumbed, Emmy herself added fuel to the 'triangle' debate
with the publication of her own memoirs in English:

> The first time I met Hermann Goering, he covered me with stones and mud. Our company
> was traveling in an open motorcoach [car] to give a special performance for a party of
> specially invited guests, among whom were Goering and his former wife, Carin.
>
> A car traveling at high speed passed our motorcoach. The road was bad, and a veritable
> shower of stones and mud bespattered us. We did not recognize Hermann Goering…
>
> Later that evening, Hermann was introduced to me after the show. I cannot say on that
> evening he made any profound impression on me, but his wife fascinated me. Sitting on a
> bench in the park during the interval, she looked ill, but there emanated from her a charm
> that I could not resist.
>
> I would like to have chatted with her, but I did not have time, because we had to repeat
> the performance … I had to go back to the stage. I afterwards regretted very much that I
> had not had a chance to hear Carin's voice at least once.
>
> I still have today her picture in my home, and I often feel it is that of a sister. I was not
> to see Hermann again until a year later, in the spring of 1932. I had then already been on
> the stage for 20 years, eight of them in the Weimar National Theater, where I played roles
> of romantic and society women.
>
> A new life had begun for me there. Before that—in Stuttgart—I had been divorced from
> my first husband, but even today, we remain good friends … I lived in three furnished rooms
> … Masculine visitors were strictly forbidden…

Comparing the accounts of Dr Kelley and Emmy, it is not impossible to believe that
a separated Hermann may have been seeing Emmy while Carin was still alive. Such a
situation may have encouraged Carin's elder sister, Fanny, to publish a biography of her
late sister. *Carin Goering* was published in 1935—the very same year of Hermann and
Emmy's elaborate state wedding, which was, oddly, attended by the von Fock family
en masse. As well as casting a veil over any illicit love triangle, the book became the
virtually sacred text of 'the love of Hermann and Carin' that all biographers—until
now—have accepted as fact.

According to Emmy, in spring 1932 Goering and Pilli Korner came up to the Weimar Imperial Café, where Emmy and her girlfriend Herma sat, about to leave for a walk. 'May we come with you?' Hermann asked. Emmy picks up the story:

> So all four of us strolled in the park for nearly two hours. For the first time in my life, I forgot the theater, my parts, and everything else.
>
> I listened to Hermann Goering ... He spoke of his wife—who had recently died—with such love and genuine sadness that my esteem for him grew with every word....
>
> 'You know,' I said to Herma, 'I am really very happy to have met—after so many years—a man whom I like so much. I feel as though I had known him a long time, although we have talked for only two hours.'... Herma ... had never heard me talk like this before. She asked me outright, 'Could you be in love with that man?' I said happily, 'Perhaps.' ... And thus I found a happiness that even today I am infinitely grateful to have experienced in such a complete way...

Soon the couple went on their first dinner date, where they were chaperoned again by Pilli and Herma. Emmy recalled:

> It was a thrilling evening. I felt that my life was about to be transformed... He walked back alone with me to my door and left me. The walk was not long, but it decided the rest of my future life.... [After a Berlin reception] Hermann took me to the station. He held my hand in his until the train began to move, did not let it go, and ran alongside the train. Then—suddenly making up his mind—he jumped on the running board of the train, and on that cold April day, traveled with me to Weimar, without a coat or a hat.

Hermann saw Emmy perform as Clarchen in *Egmont* at the Weimar National Theater. Arriving late, she saw him enter his box as she addressed her on-stage mother, 'Ah! I ask myself only if he loves me.' Forty years later, she recalled: 'The people of Weimar … knew of my friendship with Hermann, so there were broad smiles on many faces in the audience.' She mused:

> We met as often as we could. Hermann made some very dangerous night trips in the car between Berlin and Weimar … In those weeks and months, I was certainly burning the candle at both ends … A woman in love thinks only of her partner's success, and it is of little importance to her how he obtains it. It is enough for her to see that the man she loves is happy.

Election to Reichstag President

Goering was initially elected as Reichstag President on 30 August 1932, with 367 right-wing votes to the socialist candidate's 133, and eighty for the communist KPD contender. Referring to his NSDAP Deputy Delegation, Hermann stated, 'We are fighting the State legally!'

Goering was the first non-left chamber president in fourteen years, replacing the Socialist incumbent, Paul Lobe, who had been in the chair since 1918. His first act was to send Emmy a note on his new stationery, in red pencil, reading: 'I love you. H.' She still had the note in 1951. In his maiden speech as Speaker, Goering asserted, 'The honor of the people, the safety of the nation, and the freedom of the Fatherland shall be the chief guiding stars of all my actions.'

In 1949, an eyewitness to Goering's election, André François-Poncet, wrote this account of the scene:

> Traditionally, this body inaugurated its activities under the Presidency of its oldest member … This time the dean was [Jewess] Klara Zeitkin, 84, the communist … an old lady, [she] had to be supported under either arm; she climbed painfully in the Chair. In thin, monotonous tones, she read a long, scarcely audible speech, praying for the day when German Soviets might fill this hall [she had reportedly traveled to Berlin from Moscow for the event....
>
> The Nazi deputies—wearing brown shirts with the swastika armband, black breeches and boots—sat in the hemicycle, a very model of good manners … but they were beside themselves with fury … Goering was elected by 367 votes, the Catholics supporting him … Goering climbed blithely into the Chair. His clear voice resounded through the hall. With surprising ease, he assumed his functions as though these were long familiar…

When Hitler named Hermann Prussian Prime Minister, Poncet's apt comment describing this event was, 'The true Vice Chancellor was now Goering, not Papen.' Four decades after the event, Emmy recalled:

> In becoming President of the Reichstag in 1932, he had taken an office in the building. As it was furnished in such bad taste, he asked me to help him give his office a personal character … He put into it two Gobelin tapestries inherited from his father, a very attractive antique desk, an impressive armchair, and some family pictures that he particularly treasured.

Indeed, on the night of the infamous Reichstag Fire, Goering was more concerned with saving his own office than the rest of the historic structure. For this reason, Emmy argues in her memoirs that her husband could not have had any part in setting the fire.

The Papen Flap, 12 September 1932

The Papen Flap was later celebrated as one of Reichstag President Goering's stellar moments in the Speaker's Chair. Ironically, it occurred on the first and last day of that season's Reichstag sitting. Both the KPD and the NSDAP wanted to end the Chancellorship of Franz von Papen, and decided to jointly vote on a resolution of no confidence that would force his resignation and thus also the overthrow of his Reich cabinet.

The Chancellor had prepared for this, however, by having his friend Reich President von Hindenburg sign a decree dissolving the body before it could vote; that being accomplished, there would also be no new elections, which both the radical parties wanted to have.

Calling for a vote on the measure, Goering famously avoided both seeing or hearing von Papen's repeated requests to be recognized so that he could personally deliver the red-leather dispatch box containing the dissolution order to the Speaker's dais. Indeed, even as the voting was in progress, the Chancellor strode angrily up to the podium and flatly slammed the case down on Goering's desk, directly in front of him. Nevertheless, Goering got the vote that he both wanted and expected—a majority of 481 Deputies, legally ending the Papen Chancellorship.

That particular Reichstag never met again, with a new one elected on 6 November 1932; in this election, the Nazis lost both votes and seats. As he observed his paladin campaigning hard, Hitler opined admiringly, 'Give him a full belly and he really goes after them!' However, the NSDAP failed yet again to attain the Reich Chancellery—it instead went to von Papen's former mentor, Gen. Kurt von Schleicher.

Machtegreifung *(Seizure of Power), December 1932–January 1933*

Despite the disdain for Goering within the Old Fighter ranks in the working class NSDAP, Hitler had sent exactly the right man to Berlin to negotiate with the capital's archconservative social 'swells' in government—big business, the military, the royals, and high finance. Indeed, by all accounts Goering proved himself to be one of the principal negotiators during the critical period of December 1932–January 1933. In the end, this resulted in Hitler being named Chancellor of the German Reich by President von Hindenburg, the very man who had twice defeated the upstart Nazi Führer for the Presidency in 1932.

However, prior to this, in December 1932, the new Reich Chancellor, 'Red' Gen. von Schleicher, tried to split the Nazis by offering Gregor Strasser the Vice Chancellorship in his own cabinet. Strasser was keen to accept; had he done so, a sizeable part of the NSDAP might have gone with him.

Goering reportedly met with von Schleicher in private, attempting to prevent his rival, Strasser, being selected for office instead of him. On 3 December 1932 Goering even asked the new Chancellor to name him Prime Minister of Prussia, but von Schleicher stuck by his choice of the Nazi pharmacist; this could be a key reason for his murder during the 1934 Blood Purge.

Goering was reelected as Reichstag President that same December 1932, and therefore remained the official, elected face of the Nazi Party within the halls of government. In a stormy party conference at the *Kaiserhof* on 5 December, Hitler repudiated Strasser on the combined advice of his two top Berlin lieutenants (Goering and Goebbels). Raging, Hitler called the proposed pact a 'betrayal'. He feared the internal collapse of the party, threatening to shoot himself if that occurred, but Strasser himself presented this by resigning from all of his NSDAP posts on 8 December. As he prepared to leave for a vacation in Italy, Strasser asserted, 'I am a man marked by death! Mark what I say: From now on, Germany is in the hands of an Austrian, who is a congenital liar; a former officer [Goering] who is a pervert and a clubfoot.' Meanwhile, the rest of the party leadership rallied behind Hitler and the flashpoint of crisis passed.

One point that has never been considered, however, is this: what would have happened had Gen. von Schleicher offered the post of Vice Chancellor to Goering? Both were fellow officers, and as Vice Chancellor and Reichstag President, Goering would have had a unique double access to their Reich President, the revered field marshal. Hitler, meanwhile, would be nothing more than what he had been since 1924—an elected Reichstag deputy who never attended its sessions, and the leader of a civilian political party.

Indeed, von Schleicher could easily have sweetened the deal for Goering by also having him named both Aviation Minister and (the already discussed) Prime Minister of Prussia, also putting him in line for eventual succession as Reich Chancellor. Might Goering—Hitler's much-touted 'faithful paladin' to his Führer—have been tempted to accept just such a deal?

Through all of this political negotiating back and forth, Goering emerged as the party's chief and most successful fundraiser, inducing both Fritz Thyssen and fellow steel magnate Albert Vogler to bankroll all of Hitler's electioneering money for 1933. In return, Reichstag President Goering promised the steel industry vast new orders for its product once the Nazi regime was in office—and he delivered on his promise too.

On 29 January 1933, Goering got wind of an alleged plot by von Schleicher to call out the German Army's Potsdam garrison, kidnap Reich President von Hindenburg, and thus prevent him from naming Hitler as Chancellor. Afterwards, the wily general allegedly planned to install himself as the Weimar Republic's first military dictator.

However, Goering nipped this in the bud by going straight to the old field marshal and his trio of top advisors—his military adjutant and son, Col. Oskar von Hindenburg, State Secretary Otto Meissner, and former Chancellor Franz von Papen. Quietly and effectively, the President's cabal countermanded any secret orders that von Schleicher might have given, and the revolt fizzled out. The General had already resigned as Chancellor the day before, opening the door for Hitler to succeed him.

Sieg Heil*! (Hail Victory!)*

On 29 January, a jubilant Goering personally delivered the news to Hitler that he would be named head of government the very next day. Even his own rival for Nazi power in Berlin, party propagandist Dr Goebbels, gave Goering his due in a post-victory entry in his personal diary:

> That was decidedly Goering's most glorious moment … He has prepared the ground for the Führer with diplomacy and skill by negotiations that have lasted for months … even years! His prudence, his strong nerves—above all his strength of character and loyalty to the Leader were real, strong, and admirable.

This was high praise indeed from the waspish, negative Dr Goebbels. He continued:

His face became a mask of stone … His soul was wrung with anguish when—in the very thick of the difficult campaign—his beloved wife was snatched from his side by death, yet never for a minute did he flinch, but continued grimly and resolutely on his path, an unswervingly faithful shield-bearer for his Führer.

And this upright soldier with the heart of a child has remained consistent in his loyalty, and today he stands before his Führer and brings him the most joyful tidings of his lifetime.

Left: Back in Germany following a four-year exile abroad, a now portly Goering (left) appears wearing early SA kit at the September 1927 Nuremberg Nazi Party Congress. Thus began a difficult five-year reinstatement process back into Hitler's good graces. Regarding the cap he wears here, Littlejohn states: 'The kepi as introduced in 1925 had one (or two) silver buttons on the front, otherwise no insignia'. His heroes were Hitler, the Kaiser, Bismarck, Napoleon I, Mussolini, and, later, Balbo. (*HHA*)

Below: The so-called Harzburg (Nationalist) Front demonstration of 11 October 1931, around the time of Carin's sad demise. One source notes that 'Carin had been left to die in Stockholm in order that Goering might attend this function', while others insist that it was so that he and Hitler could be received officially by President von Hindenburg. From left to right are an unknown SA man, Viktor Lutze, Hitler (saluting from car), SA Staff Chief Ernst Röhm, Goering, and two other unidentified men. Note that Röhm and Goering appear to be about the same weight— at least from the waist up. (*HHA*)

Above: Dr Paul Josef Goebbels (1897–1945) (in the front passenger seat) was Hitler's choice to be Nazi *Gauleiter* (Regional Leader) for Berlin during the drive for office before 1933. However, the Führer still sent Goering (in the rear seat) to Berlin to act as his 'salon Nazi', wining and dining important industrialists and military officers—a role in which Hermann excelled. (*HHA*)

Right: Hitler and Goering talking at Berlin's Tempelhof Airport in July 1932, after the suicide of Hitler's niece—and reputed lover—Geli Raubal and the death of Carin. Significantly, Goering wears a black mourning band on his left coat sleeve, while his Führer does not. Hitler's relationship with his dead niece was thereafter a closely guarded secret. Note also that Goering wears his hat in the then popular 'Potsdam style'—rear flap down and front flap tilted upward for a rakish look. (*HGA*)

Seen at the same Tempelhof meeting are (left to right) Ernst Franz Sedgwick 'Putzi' ('Little Fellow') Hanfstangl (1887–1975), Hitler, and Goering. Hanfstangl served officially as Hitler's first foreign press secretary. During this period the Nazis and the communists battled each other in city backyards and on crowded tenement landings in slums; 70 per cent of all NSDAP members were working-class men. (*HGA*)

Left: Goering's main government foe during the *Kampfzeit* (Time of Struggle) in Berlin before 1933 was German Army Gen. Wilhelm Groner (1867–1939), the man who had told the Kaiser in 1918 that he must give up his throne; he also proved to be a worthy opponent for Goering. In a speech at Berlin's Circus Crown Hall on 8 August 1928, Goering suggested that Gen. Groner should 'wear a peacock's feather out his ass'. A court fined him 300 RM, but his audiences loved it. The NSDAP referred to 1918–33 as *'Systemzeit'* ('The Time of the System'). (*HHA*)

Right: Proof positive that Goering visited the former Kaiser, Wilhelm II, at his place of exile in Doorn, Holland. Goering leads the way down the building's front steps, followed by Empress Hermine (in rain gear, with dogs), and His Majesty himself (with cane, at the top of the stairs). The former Kaiser reportedly considered Goering to be 'a vain creature who would be consigned to obscurity once the Kaiser remounted his throne'. As for the other Nazis, Wilhelm contended, there 'would be no place for them' in the Second Wilhelminian Reich. Goering's two known visits here took place on 18–19 January 1931 and 20–21 May 1932. Despite his relationship with the former Kaiser, Goering publicly rejected any restoration of the monarchy on 26 June 1934, in a speech to a Nazi convention in Hamburg. He stated, 'We who are living now have Adolf Hitler!' (*Doorn House Museum Collections, Holland*)

Above: Hitler and his lieutenants at Obersalzberg, before the big Schleicher-Strasser rift of late 1932. From left to right are Gregor Strasser (1892–1934), Ernst Röhm, Hitler, Goering, and Wilhelm Bruckner. All except the Führer wear the traditional Bavarian *lederhosen* outfits. Of the five men, only Bruckner died of natural causes (in 1954). Strasser and Röhm were shot, while Hitler and Goering both committed suicide. Gregor and his brother, Otto (1897–1974), had both been officers in the Kaiser's Army in the First World War; they had seen through Goering, and at least Otto felt that Goering had achieved his Blue Max through underhanded means. Otto Strasser would outlive them all. (*HGA*)

Right: Reich Chancellor Gen. Kurt von Schleicher (1882–1934) blocked Hitler and Goering's paths to office from 1932–33. Here, he (on the left) is seen with Franz von Papen (right, in the bowler hat) at Berlin's famed *Grunewald* (Green Forest) Races. A contemporary joke in Berlin ran: 'Gen. Schleicher ought really to have been an admiral, for his military genius lies in shooting underwater at his political friends!' In 1932, Schleicher reportedly told an enraged Goering, 'I do not see you as a man fit to be appointed to a ministerial post.' The general and his wife were murdered during the Blood Purge—possibly on Goering's orders. (*HHA*)

Left: Emmy Sonnemann wearing braided hair for her role as Margareta/Gretchen in Goethe's *Faust*. Goering's valet, Robert Kropp, related the following story: 'I was to drive her somewhere that the Chief was to join her for the weekend, I think it was Weimar. The Chief had given me a sealed envelope that I was to hand to her with strict instructions that she was not to open it until we arrived. She took the envelope … but she opened it at once. I saw her beam with delight. She jumped straight out of the car before we started, rushed back into the house … and threw her arms around Goering. Only later did I learn what was in the letter—just two words in the Chief's handwriting, '*Wir heiraten*' ['We are getting married'].' That was Hermann's 'proposal'. (*HGA*)

Right: Emmy (left) in costume for the role of revered Prussian Queen Louise in *Prince of Prussia*. According to Munn, her film career began at the age of thirty-eight, appearing in *Goethe Lived* in 1932 and starring in *William Tell* (alongside famed actor Conrad Veidt) in 1934. According to Irving: 'What [Goering] felt for Emmy was probably not physical attraction. At the end of 1935, he would reveal to State Secretary Milch his belief that the groin injury had left him impotent. Probably he regarded his blonde fiancée as merely another dazzling bauble for his collection.' (*HGA*)

Emmy's first husband, fellow thespian Karl Kostlin, whom she married on 13 January 1916. She divorced him in either 1924 or early 1935—accounts differ. She married Goering as his second wife on 10 April 1935, when both were forty-two. As an actress, she probably understood his flamboyance better than anyone else. She and Hermann had a decade of marital bliss before he was arrested in May 1945. Bewley claimed that Hitler liked her, and one later rumor had them being secret lovers who even had a child together. (*LC*)

Left: A formal portrait of Emmy Sonnemann Goering as First Lady of the Third Reich after 10 April 1935. Dr Gritzbach stated: 'In her favorite role as Minna von Barnhelm—a play by G. E. Lessny—she said farewell to the stage that had also been her world … at the zenith of her career … Despite all her joy and glory, she felt in her heart the bitterness of seeing her "last curtain" rung down.' She had given up on being known in her own right, becoming 'Mrs Goering' instead. Today, few know her name, while that of Eva Braun reverberates around the globe with recognition. (*HGA*)

Right: A candid snapshot of Emmy as she appeared more naturally. All who met her agreed that she made a perfect wife for Hermann Goering. Irving claims that they lived together from 1932 until her divorce early in 1935. In 1938, Dr Gritzbach wrote: 'His wife was always his best companion … They frequently conversed about opera and drama until late into the night. They discussed technicalities about production and layout, as well as more abstract questions about the present and future of art and artists.' (*HGA*)

Below: After his election to Reichstag President on 12 September 1932, Goering christened his official stationery with a note to Emmy, reading: 'I love you. H.' She kept it until her death, forty-one years later. On 30 March 1948, Hitler's former Munich housekeeper, Mrs Anni Winter, told American naval officer Judge Michael A. Musmanno, 'Hitler did not like Emmy Goering. She acted too much "the high lady", the First Lady of the Reich. Hitler did not like such women who called themselves by the titles of their husbands.' (*HGA*)

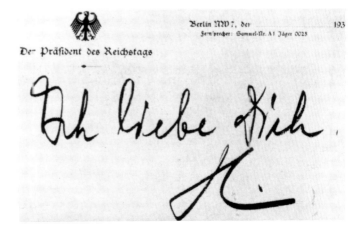

The Goerings (center) out on the town during Hermann's early time as Prime Minister of Prussia. As far as we know, Goering never cheated on either of his two wives—unlike Goebbels. After 1933, Goering boasted and laughed about foreign press reports that he was trying to overthrow Hitler. 'I am the first to bring the name of Goering into the history of the world!' he crowed. When Hermann met Emmy, she was making her own money—10,000 RM per year. (HGA)

Hermann and Emmy with Josef and Magda Goebbels at the annual Press Ball in the Berlin Opera House on 2 February 1935. Dr Goebbels smiles (seated, center), with Goering laughing (right), while their two wives—Magda (left) and Emmy (right)—chat at the rear. Until Hermann married Emmy in 1935, Magda Goebbels served as First Lady of the Third Reich— on Hitler's order, Emmy took her place. At the left is Goering ally Dr Walther Funk, and peering over at the two couples (below, at center) is the bespectacled Dr Erich Gritzbach, one of Hermann's top aides. (HGA)

Left: Like Hermann, Emmy was also a fashion plate in her day. She is seen here wearing a snappy-looking leopard-skin overcoat with a fur cap and muff, pictured during the rebuilding of Carinhall on 11 December 1936. (*HGA*)

Right: Emmy (left) visits Reich Chancellor Hitler on his birthday, 20 April 1936, with little Roswitha Huber, one of Hermann's nieces. A fan of Carin's, Hitler was generally more reserved with Hermann's second wife. Hitler knew all about Hermann's enforced stays in Swedish asylums, and heard Röhm refer to Goering as 'this crazy *kerl* [guy]'. Nevertheless, after 1932 Goering rarely spoke before crowds of less than 20–40,000 people. (*HHA*)

The Nazi Big Three enjoy a night out on 1 February 1936; Hitler stands, applauding, flanked by a grinning Goebbels (right) and smiling Hermann and Emmy Goering (right). Otto Strasser called Hermann 'The German Napoleon', while Goering saw himself as 'The Scharnhorst of the Luftwaffe'—a title that more properly belonged to Erhard Milch. When Milch sensed that Goering drugs, he simply hung up the telephone on him. (*HGA*)

Chancellor Hitler's first coalition cabinet convenes for formal photographs on 30 January 1933. From left to right: Labor Minister and founder of the German Veterans' Steel Helmet organization Franz Seldte, Gunther Gerecke, Finance Minister Johann Ludwig Count Schwerin von Krosigk, Goering, Reich Minister of the Interior Dr Wilhelm Frick, Hitler, Defense Minister Army Gen. Werner von Blomberg, Vice Chancellor Franz von Papen, and Reich Economics Minister Alfred Hugenberg. There were others not seen here. On 1 January 1933, Goering crowed to Hitler, 'The fortress has been stormed—we are in the saddle now!' (*HHA*)

'*Sieg Heil!*' ('Hail Victory!'). This photograph was taken on the night of 30 January 1933, as Nazi Stormtroopers paraded past a window at Hitler's Old Reich Chancellery in Berlin. From left to right: Hitler, Dr Frick, Bruckner, Goering, and Hess. Wary about what might happen, Hermann gave Emmy a pistol; she in turn gave it to their maid, Cilly Wachowiak. Thus began the Third Reich on this jarring note. (*HHA*)

5

FLAMES, 1933

Following their joint entry into office, Goering rushed outside to be the first to tell the waiting crowd, 'Adolf Hitler has become Reich Chancellor!' As one of only three Nazi Party members of Hitler's first cabinet, Goering would become its most important minister by June, a mere six months later.

On Hitler's inaugural night as Chancellor, there was a famous Nazi torchlight parade past the Presidential Palace and the Reich Chancellery, and Hermann booked a room with a view of it all for Emmy at the Kaiserhof. She later wrote:

> ... he did not seem very sure of the sentiments of the crowd. He handed me a revolver with the remark: 'Here, take this, in case anything happens.' I had never held a gun in my life ... Terrified, I slipped it into my muff and passed it on a few minutes later to my maid, Cilly [Wachowiak, who stayed on with Hermann after Carin's death].

At 5 p.m., she also witnessed Chancellor Hitler's first cabinet meeting:

> At Hitler's side, there was no longer Captain Goering, but the Minister of the Interior of the Third Reich. In the distance, one could hear the singing of the Storm Troopers as they assembled for the torchlight procession. It was a prodigious spectacle ... Hitler—with Hermann and a few of his other collaborators—stood at a window of the ... Chancellery, where, from now on, the history of Germany would be made.

On that first day, Goering was named both Reich Minister without Portfolio and Prussian Police President/Chief of Police under Nazi Interior Minister Dr Frick. His NSDAP memoirist and biographer Dr Gritzbach wrote that Goring worked, lived, ate, and slept at the Prussian Interior Ministry office during almost all of his first two months in office, February and March 1933. His two personal secretaries were Miss Gisele Limberger and Mrs von Kornatzki, aided of course by various other staffers in the many offices Goering held. Another secretary—a Miss Grundberger—took the call that informed the office that the Reichstag was on fire.

As Prussian Interior Ministry Police Chief, Goering succeeded its previous (socialist) manager, Karl Severing. Goering's oft-expressed law-and-order philosophy and actual operational practicality was spelled out in a number of now-infamous orders and public speeches. His basic mantra was to do what he knew or believed Hitler wanted him to do: 'I have no conscience! My conscience is Adolf Hitler.'

On 2 February 1933—a mere three days into his governmental tenure—he ordered, 'Each bullet that now leaves the barrel of a policeman's revolver is my bullet! If you call that a murder, it is I who am the murderer! These are my orders, and I give them my full support. I assume the responsibility, and I am not afraid.' When an angry von Papen told his subordinate Goering to resign, the latter exploded, 'You will only get me out of this room flat on my back!' Hindenburg's choice as Foreign Minister—the Wilhelminian Era Baron Konstantin von Neurath—branded Hermann as 'a dreadful man'.

Goering told his policemen to cease troubling NSDAP members and uniformed SA and SS, and to instead go after communists and socialists. Goering again received praise from Dr Goebbels in his diary entry of 14 February 1933: 'Goering is setting things to right in Prussia with splendid energy. He is the sort of man who does a thing radically, and his nerves are made to stand a hard fight!'

On 15 February 1933, Goering named NSDAP Reichstag Deputy Adm. Magnus von Levetzow as Chief of the *Orpo* (Regular Police) to help him clean out all the pro-Weimar Republican members within the various police departments. On the 20th he lectured his police, 'I must hammer it into your heads that the responsibility is mine alone. If you shoot, I also shoot!'

On 21 February 1933, Goering simply 'added' to their ranks fully 50,000 *Hilfspolizei* (Auxiliary Police)—members of the SA, SS, the German national veterans' organization *Stahlhelm* (Steel Helmet), and German National Peoples' Party *Kampfring* (Battle Front) troops (wearing white armbands over their red-white-and-black swastika armlets). They served as such until 8 August 1933. The first 200 Auxiliary Policemen were duly armed with pistols, and were under the command of Berlin SA leader Count Wolf von Helldorf; in Berlin alone, there were later an estimated 1,500–2,000.

Five days later, Police Chief Goering ordered his Orpo to raid and seize the national communist KPD headquarters, the *Karl Liebnecht House*, over which the Nazi swastika was raised.

On 3 March 1933, during a speech in Frankfurt, Goering asserted:

I am not called upon to render justice. My measures will not be crippled by bureaucracy! My mission is to destroy and exterminate—nothing more! The fight to the death—in which my hands will wring your neck—I will carry out with the help of the Brownshirts.

On 11 May 1933 in Essen, Goering boomed out:

I have only just begun my purge! It is far from finished. For us, the people are divided into two parts—one that professes faith in the nation—the other that wants to poison and destroy.

I thank my Maker that I do not know what objective is! I am subjective. I repudiate the idea that the police are a defense force for Jewish department stores! We must put an end to the absurdity of every rogue shouting for the police.

The police are not there to protect rogues, vagabonds, usurers, and traitors! If people say that here and there that someone has been taken away and maltreated, I can only reply: you cannot make omelets without breaking eggs!

One of Goering's first acts had been to replace the former police batons/night sticks and rubber truncheons with revolver pistols.

Do not shout for justice so much, otherwise, there might be a justice that is found in the stars, and not in your paragraphs! Even if we make a lot of mistakes, we shall at least act, and keep our nerve. I would rather shoot a few times too short or too wide, but at least shoot!

As he notoriously ordered his policemen, 'Shoot first and inquire afterwards! If you make mistakes, I will protect you.'

He was equally ruthless in 'reforming' the Prussian Police, replacing all the anti-Nazi members with pro-party SA and SS men, and reportedly firing twenty-two out of thirty-two police chiefs, hundreds of inspectors, and thousands of sergeants within his first month in office. 'The "System" big shots were thrown out,' he explained. 'This cleansing process extended from the supreme police chief to the doorkeeper.'

Goering Explains the Nazi Revolution, 9 April 1933

In a formal address to the NSBO (National Socialist Workplace Cell Organization) in the cavernous Berlin Sports Palace on 9 April 1933, Goering explained how he saw the ongoing Nazi Revolution:

My dear citizens! We are living through a National Socialist revolution … Just as nationalism protects a people from outside forces, so socialism serves a people's domestic needs … Previously the two fought each other, divided by hatred and unfortunate enmity. Nationalism and socialism stood opposed: the middle class supported nationalism, the Marxists socialism. The middle class fell into a barren hyper-patriotism, lost in pacifistic cowardice.

On the other side, a Marxist layer of the people—a Marxist class—wanted nothing to do with the Reich or a people. There was no bridge between them. Marxist socialism was degraded to a concern only with pay or the stomach. The middle class degraded nationalism into barren hyper-patriotism … Our idea grew out of the people, and because it grew from the people—led by the unknown corporal of the World War—this idea was destined to bring an end to fragmentation, and forge once more a unity among our people.

Outwardly, the Reich was weak, existing only on paper. Inwardly, the people were torn apart, bleeding from a thousand wounds. At home, strife dominated between parties, occupations, groups, classes, and religions.

Our Führer … saw that the Reich could survive and grow strong only if one achieved unity within the German people. That was the work of our party over the last fourteen years: to make once more one German people from a people of competing interests … of differing religions, occupations, groups, and classes…. And when the Reds claim that we are now the bigwigs, we answer, fellow citizens … We have not had the time to become bigwigs! … We want only to be the workers in German construction, masons on German projects…

The parties are finished! … The System was cowardly, and it left in a cowardly way! … We have slowly begun to create unity from the chaos of parties … One shakes one's head that such things ever existed in the German Reich… Now, my national comrades, you members of the factory cells are now the blacksmiths who are forging our German people …

To be sure, we have won a great victory … We must be cautious! Clothing is not enough to make a National Socialist, nor the badge for which we were persecuted for a decade, nor the *Heil* greeting.

The heart alone determines whether one is a National Socialist. We want no fighter, no NS, of the mind! … We also should be generous … We are, after all, the victors. What difference does it make if someone who once called us criminals, or brown bandits, or something else! … Where real crimes were committed against the people, there must be pitiless and just revenge … The big ones must be caught, not the little ones. We want to let the little ones alone, but we must settle accounts with the big ones … They must receive just revenge with pitiless hardness …

This is the context in which we have to understand the new Civil Service Law, as everything is being cleansed, purified, and rebuilt … This is a hard law … It shatters careers if falsely applied…. Whether it concerns the fate of a worker, a porter, or a state secretary, makes no difference. Everyone is affected equally…

Millions of Germans throughout Germany over these years had no idea what National Socialism was. They saw the brown columns, they read terrible things about those columns each day in the Jewish press, they read how bad National Socialism was, they read that it would destroy everything, that it would ruin everything, that it could lead to anarchy, to collapse.

They did not know us … And then, suddenly, the movement came, tearing through the clouds, suddenly, there was light again, the sun shone. Hundreds of thousands—even millions—of people suddenly woke up. The scales fell from their eyes, and they saw something wonderful … new joy, new hope …

Men and women of the factory cells … You must make clear to the former Marxist or communist that work is no curse, but rather a blessing … A small but disciplined unit will always overcome and defeat a larger, undisciplined mob … Get to work, and may God bless our labors!

Goering's Mission to Fascist Italy; Prussian Prime Minister, 10 April 1933

In 1931, Goering, at Hitler's behest, had made a party-business trip to Rome that had not accomplished much. On 10 August 1933 he embarked again—as an official representative of the sitting German government—and had greater success. Decades later, Baur recalled:

Our trip had a little background story concerning our clothing. We were to wear the new uniform of the German Air Force that was just being organized. A well-known Berlin uniform tailor, Holters, was sent to our homes to take measurements, so Goering, Korner, Milch, my crew, and I went to Rome in our new finery.

It was termed 'a vacation' by some. He was finally given access to both Mussolini and also the Fascist Air Minister Marshal Italo Balbo, and he reveled in his role as Hitler's special envoy to Rome. He was even given a guided tour of the impressive *Regia Aeronautica* (Royal Air Force) Ministry Building in Rome. This former-Fascist structure still stands today—minus its fascist and swastika emblems, of course. Balbo's Air Ministry spurred Goering on to build his own in Berlin, as soon as he could.

Upon his arrival at Rome's airport, he had received a telegram from Hitler naming him as the replacement for his former boss, von Papen, as Prime Minister of Prussia. The news was handed to him by the German Ambassador, Ulrich von Hassell, and greatly enhanced Goering's official status in the eyes of his Italian hosts—just as Hitler had planned.

As Prussian Prime Minister, Goering also took over the Prussian State Police. Unlike most criminals, he was able to read his own police file; it was provided to him by his deputy, Rudolf Diels. Inside, there was a questionable allegation against the new Prime Minister:

> He exhibits many of the signs of a suppressed homosexual, and is given to flamboyance in dress and the use of cosmetics. There is, however, no evidence that his close friendship with Paul Korner is anything but normal.

While Goering was in Italy, von Papen negotiated with the Vatican (as Germany's foremost Catholic politician) for a concordat between Germany and the Pope—similar to that signed with Mussolini in 1929, known as the Lateran Accord. Hitler had Goering accompany his Vice Chancellor because he did not entirely trust von Papen. Thus, while officially meeting with Marshal Balbo, Goering also managed to have a group picture taken with Cardinal Angello Giuseppi Roncalli, the future Pope John XXIII.

Hitler's own personal pilot, Col. Hans Baur (1897–1993), was present on the epic flights to Rome. He published his memoirs in 1958, in which he described the trip:

> I flew Goering on his first visit to Air Marshal Balbo in Rome. It was April 1933 ... and off we flew to Rome in our brand-new uniforms. Goering sat next to me, and flew the plane. We had not been more than 10 minutes in the air when his valet arrived with ham laid on bread and butter, and I took over while he ate.
>
> After that, there was coffee with cakes, a Steinhager liqueur, and then oranges ... every now and again he appeared with sandwiches, coffee, cakes, and so on, and Goering steadily ate his way to Munich ... Goering then had his first flight over the Alps...

Once aground, the German delegation was treated to a banquet in a nearby military barracks, 'where a huge table was loaded with every possible delicacy. Goering's eyes sparkled, and he set to with a will—the colossal quantity of food that man could put away was astonishing!' Baur was recalled to Berlin, so the Goering entourage came home without him. Goering later told him, 'Baur, I thought I was going to die on that return flight!' Goering had great trouble breathing over the Alps, using up all the available oxygen. As Baur was told, 'Milch hurriedly came forward to the pilot and ordered him to fly lower because Goering was going blue in the face and gasping for breath,' but the pilot turned back for Venice instead. On the second try for home, 'Goering turned blue again and looked as though he were dying ... As soon as they flew lower, Goering recovered. Instead of two hours, the flight to Munich had taken four'.

Back home, Hitler asked Baur how he would have handled the situation. Bauer replied, 'You just KO him, and that is what I would have done to Goering, by flying still higher. He would then have lost consciousness altogether, but no harm would have come to him ... As soon as we were able to fly lower, he would have been all right. I have had that experience time and time again.'

Hitler snorted, 'You are a brutal fellow, Baur!'

Actually, the situation was rather more serious than even Baur recalled, as related by eyewitness Erhard Milch, who entered the pilot's cabin and found his boss, Goering, flat on his back, on the floor, eyes staring and mouth frothing for lack of oxygen. 'No wonder!' Milch recalled. 'He had been taking it since we reached 1,500 feet,' and the crew had not stored any emergency supplies. Opening Goering's collar, Milch splashed his face with cold water, but Goering remained blue and only partially conscious. Worse than that, however, was that by now the crew had also become disoriented, and they simply felt their way through the air, without radio bearings, to land safety at Munich.

Had Goering died, or had the plane crashed and killed both him and Milch, who would have succeeded them to head the Luftwaffe? Hitler probably would have chosen Wever over Wilberg, but had the former still died in his own crash in June 1936, would the Führer have then named the Jewish Wilberg to succeed him? It is difficult to say. As for the possibility of an Alpine crash occurring, that is precisely how former-Luftwaffe airman and wealthy industrial magnate Harold Quandt—the stepson of Dr Goebbels—died in 1967.

Later, Goering presented Hitler with a brand new Ju-52 for the Führer's use, complete with green suede-upholstered seating. Hitler chortled, 'Wonderful Goering, wonderful! Very beautiful, indeed!' but then told Baur later, 'That machine would suit Goering very well, but it does not suit me ... We will stick to the old, simple, well-made things. What would my friends think if I started flying around in a luxuriously equipped plane like that?'

On another occasion, Baur suggested that Hitler do his personal Christmas gift shopping the way that Goering did: 'Go to a shop after closing hours and have the whole staff waiting on him. Hitler laughed, and said that such a method ... no doubt suited Goering, but ... it did not appeal to him.' Thus, Hitler was well aware of many of his paladin's shortcomings, but—as later, during the war—chose to overlook them until it was too late.

Reich Commissar for Aviation, 2 February 1933

On 2 February 1933, Reich President von Hindenburg named Goering Reich Commissar for Aviation. In turn, Goering himself named his former Lufthansa briber, Erhard Milch, as his air deputy. Thus began a near-unique relationship that endured for eleven years, into 1944.

As he would time and again, Goering designed his own first blue-gray uniform as Reich Air Commissioner, somewhat modeled on the RAF walking-out dress kit of 1933 as well as on that of the Christiansen/Keller DLV/German Air Sports Association uniform. The new Air Commissioner was so pleased with it that he wore it when piloting his own plane to Rome on 10 May 1933, to show it off to both Mussolini and Italian Air Marshal Italo Balbo.

From the former Prussian *Landtag* Building, Goering created his future *Haus der Flieger* (Airmen's Club)—not to be confused with the later Reich Air Ministry, which was, again (like his two Berlin palaces) a separate building altogether. The latter was projected to be a 5,000-room structure, complete with a rooftop landing pad.

In addition—after an long hiatus—Goering decided he had to re-learn his pilot's craft to bring himself up to date. Accordingly, a Captain Hucke trained him, also showing Goering the more modern night flying in 1933, in time for his April flight to Fascist Italy and back.

Contrary to some accounts, he also was open to the concept of long-range bombing, the lack of which helped defeat his Luftwaffe in the Second World War. 'I regarded it as my duty to take all possibilities into account,' he asserted, but he changed his mind in 1936, when Hitler stressed instead his own air-to-ground combat liaison concept of the Air Force with the German Army's early Blitzkrieg tactics.

On 26 April, Goering announced to the Prussian State Council that he had established his new Prussian Secret State Police, known by its bureaucratic office acronym of 'Gestapo', with Dr Rudolf Diels as his hands-on administrative deputy. Thus was born an agency that struck fear into millions of hearts across the crowded twelve-year Reich of 1933–45. It gained full official recognition in June 1933.

The Goering Administrative Team 1933–45: Paul 'Pilli' Korner (1893–1957)

Paul Korner (nicknamed 'Pilli') was born on 2 October 1893 in Pirna, Saxony, and died on 29 November 1957 in Tegernsee, Bavaria, aged sixty-four. He was the son of Saxon Army General Physician Paul Theodor Albert Korner; in testimony at Nuremberg during his own 1948 Ministries Case trial, Pilli stated:

> On my father's side, I came from an old theological family that from the Reformation until my grandfather's time, produced scholars and theologians. My father was the first one in the family who broke this tradition, and became a doctor … My mother … came from an old commercial family … I was brought up in a purely nationalistic and Christian way. This … education resulted from my father's position, and from the traditions of my family.

In general, Korner has gotten rather short shrift from Goering's biographers. He was an accomplished person in his own right, and played a major role in the career of our subject. Indeed, throughout 1933–45, Korner was one of Goering's top aides, and also testified in his defense at the March 1946 International Military Tribunal in Nuremberg. According to his SS Personnel File at the US National Archives at College Park, MD, USA, Korner began the First World War in a Saxon field artillery regiment, was later promoted to battery chief, and ended the war as a General Staff officer in 1917–18.

At Nuremberg, Korner (a former law student) testified on his own behalf:

> I took part in all the battles that took place on the Western Front throughout 1917. At the end of 1917, I was transferred to the General Staff for meritorious service … [and] was adjutant to the Chief Deputy of the General Staff of the Army.

Unlike his later chief Hermann Goering, veteran Paul Korner served in the Lutzow Free Corps, fighting the communist uprising in Berlin into mid-1919, having left the Army formally that spring.

In *Hermann Goering and the Third Reich* (1962), Charles Bewley refers to Korner only as 'Goering's chauffeur' prior to 1933; in fact, during 1919–30, Pilli both co-founded and was chief executive officer of the wholesale tool and tool-making firm Korner & Siebel, set up by fellow Army war veterans like himself. The business also took over the management and sales of the Siebel aircraft manufacturing company, providing Korner an entrance of his own into the aviation industry.

During his IMT testimony on 29 July 1948, Korner recalled his first meeting with Goering:

> I made his acquaintance on the day he arrived in Germany [in 1927] through a common friend. Goering immediately made a deep impression on me.

Korner went on to help Goering in his 1928 Reichstag campaign, and after the equally successful 1930 election, became a member of the Deputy's staff full-time. He later said, 'I separated from my firm so that I might be completely independent, and devote myself wholly to Goering.' Korner joined the Nazi Party on 5 December 1931, and in 1932 he also enlisted in the SS. Of Goering, Korner said, 'Despite the failings that he had that are well-known, I had a deep inclination and respect, and … Goering felt toward me the same sort of friendship.' Despite his devotion to Goering, Korner kept a foothold in the business world from 1930–33 as the director of a taxicab firm in Berlin—probably in case the Nazis never took office.

From 1931–33 Korner was titled Adjutant and Private Secretary to Hermann Goering, but fifteen years later he claimed:

> Goering insisted on having his own way … Goering discussed many things with me that he did not discuss with others … I had no influence on any decisions that Goering arrived at … [He] listened to my opinion and accepted it or turned it down … Anyone who knows

Goering will corroborate the fact that he was the one who did the deciding ... in the Prussian State Ministry, and then, after 1936 ... in the work for the Four Year Plan ...

In human matters, I was certainly his confidante, but in official matters—particularly ... that were discussed between Goering and Hitler—Goering never discussed secret matters with me that he had discussed with Hitler.

In February 1933 Korner was named Personal Advisor to the Prime Minister of Prussia, and that May he was also elected as a Member of the Reichstag himself, representing Election District Dresden-Bautzen. From 22 April 1933 until May 1945, Korner served as State Secretary to the Prussian State Ministry—in effect, again, as Goering's personal deputy. On 30 January 1942 Korner was promoted to SS Obergruppenführer as well.

Korner was Deputy Plenipotentiary for Prussia on the Reich Council during 1933–34, and on 10 April 1933 he established the secret *Forschungsamt* (FA, or Research Office), which was Goering's personal intelligence and telephone-wiretapping agency; Korner was its general manager. His mission was to spy on SA Staff Chief Ernst Röhm and his top lieutenants (among others) leading up to the Blood Purge of 1934. It was Dr Diels who had first brought telephonic tape recording to Goering's notice as a powerful tool for the future, as it indeed would be under Korner and his successors.

From 1937–45 the FA was officially transferred to Goering's Reich Air Ministry so that he would not leave it behind for SS Reichsführer (National Administrator) Heinrich Himmler, who became Chief of the German Police from 1936–45. Another factor was the rising costs of the FA, leading Goering to place it under the official Luftwaffe budget. All its staff members thus donned Air Force grey-blue uniforms to blend in at the RLM headquarters in Berlin. By 1937 fully 500 wiretaps operated twenty-four hours a day in Berlin alone, focusing mainly on foreign embassies and legations, newspaper people and broadcasters, and other anti-Reich suspects. According to the transcripts of Albert Speer's 1945 pre-IMT interrogation:

Its function was the tapping of telephone conversations. The results were reported in the so-called 'Brown Sheets' ... circulated to all Ministers ... bearing on their jurisdictions. Hitler had issued a strict ban on the tapping of conversations by the Reich Ministers themselves, but I do not know if this was observed.

Most of the listening in was done on big industrialists and businessmen, but it was said that embassies and legations were also tapped ... Sometimes the reports were very instructive.

On 16 March 2006 *The Baltimore Sun* published an article by Niels C. Sorrels entitled 'Germany's Lessons on Use of Wiretap', which asserted the Fourth Reich maintained 29,071 separate wiretaps in 2004 in the Allied war on terror; another part of the overall legacy of Hermann Goering is both alive and well.

According to Robert Kropp, Goering's happiest hour of his working day was at its very start, when he read over the latest FA Brown Sheet transcripts of the night before, which made him the very best informed man in Nazi Germany.

From 1933–34 (the most important part of the Nazi seizure of the German government and its agencies from within) Korner also served Goering as Deputy Chief of the

Prussian Secret State Police. After the war, the IMT noted that Korner 'participated with Goering in setting up the Gestapo as an instrument of force and terror. He was the administrative head of the special "spying agency"—the FA—an organization that monitored conversations of Germans'. In sum, Paul Korner was rather more than just Goering's former driver!

SS Standartenführer Dr Rudolf Diels (1900–57)

One of the more interesting characters of this first period of Goering's rule was Dr Rudolf Diels (16 December 1900–18 November 1957), first Chief of the Gestapo from 1933–34. Diels was born in the Taunus Mountains, the son of a farmer, and served in the Imperial Army during the First World War. In 1919, he began studying law at the University of Marburg. On 17 June 1934 von Papen would give a famous anti-Nazi speech there that would almost get him killed—it cost him the lives of two of his top aides during the Blood Purge.

As a student, Diels quickly gained a reputation as a duelist, a heavy drinker, and a rampant womanizer; the latter characterization was still true in 1933, despite his first marriage. Dueling scars marked his face when he joined the Prussian Interior Ministry in 1930; he soon found his niche in the political police, especially in gathering sensitive intelligence on the era's two most revolutionary parties, the NSDAP and the KPD.

Some time before Hitler took office, Dr Diels came into secret contact with Goering. He became his spy within the Prussian Police Department, as he had been before for Gen. Wilhem Groner—the man who was probably the most dangerous governmental foe Goering ever had. When Goering was made chief of the Prussian Police Department in 1933, Dr Diels was named as his deputy; in April 1933 Goering also appointed him as the Chief of the new Prussian State Police Department 1A—the Gestapo.

In this capacity, Dr Diels became one of Goering's main men in arresting communists in connection with the Reichstag Fire. He was twice fired and replaced as chief of the Gestapo; the first time was in September 1933, when he was replaced by Paul Hinkler only to be restored to office the following 1 December, with a new title from Goering. This was as Inspector of the Gestapo, which in Nazi parlance meant a kick upstairs.

Ulrich Grauert and Hans Gisevius had undermined Dr Diels, and after the war the latter claimed that Diels had actually blackmailed Hermann in order to be reinstated. In 1949, Dr Diels claimed that from January 1934 Goering ordered him to start preparing for the eventual murders of Röhm, Gregor Strasser, and the man they called The Field Gray Eminence—Gen. von Schleicher, via Artur Nebe. Ironically, as Dr Diels had many enemies, he was also nearly a victim during the Blood Purge, but he was saved as Goering's protégé. Indeed, he remained safe for the rest of the Third Reich, even making Goering's cousin and widowed sister-in-law Ilse Goering his second wife (following his own divorce in 1936).

As part of Goering's alliance with RFSS Himmler versus the Röhm-Strasser cabal, Dr Diels was fired as Gestapo chief on 1 April 1934, being succeeded on the 20th by Himmler's deputy, Reinhard Heydrich; Heydrich remained in the role until 1942. As a sop, Diels was given the position of Deputy Police Chief to Count Wolf-Heinrich von Heldorf in Berlin; he retained this job for five weeks before being transferred to Cologne, in the Rhineland, for his own safety. He was appointed as Reich Governor, and was later sent to Hannover to take the same position. In 1941 he was named Director of Shipping for the Hermann Goering Works steel conglomerate.

Kurt Daluge

Kurt Daluge (15 September 1897–24 October 1946) rose to the ranks of SS Obertgruppenführer and Generaloberst (Colonel General) of Police as of 20 April 1942, and served as chief of the national uniformed regular police from 26 June 1936 to 31 August 1943. Prior to Goering's ascendancy in Berlin in 1932, Daluge had served as SA chief under Gauleiter Dr Goebbels, but when Hermann reorganized the Prussian Police, Daluge became his Chief of the Ordnungspolizei/Orpo (Regular Police).

When Goering gave up the Gestapo to Himmler in 1934, Daluge changed allegiances once again, shifting over from Hermann to the new power, the men in SS black; he thus became Chief of the Reich Orpo under them in June 1936.

Landespolizei General Goering, *1933–35*

As General of Infantry from August 1933, Goering was also *General der Landespolizei*. Within a month of Hitler taking office as Chancellor of the German Reich, Goering felt the need for his own, personal armed force, both as a bodyguard unit and as one that would carry out raids against the enemies of the regime. In his role as Prussian Interior Minister, on 23 February 1933 Goering thus established an armed force under Prussian Police Maj. Walther Wecke; it was named Special Purpose Police Group Wecke, a common practice in Germany from 1919 until 1945. Two days afterwards, the Major reported to his chief that the new unit comprised fourteen officers and 400 men; they were initially housed in the Kreutzberg Quarter, previously the barracks of the Prussian Queen Augusta Grenadier Guard Regiment No. 4.

Early on 2 March 1933, Goering led this new unit on a raid against the Communist Party headquarters in Berlin; within two hours, fully twenty-seven KPD leaders had been arrested, and a large cache of weapons was also confiscated. In subsequent daily raids, Police Force Wecke continued to arrest KPD members to continue the destruction of the KPD organization throughout Berlin. These raids increased in intensity until April 1933, with fifteen carried out in all.

The new unit also participated in public-relations-oriented events, receptions, and formal parades. Police training was followed by military exercises as well, with machine gun and trench mortar companies being added; thus, ironically, the force became the first of the wartime paratroop units and full-scale Luftwaffe Field Divisions.

On 17 July 1933 the *Landespolizei* was officially renamed as *Landespolizeigruppe Wecke z.b.V*, thus becoming the first State Police of the Third Reich. On 15 September

1933, Prussian Minister-President Goering presented his unit with seven new State Police colors, with the party's swastika at its center. According to Nazi propaganda, the unit:

> …was in the stormy days of the NSDAP Revolution a concept that pursued the enemies of the State like a nightmare. It was Col. Wecke—who with his quick Police Formation—was the sword of the Secret Police that cleaned out the last shady Communist hiding places.

During the Reichstag Fire trial, Goering himself called Col. Wecke 'his dependable police officer'.

Bernhard Walther Wecke (1885–1943)

Walther Wecke held a trio of top posts under Goering—State Police General, Army Major General, and Luftwaffe General. The son of a train station manager, he was born on 30 September 1885 in Nennhausen, near Rathenow, and died on 16 December 1943 in Gotha, with the Third Reich still surviving and occupying most of Continental Europe.

Finishing junior high school as an average student, young Wecke already saw himself as a future soldier; he wanted to follow his father, who at eighteen, during the Franco-Prussian War, had taken part in the famed 'death ride' as a member of the 16th Uhlan Regiment in the Battle of Mars-la-Tour in 1870. On 16 October 1903 Walther enlisted for two years in a field artillery regiment in Brandenburg, on the Havel River, remaining with them until September 1909; he had been promoted to non-commissioned officer on 27 February 1905.

From 1 October 1909 to August 1910, Wecke served at Spandau's Ammunition Depot, and later on in the same service at Darmstadt and on the Neisse River until the First World War broke out. His combat artillery service continued until 22 May 1915, when he was promoted to the officer grade of Lieutenant, and on 3 March 1916 he was again posted to an ammunition depot. From 29 March 1917 until December 1918, he served in a foot artillery battalion. He saw combat service on the Western Front, as well as in Romania and Macedonia, and was awarded both the first and second-class versions of the Iron Cross. On Christmas Eve 1918 Wecke was assigned to the Regiment Reinhard, seeing action against the communist Spartacists during the revolt of 6 January until the end of February 1919. Since 1 January of that year he had been posted officially at Spandau, outside Berlin, and he continued here until 24 June.

After being assigned to Group North, Wecke attended the Police School in Potsdam from 29 September until December 1920. Under the socialist Weimar Republic system, he was promoted from Police Lieutenant to Major in 1927.

He came into closer contact with NSDAP elements from 1930 onwards, effectively acting as a secret political informant for the Nazis and providing them with information on police business from within. In 1932, Wecke (in civilian clothes) accompanied Hitler to a Berlin stadium for a party rally. In March of that year he even compiled a list of names in his department whom he felt should be fired once the Nazis took over, and in November 1933 he joined the party himself.

On 5 January 1933 Wecke was chosen as the leader of the Joint Prussian Police Officers Group, and on the 29th he learned of the military's 'Potsdam Plot' to prevent the Nazis from taking office the next day. On the night of the 30th Wecke's new chief, Goering, told him to be prepared for an attack by the Potsdam Police garrison; in the event, this did not materialize. As Chief of the Prussian State Police, on 2 February Goering ordered Wecke, Rudolf Diels, and Kurt Daluge to begin the long-planned purge of 'unreliable elements' from the Prussian Secret Police, the regular police, and the Police Officer Corps—who were believed to be hostile to the Nazi takeover.

During Goering's anti-communist raids, Wecke's motorcycle troops were known as the feared 'Black Hussars'.

On 1 February 1933 Wecke was named as President of the Technical Institute for Traffic and Transportation of the Prussian Police. The Wecke Police Group morphed into the Wecke Staff Watch in July 1933, and on 22 December it was renamed as State Police Group General Goering; in September 1935 it became Regiment General Goering, with a strength of six full battalions housed on Berlin's Friedenstrasse.

In June 1934 Wecke was made head of the National Police Brandenburg Inspectorate, in which Berlin was located; however, on 6 June he was succeeded in command by State Police 1st Lt Friedrich Wilhem Jakoby. During the Blood Purge of June–July, Wecke and Jakoby's men guarded Goering's Prussian Ministry, placed Vice Chancellor von Papen under house arrest (on Goering's orders), and helped 'cleanse' the doomed Berlin SA. Indeed, for a few weeks in July Wecke himself was placed in command of the late SA Commander Karl Ernst's own SA Group III, Berlin-Brandenburg, after Ernst's execution.

Martin Heinrich Sommerfeldt (1899–1969), Goering's First Press Chief

During the dozen years of the Third Reich, Goering had two press secretaries. The first was Martin Sommerfeldt, and he was succeeded by Dr Erich Gritzbach. Sommerfeldt had succeeded von Papen's man, Herbert von Bose, Chief of the Press Office in the Prussian Government Ministerium.

Martin Henry Sommerfeldt was born on 5 February 1899 in Glucksburg, and died, aged seventy, on 10 April 1969, after a career as both a journalist and State government official. The son of a court preacher, he attended both grammar and high school in Flensburg, North Germany. He enlisted in the German Army in 1916, in the middle of the First World War. After the war, Sommerfeldt took part in the failed March 1920 Kapp Putsch in Berlin (unlike his future boss, Goering). On 11 November 1920 he married Udi von Buch (1899–1945), but the couple divorced on 26 February 1926.

As a journalist, Sommerfeldt covered the Reichstag, becoming chief editor at the *Daily Review* newspaper. In 1932 he published the books *Hermann Goering: What Are You Thinking?* and *Hermann Goering: An Illustrated Life*, which were also printed in Swedish. It was actually Goering who approached the young journalist to write his first-ever biography, and it was the only one not to be published by the Nazi press,

Eher Verlag of Munich. After the request, Sommerfeldt duly composed a sixty-page, martial-themed essay on Goering's exploits as a warrior, rather than concentrating on Hermann's political ambitions. It was published by the Berlin publishing house E. S. Mittler & Son. Sommerfeldt made some astute observations:

> Despite his corpulence, he surprised one by his great physical endurance and power. He was charged with energy and sparkled with vitality… and placed much value in his descent from a 'good family'…

Of course, Goering's family virtue was actually tainted by his mother's extramarital affair.

A year later, Goering had the book banned—perhaps because of Sommerfeldt's too-close-to-the-mark observations on his varied dualities. He was a 'bloke' but desired the throne for himself, and the 'second man in the Reich' but always aiming to be first. At this time, however, Goering was portraying himself as nothing more than his Führer's 'faithful paladin'.

In 1998, the term 'paladin' was thus defined by Paul:

> [Paladin:] As a hero or loyal follower was formerly called in the days of Charlemagne/ Charles or Karl the Great. The term 'paladin', however, derives from 'palatin', a bondsman of the palace, a chattel of the King's.

Despite banning the earlier book, in 1933 Goering duly hired Sommerfeldt to work in his Prussian administration, for which Sommerfeldt wrote biographical sketches of other Nazi leaders—running into fourteen editions by 1937. After clashing with Goering over differences between their press releases about the Reichstag Fire on 28 February 1933, Sommerfeldt's tenure came to a swift end with him being fired and replaced by Dr Erich Gritzbach in March 1933. By October 1934 Sommerfeldt had completely retired from Prussian government service, at the tender age of thirty-five. He had been amazed by the change in Goering from 1933 to 1934:

> It took only about one year of sovereign power to change Hermann Goering … into one of the strangest and most striking characters of the Hitler Era. In a virtual somersault, he hurled himself into the other side of his dual nature …
>
> What until then had only appeared rarely—and among the most intimate circle—as the belated and playful phantasy of an immature boy, now broke out with an intensity that made his friend deeply uneasy, but for the time being only amused the public.
>
> It is in no way true that Goering paid 5 Marks for any good joke about himself. I had invented this white lie as a means of countering Goebbels' poisonous sarcasm. In reality, anybody who dared to recount the newest Goering anecdote to the Minister President was in for trouble.

In 1933 and 1934 Sommerfeldt ghostwrote the illustrated biography *Carin Goering* with Carin's elder sister, Fanny, and this was published by Martin Warneck in Berlin.

Dr.sc.pol Robert August Erich Gritzbach

Another of Goering's top men within the Prussian State Ministry was Dr Erich Gritzbach (12 July 1896–approximately 1955, aged fifty nine), State Civil Service and SS Führer; he is rarely chronicled in Goering's biographies except as Goering's second NSDAP German-language biographer. The son of painter August Gritzbach and his wife, Flora Simon Gritzbach, on 8 May 1924 he married Sophie Wessel (born 1897), but they divorced on 12 August 1941. On 17 December 1941 Dr Gritzbach married Hildegard Hinnenberg (born 1910.

Gritzbach attended primary and secondary school in Forst, on the Lausitz, and he joined the Imperial German Army in August 1914; on 5 November he was severely wounded near Langemark, in Flanders, only returning to front-line service in April 1916. He was again badly wounded on 14 July 1916—this time by a bullet in the head. After being promoted to Reserve Lieutenant, Gritzbach earned both classes of the Iron Cross and also the Austrian Medal for Bravery. He was discharged from the Army in January 1919.

After the war, Gritzbach graduated from Berlin's Konigstadt High School on 19 April 1919. Unlike his future boss, Goering, he joined Border Patrol East until May 1920, acting as commander of a rifle company in the 9th Regiment. He then served in Silesia, East Germany, with Reich Protection Regiment 93. From 1920–22 he was Assistant Director of German Medicine Tool Factories, a trade organization; simultaneously, he studied both law and political science at the Universities of Berlin and Tubingen. He undertook his doctoral dissertation at the latter, achieving his degree in political science in 1924. His dissertation was entitled *Price Estimation in German Machine Tool Construction*.

Until 17 April 1924, when he joined the Prussian Interior Ministry, Gritzbach had been a member of the German National People's Party (the DNVP). After being promoted to the Prussian Administrative Council on 29 July 1932, on 1 October Gritzbach was again promoted, this time to the Prussian State Ministerial Council—all before the advent of Goering. In February 1933 he found himself in the role of Personnel Departmental Director for Reich Commissar and Vice Chancellor Franz von Papen, remaining in this post after Goering took over.

On 24 March 1933 Gritzbach succeeded Martin Sommerfeldt as Goering's formal press secretary. Like his predecessor, he also authored an official biography of Goering—1937's *Hermann Goering: Work and Man*. The following year he also edited *Hermann Goering: Speeches & Essays*. 1933 also saw Gritzbach as the Head Commissioner of the 1936 Berlin Olympics, preparing for the winter and summer games of that year.

On 25 September Gritzbach joined Himmler's SS, serving on the RFSS's staff, and he was promoted to SS Oberführer on 20 April 1938—Hitler's forty-ninth birthday. He had joined the Nazi Party in 1936, at Goering's request, taking a position on Goering's Prussian State Council. From 1933–45 Gritzbach served as Goering's principal administrative aide—as Chief of the Minister's Office from 1933–38, and Chief of the Prussian Minister-President from 1936–45.

The Reichstag Fire, 27 February 1933

The Nazis despised the Reichstag as the 'talk shop' of the hated socialist government 'system', and only served there so as to destroy the republic from within. With Goering's election on 30 August 1932 as the body's official president, the Nazis took a giant step forward in realizing this goal.

On the evening of 27 February 1933, police and firemen were summoned to the scene of an astounding sight—the Reichstag was ablaze! To this day, both Nazis and their opponents believe that Goering's men set fire to the building, secretly entering it via an underground tunnel that connected the house of legislature to Goering's Presidential Palace on Potsdammerplatz. In 1934, Goering wrote:

> If I am further accused of having myself set fire to the Reichstag in order to get the communists into my hands, I can only say that the idea is ridiculous and grotesque!
> I did not need any special event to enable me to proceed against the communists ... The firing of the Reichstag did not—as a matter of fact—at all fit in with my plans ... I knew that people would probably say that—dressed in a red toga and holding a lyre in my hand—I looked on at the fire and played while the Reichstag was burning.

On 20 April 1942, at the Führer's wartime military headquarters in East Prussia, Goering famously even joked about it. Chief of the German General Staff, Col. Gen. Franz Halder, was quoted at Goering's trial at Nuremberg:

> At a luncheon on the birthday of Hitler in 1942, the conversation turned to the topic of the Reichstag building and its artistic value. I heard with my own ears when Goering interrupted the conversation and shouted, 'The only one who really knows about the Reichstag is I, because I set it on fire!' With that, he slapped his thigh with the flat of his hand.

Asked for his response to Halder's charge, the defendant testified:

> I had nothing to do with it! I deny this absolutely! I can tell you, in all honesty, that the Reichstag Fire proved very inconvenient to us. After the fire, I had to use the Kroll Opera House as the new Reichstag, and the opera seemed to me much more important than the Reichstag! I must repeat that no pretext was needed for taking measures against the communists. I already had a number of perfectly good reasons in the forms of murders, etc.

Goering arrived at the scene of the blaze at 9.35 p.m. in his Mercedes. He had been driven there from his Prussian Interior Minister's office, on Unter den Linden, with his bodyguard, Walther Weber, just thirty minutes after an arsonist had been spotted on one of the building's balconies. A reporter from *The Times* of London arrived simultaneously, and saw Goering throw another reporter (who had been telephoning his office) down the steps of the building. Reed went inside with Goering, rather than ahead of him.

One eyewitness recalled Goering wearing 'a furry, gray felt hat, and an IRA-like trenchcoat'. Another reporter present was Willi Frischauer, who would write a biography of Goering in 1951. He recalled: 'As he passed us, I saw that his face was a purple red … "A crime, an unheard-of crime!" he thundered … He screamed, "To the gallows with them!"' Both Hitler and Dr Frick wanted to hang the suspect, Marinus van der Lubbe, right there and then, but the Berlin police simply ignored them. Frischauer was one of those in the press who was thoroughly convinced of the guilt of Goering and the SA, and published those allegations in his story. His and other accounts went worldwide, thus providing Goering with global notoriety for the first time.

Goering himself later recalled, 'It never even occurred to me that the Reichstag might have been set alight. I thought the fire had been caused by carelessness.' However, he later claimed that as he entered the building, he heard the word 'arson' from the gaping crowd. Thereafter he almost immediately changed to a political narrative, stating, 'In this moment, I knew that the Communist Party was the culprit.' Indeed, when his nominal boss, von Papen, arrived, Goering shouted, 'This is a communist crime against the new government!'

Sefton Delmer: A Fly on the Nazi Wall

In *Manchester Guardian* reporter and British propagandist Sefton Delmer's 1961 memoirs, he recalled one of Hitler's unique ways of avoiding making a decision that Goering pressed him for—he would excuse himself, claiming that he needed to answer the call of nature, and then simply leave the building altogether. A flabbergasted Goering only found out how he had been outfoxed after half an hour.

Delmer and Goering got on well. Trying to impress the journalist, Goering told him of how he had arrested the cabinet Minister for Unemployment (Compensation) Dr Gunther Gerecke for both embezzlement and bribery. Goering stated, 'That will prove to the world that we Nazis are not afraid of arresting even cabinet ministers if they are guilty of crimes!' Later, Selmer would recall:

> Goering was a good guest. To demonstrate his love of animals, he took Popitzshka, my parrot [possibly named after Goering's Prussian Finance Minister, Johannes Popitz], and put him on his shoulder … He just laughed when Popitzshka treated the future Reich Marshal's elegant dinner jacket as a guano depository.

Delmer was also a witness to the Reichstag Fire:

> I saw the … fire not only from the outside, but the inside—in all senses of the word, and as a result, I formed a view of its origin very different from the legend accepted by historians.

Since he had no vehicle, Delmer simply ran all the way from his office to the burning building—1.5 miles—and arrived at 9.45 p.m., about forty minutes after the first fire alarm had sounded outside Portal No. 2.

An excited policeman told me, 'They have got one of them who did it, a man with nothing but trousers on. He seems to have used his coat and shirt to start the fire, but there must be others still inside. They are looking for them there.

When Hitler arrived, Delmer was allowed to go inside alongside the Führer's entourage.

Inside the entrance stood Goering, massive in a camel hair coat, his legs astride like some Frederician guardsman in a [*sic*.] Ufa film. His soft brown hat was turned up in what was called the 'Potsdam' fashion. He was very red in the face and glared disapprovingly at me … Goering made his report to Hitler, while Goebbels and I stood at their side, listening avidly. 'Without a doubt this is the work of the communists, Herr Chancellor! A number of communist deputies were present here in the Reichstag twenty minutes before the fire broke out. We have succeeded in arresting one of the incendiaries,' he said with that thin shark's mouth of his.…

Then Hitler asked … 'Are the other public buildings safe?'

'I have taken every possible precaution … I have mobilized all the police. Every public building has been given a special guard. We are ready for anything!' … Both Hitler and Goering then still feared the possibility of a communist coup …

Someone opened a yellow varnished oak door, and for a moment, we peeped into the blazing furnace of the Debating Chamber. It was like opening the door of an oven. Although the fire brigade was spraying away lustily with their hoses, the fire was roaring up into the cupola with a fury that made us shut the door again in a hurry.

Goering picked a piece of rag off the floor near one of the charred curtains. 'Here, you can see for yourself Herr Chancellor how they started the fire. They hung cloths soaked in petrol over the furniture and set it alight.' [Delmer noticed straight away that Goering always said 'they' and never 'him']. There had to be a gang of incendiaries, but as I looked at the rags and the other evidence, I could see nothing that one man could not have done on his own...

Goering's main concern was that his precious Gobelin tapestries had not been burned. When Vice Chancellor von Papen arrived, he asserted, 'I trust the Gobelins have escaped, and that the Library … has not been touched either.'

Hans Bernd Gisevius later noted that 'Goering [knew] the House [contained] two irreplaceable treasures: the Library and the Gobelin tapestries that were kept in a room behind the Diplomat's Box. "The Gobelins must be saved!" the Minister cried. His first care was for these irreplaceable works of art'.

Inviting his formal deputy to attend a strategy meeting in Goering's office, Hitler was surprised when von Papen demurred, hurrying off instead and stating, 'I must go and report to the Field Marshal [Hindenburg] first.'

Marinus van der Lubbe (1909–34)

The Berlin police had already arrested a twenty-four-year-old Dutch former communist, Marinus van der Lubbe, who immediately told them that he alone had set the blaze. He never changed his story, neither at the police headquarters nor during the long trial that followed. He stated:

> I acted alone … No one at all helped me, nor did I meet a single person in the Reichstag. The fact is that I did set the Session Chamber on fire with only my jacket! They [those who disputed the story] are experts, but I was there, and set the fire. All I ask for is a verdict. I did it alone. I was there, I know. I set the fire, and it spread by itself.

In fact, he asserted, he had not even decided to burn the building until his arrival out-side it at noon on 27 February 1933, the day of the conflagration. He stated, 'I decided upon the Reichstag as the center of the whole system,' thus using the exact Nazi term to describe the former socialist rule in Weimar Germany during the fourteen years of 1918–33—'the system'.

The blaze was not van der Lubbe's first attempt at setting fire to state buildings, but merely the fourth in a full series that had taken place over the preceding days. First had been a government welfare office at Neukolln-Berlin, next a failed attempt at City Hall, and then the former Berlin palace of the exiled Kaiser Wilhelm II. He had started the Royal Castle fire on the previous day, the 26th, setting fires on the sixth floor and the roof. Discovered by the Berlin Fire Department, both conflagrations were soon extin-guished; van der Lubbe escaped, as he had done after the previous two attempts. His stated goal, he asserted, was 'to spark a workers' rising against the State', and at least in this respect van der Lubbe suited Goering's precise description of him—a politically motivated incendiarist, pure and simple. Part of van der Lubbe's motivation was that he hoped that the revolt of the workers would stop the world war he believed was coming—his prediction of conflict was proved to be accurate in 1939.

Born on 13 January 1909, van der Lubbe was a modest, intelligent boy who enjoyed reading the travelogue books by Swedish pro-German explorer Sven Hedin, who was also admired by both Goering and Hitler. He had worked as a construction worker in Holland, but was partially blinded after a prank played on him by coworkers had left him with lime in his eyes; afterwards, he lived on monthly disability payments from the Dutch government. Despite four operations, he was legally declared partially blind in both eyes.

He held numerous manual labor jobs, working as a waiter, a potato trader, a dredger, a butcher, and a messenger boy. He was intelligent and physically strong at 5 feet 10 inches and 151 pounds. During his early socialist-communist phase, van der Lubbe asserted himself both in speeches and by throwing bricks—thus becoming well-known to the Dutch police. Clearly eccentric, in 1930 he considered swimming across the English Channel from the French coastal port of Calais, but bad weather prevented his attempt; he hitchhiked across Europe instead.

In September 1931 van der Lubbe began to walk to China via Austria and Hungary, but he was halted in Yugoslavia. On a follow-up trip to the USSR in September 1932, he was halted at the border and turned away by Polish frontier guards. Returning home to the Netherlands, van der Lubbe lived in a government workmen's compensation camp until setting out on yet another cross-country trek to Berlin, where he first arrived on 18 February 1933 after a fifteen-day hike. Upon his arrival, German communists thought he was a spy for the hated Nazis, and that he had been sent to infiltrate their ranks. In the 1933 communist-produced, anti-Nazi *Brown Book*, it was alleged that van der Lubbe was a homosexual, and had either been pimped into Germany to become Röhm's lover or already was. Neither allegation was proven.

Just prior to setting the Reichstag ablaze, van der Lubbe had walked to neighboring Spandau (which would be home to the Nazi war criminals from 1947–87), and then walked back home to Berlin again.

To accomplish his nefarious plan, van der Lubbe bought four packages of Oldin-brand matches—a mix of sawdust and naphthalene used to start residential coal fires, showing a red flame when lit. Van der Lubbe simply climbed through a Reichstag window into the building's restaurant, where the elected deputies and various staffers ate; he set his first fire there. Later, it was charged that he had set this fire in order to distract the firefighters from the main blaze in the Session Chamber. If this was his plan, he succeeded, with the latter being totally devastated.

Entering the cavernous, ornate Session Chamber, he torched a curtain of old draper-ies behind the Speaker's chair, the very same occupied during meetings by Reichstag President Hermann Wilhelm Goering. He used his sweater to torch Goering's own chair 'as a protest', he later avowed. Because of the age of the curtains, they were no longer flame-retardant, and burned right away. Van der Lubbe later asserted that he used his overcoat, vest, shirt, and then 'a bit of burning tablecloth' as kindling. The curtain fires spread to the wooden desks of the deputies and then onto the walls.

At this point van der Lubbe could hear voices outside the chamber, and so he stopped in the hallway of the Bismarck Room at 9.25 p.m., awaiting certain arrest. By now he was shirtless and sweating heavily. Meanwhile, the Berlin police were certain that they were dealing with arson, mostly likely carried out by seven men or more; their loaded pistols were out of their holsters, and one had even taken a shot at the arsonist, but he missed.

The extraordinarily rapid spread of the fire been ongoing for but six minutes, from 9.21 to 9.27 p.m., when the massive, magisterial, glass-dome cupola above the Session Chamber simply exploded from the pent-up gases that had gathered down below. In Hett's *Burning the Reichstag* (2014), he describes how the flames poured up and outward with 'a rush of air'. To the police and the firemen on the scene, the Session Chamber appeared as 'a sea of flames'; later, experts such as Prof. Karl Stephen, Gustav Wagner, Emil Josse, and Dr Franz Ritter would unanimously conclude that 'some kind of flammable liquid—probably kerosene or heavy gasoline—had been used' to make the oak and pine 'hot enough for ignition temperature'. Another theory was that van der Lubbe had used the deputies' cardboard nameplates, sitting on their desks, to help spread the flames from the curtains to the oak, but the experts insisted that this might only have worked if they were piled up in stacks, campfire-style; nonetheless, photo-graphs taken at the time showed burnt and singed nameplates amongst charred debris.

The explosion at 9.27 p.m. had been caused by 'generating gases', causing the fire 'to spread like lightning across the whole room', as described by Fire Officer Waldemar Klotz. He later testified that he had to hold on to the chamber's door handles to prevent being sucked into the maelstrom, so strong was the force inside. Later, the various court-ordered experts (engineers, firefighters, chemists, and specialists in thermody-namics) consistently agreed that:

> Only burning gas and kerosene could have generated enough explosive gas in the time available for the flames leading to the smoke of a shouldering fire and its outward draft in succeeding phases.

In what was termed as 'the most reliable evidence produced', the fire was centered on the 'stenographic enclosure' and the steps that 'led from the enclosure down to the lower floor'. The experts also agreed that the fire site 'had been prepared with gas-soaked rags on the deputies' desk seats, and then were connected to the primary fire with either match cord or filmstrips'. It did not help the Nazis' later pleas of innocence that the Berlin SA had a unit for 'special missions' like these at the time of the fire; it was also simply not believed that one man could have had enough time to accomplish all that destruction in the six minutes he had between being sighted and being arrested. The experts argued that if van der Lubbe had ten minutes (at most) inside the building, he could not have got the sturdy oak chairs to burn in that time.

Additionally, no liquid agent was found on his person upon apprehension, nor did he credit the cardboard nameplates for helping set the blaze. A 1970 re-opening of the investigation again concluded that the fire must have been caused or aided by kerosene or gasoline. Tobias claimed that the burning curtains ignited the wooden wall paneling, and that these combined fires resulted in an 'enormous upward pressure with a cor-responding draft'; however, the restaurant fire still required 'some kind of petroleum or self-igniting fluid'. Another expert at the 1933 trial argued, 'The only way to get the oaken seating to burn was via a fire started with a self-igniting phosphorous solu-tion', which again seemed to indicate it was impossible that van der Lubbe could have achieved the fire on his own. One eyewitness claimed to have seen 'fifteen to twenty' small fires raging, while others argued that these were simply reflections of the main fire on the smooth desktops.

The very night of the fire, Berlin Police Chief and Nazi member Count Wolf von Helldorf, Dr Diels, and Maj. Wecke began a wide crackdown on KPD and Socialist party activists. Over 4,000 were arrested, selected from lists already compiled by Diels for Chancellor von Papen in summer 1932. As a Nazi spy within the Weimar Republic, Diels had already made the list's existence known to Goering. Goering later asserted, 'Whenever you use a plane, you cannot help making splinters!'

For the trial, van der Lubbe was taken to the Reichstag and asked to retrace his exact route, which he did precisely—in a building which he had never been in before the night of the fire, and in the dark, no less. It was suggested that his lack of reliable eyesight had been supplanted by a sixth, guiding sense that he used twice—once on the night of the fire, and again during the reenactment. He showed how he entered the chamber from behind the president's desk—just as Goering would—and set fire to the curtains only, and not to any other items. He testified that he set two curtains on fire at both the front and rear of the chamber, and then ran through it, back to front, dragging a burning curtain.

The prosecution alleged that van der Lubbe was covering for alleged communist accomplices who had escaped, just as Goering had claimed from the start—and the court agreed. Conversely, the communists and almost everyone else accused Goering of commanding the arson via SA Maj. Gen. Karl Ernst (1904–34), who was in charge of the Berlin-Brandenburg SA (although actually under the command of Goebbels, as Berlin Gauleiter, and SA Staff Chief Ernst Röhm. Those who alleged Nazi involvement claimed that Goebbels had the idea, Goering planned it, and Karl Ernst executed the operation, entering and leaving the Reichstag through the tunnel, disappearing before van der Lubbe was arrested.

Much of the free world accepted this narrative until more than thirty years later, when German journalist Fritz Tobias (1912–2011) turned the theory on its head with the publication of his groundbreaking work *The Reichstag Fire*. On first reading, the author's claim that van der Lubbe had the time and the necessary materials to act alone is convincing; in 1972 R. John Pritchard's *Reichstag Fire: Ashes of Democracy* endorsed Tobias's findings.

In 2014 Benjamin Carter Hett's superb revisionist history, *Burning the Reichstag: An Investigation into the Third Reich's Enduring Mystery*, was published, and raised new questions about Tobias's theory. Hett lays blame in the same manner as the anti-Nazis of 1933 and beyond, holding Goebbels, Goering, Ernst and Edmund Heines responsible. Tobias's research was acclaimed for fifty years, and the author was still living when Hett was researching the new book—however, Hett's argument is by far the most convincing.

Goering v. Sommerfeldt

Goering's first press secretary, Martin Sommerfeldt, thirty-three, drafted a matter-of-fact, official press release about the fire for the Prussian Press Service, not mentioning any plot. At 1 a.m. on the night after the fire, Goering read the document and exploded with rage, banging his fist down on a table and roaring out, 'This is sheer bullshit! It may be a good police report from the Alex [the Berlin nickname for the police headquarters located on the Alexanderplatz], but it is not at all the kind of political release that I have in mind!'

The young press aide was taken aback, later recalling: 'His tone was insulting. No one had ever dared to speak to me in that way.' Goering then took out a blue pencil and began editing his aide's first draft.

'One hundredweight of incendiary material? No, ten—or even 100!'

Sommerfeldt stood his ground. 'This is quite impossible, Minister! No one can possibly believe that a single man could have carried that load!'

'Nothing is impossible!' Goering barked back. 'Why mention a single man? There were ten or even twenty men! Do you not understand what has been happening? The whole thing was a signal for a communist uprising!'

Sommerfeldt was not backing down, however. 'I do not think so, Minister! No one has mentioned anything of the sort, not even Diels … I must insist, Minister, that my report is based on the official findings of the fire brigade and police.'

Throwing down his blue editing pencil, Goering snorted, 'I shall dictate the report myself to Miss Grundtmann. You can insist all you want!' Sommerfeldt asked Goering to sign his new version. 'Whatever for?' Goering asked, astonished.

'Because this is not an official report on a fire, Minister,' his press aide replied, 'but a political document. The news agencies will only accept it from me if you sign it officially.' In silence, Goering signed a large 'G' after its last line.

When the report was published, the communists not only accepted Goering's figure of ten arsonists instead of one, but gleefully converted them from communists to Nazis. They were not the only readers who ridiculed the government's claim that the communists were responsible; Hett describes how government-employed historian Friedrich Thimme, at breakfast with his children, chuckled, 'That can only have been Hermann Goering!'

After surviving the Nazi regime and the war, Sommerfeldt published his memoirs, *I Was There*, in 1949, discussing the fire at length. Additionally, a Dr Wolff published a letter he had received from Sommerfeldt:

> From the night of the fire to this day, I have been convinced that the Reichstag was set on fire neither by communists nor at the instigation—let alone the participation—of Hermann Goering, but that the fire was the *piece de resistance* of Dr Goebbels' election campaign, and that it was started by a handful of stormtroopers, all of whom were shot afterwards by an SS commando ... in Berlin.

Dr Rudolf Diels and Karl Ernst allegedly also discussed the incident with Sommerfeldt in the spring of 1934, in which 'there was talk of ten men ... exact details about the scene and of the crime, and the identification of the ten victims'. However, Sommerfeldt did not chose to reveal this information in his 1949 memoir. His conclusion was this:

> Goebbels administered this act of incendiarism as a shot in the arm of the floating or lazy voters ... Goebbels flung Hitler and Goering into a whirlpool of profound and irrevocable decisions ... [and he] knew what he was doing.

Ernst Röhm agreed during a heated discussion with Sommerfeldt over the fire. 'What on earth did Goering have to do with the whole business?' he asked.

'Who else?' Sommerfeldt responded.

'Who but that devil, Jupp?' 'Jupp', meaning 'Joe', was a spiteful nickname for Dr Goebbels.

Goebbels' machinations were entirely possible, as he had indeed caused many political problems for Goering in the past, as Hermann had himself asserted after a conversation with Hindenburg. 'Every time I have gotten that hard East Prussian head almost soft, Jupp clubs me one between the legs!'

Someone who did not believe Goering's version of the fire was the industrialist Fritz Thyssen, to whom he had given a tour of the Reichstag's burned area on 1 March 1933. In 1941, Thyssen recalled:

The burning of the Reichstag—organized by Hitler and Goering—was the first step in a colossal political swindle ... **Two months** earlier, [Goering] had telephoned to my house to warn me that a rebellion **was about** to break out in the Ruhr, and that I headed the list of proposed hostages. He said **that he had** been informed by his spies in the Communist Party. How could I have doubted his **word?** I therefore began to collaborate openly with the regime.

The Emergency Decree for the Protection of People and State, 28 February 1933

On 4 February 1933, President von Hindenburg, at the behest of Hitler and Goering, had enacted the Decree for the Protection of the German People. A more-strident version of the legislation **was kept** in waiting, and was referred to as 'the decree in the drawer'; it was initially **drafted** for then-Chancellor von Papen by Socialist Reich Minister Karl Severing in the **summer** of 1932.

The later version was **introduced** on 28 February 1933, the day after the fire; it was the genesis of the Nazi **repression** of the Third Reich. It reads:

Sections 114–15, 117–18, 123–4, **and** 15 of the Constitution of the German Reich are suspended until further **notice. Accordingly,** restrictions of the freedom of the person, of speech, press, assembly, **and association;** interference with the privacy of letters, mails, telegraph, and telephone, **also authorized** search of domicile and confiscation and restraint of property are admissible **also outside** the limits normally set by the law.

In effect, von Hindenburg **had given** Goering a blank check to violate any and all civil rights at his whim. In **doing this,** he took a big step to becoming the dictator (under Hitler) of both Prussia **and the Reich** in total in one fell swoop.

Sefton Delmer watched **the decree** take effect on the streets of Berlin as truckloads of SA raided all known **communist** haunts, arresting both German communists and also 'lawyers, doctors, actors, **and journalists',** men and women. One KPD figure who escaped Goering's dragnet, **however,** was the later ruler of post-war communist East Germany—Walter Ulbricht. **In 1961** Delmer wrote that the half-naked van der Lubbe had been 'wrapped in rugs' **for his trip** to the Berlin Police Headquarters on 'The Alex'. Once there, the 'sole arsonist' **declared** that he belonged to an anti-Moscow, communist splinter group. Delmer insisted **that once** inside, he could see no SA men at all.

Another NSDAP Sweep at the Polls, 5 March 1933

On 29 February 1933, **Goering** gave his famed 'Red Monster Speech' in a nationwide radio address. He asked, **'What would** have happened if this communist bestiality had been given twenty-four **hours'** grace? ... We have no wish to see the German people torn to pieces by the Red Monster!'

With the alleged 'Red' arson **most** prominent in the minds of voters, on 5 March

1933 the NSDAP gathered 17.2 million votes, gaining ninety-two more seats in the Reichstag and making a total of 288 in the party's delegation. However, this was still only 43.9 per cent of the total votes cast; the Nazis therefore never even achieved 50 per cent of the votes in any free German election, but they managed to gain a dictatorship anyway. The KDP won 120 seats, with a total vote of 7.1 million, but Goering had all the KDP deputies arrested, so they never took their seats or voted.

'Jews Out!'—Goering's Anti-Semitic Pogrom, 13 March 1933

On 13 March 1933 Goering appointed Julius Lippert, a former elected member of Berlin's city council, as Mayor of Berlin. Goering ordered him to dismiss all Jewish doctors and Jews in government office. By 1 April, Berlin's Moabit General Hospital had thus been 'cleansed' of all Jewish medical staff. Later that spring, this was extended to 85 per cent of the city's Jewish physicians, lawyers, and administrators being driven out of their professions.

'The Birth of the Third Reich'—Goering Passes the Enabling Act, 24 March 1933

The Third Reich began on 24 March 1933, when the Nazi-dominated Reichstag voted to give Hitler dictatorial powers. Goering counted the votes from his chair, located behind and above the Speaker's rostrum in the Kroll Opera House.

With the communists prevented from voting, terror and intimidation persuaded enough of the remaining non-Nazi deputies to give their votes to the Nazi dictatorship, thereby also voting themselves out of existence. Machine guns reportedly stood in the halls and on the balconies as the votes were cast—shades of the 1923 Beer Hall Putsch. The result was duly announced by Reichstag President Goering—444 to 94 in favor of Hitler.

The Socialist Party was subsequently outlawed altogether in June, thus achieving at last the dream of both Bismarck and the exiled Kaiser. The liberal period in Germany of 1848–1933 had ended, not to be restored until 1955—a decade after the fall of the Third Reich.

Berlin-Brandenburg SA Leader Karl Ernst (1900–34)

Goering's February–August 1933 augmentation of the Orpo presented him with a dilemma—one which he had created himself—for it brought to the fore the commander of the Berlin SA, Lt Gen. Karl Ernst, as Berlin Police President.

A former Berlin Eden Hotel doorman and waiter in a café, Ernst wore his kepi cap at a jaunty angle and swaggered even more than the typical cocky Nazi thug. As Röhm's 'man in Berlin', Ernst was rumored to be bisexual, taking high-society women and boys as lovers—and maybe even Röhm as well. Ernst was also reportedly a fan of torture, reveling in commanding the SA's 'wild' concentration camps (the ones that Goering did not directly control).

Goering feared and hated Ernst, and with valid cause; an ugly rumor circulated that he had boasted that he wanted to cut down 'Fat Hermann's' weight by half, personally slicing off slabs of Goering's flesh with a knife and then sticking the knife in his throat.

On 3 June 1934, just twenty-seven days before he would be shot during the Blood Purge, Ernst allegedly signed what has become known as 'Ernst's Confession'—his admission of complicity in setting the Reichstag Fire. Although Fritz Tobias later claimed it was a communist forgery, it makes for fascinating reading. Ernst claimed that he chose two unidentified helpers, and travelled to the building using the Goering tunnel:

> We entered the Session Chamber at 8.45 p.m. … where we prepared a number of fires by smearing chairs and tables with the phosphorus mixture, and by soaking curtains and carpets in paraffin. At exactly 9.05 p.m. we had finished, and started on our way back … The phosphorus was fixed to go off within thirty minutes. At 9.12 p.m., we were back in the Boiler House, and at 9.15 p.m., we climbed across the wall [all of them wore civilian clothes, and not SA uniforms].
>
> The allegations published abroad against any others are false. We three did the work entirely by ourselves. Apart from Goering, Goebbels, Röhm, Heines, Killinger, Hanfstangl, and Sander, no one knew about our plan … I am writing this confession as my insurance against the evil plans of Goering and Goebbels. I shall destroy it the moment these traitors have been paid out.

And what of the alleged Nazi dupe, Marinus van der Lubbe? Of him, Ernst wrote:

> Helldorf told us that a young fellow had turned up in Berlin of whom we should be able to make good use … the Dutch communist. I did not meet him before the action … The Dutchman would climb into the Reichstag and blunder about conspicuously in the corridor. Meanwhile, my men and I would set fire to the Session Chamber and part of the lobby. The Dutchman was supposed to start at 9 p.m.—half an hour later than we did. The main difficulty was keeping to a precise timetable.

When he signed this document, Ernst did so believing that he was supporting Hitler and Röhm against Goering and Goebbels, at a time when he commanded 8,000 SA men. The 1933 *Brown Book* further claimed that van der Lubbe was one of Röhm's gay lovers, but named the NSDAP arsonists as Count von Helldorf, Heines, and Schulz. Communists also alleged that the victims of the Blood Purge died because of their intimate knowledge of the Reichstag Fire conspiracy. In 1934, future anti-Goering memoirist and IMT prosecution witness Hans-Bernd Gisevius stated, 'There was never a Röhm Putsch … but only a Goering-Himmler Putsch … not a single shot was fired by the SA.'

Goering's Alliance with the SS Duo, October 1933–July 1934

Aside from the Orpo SA, both Hitler and Goering had personal guard units of Röhm and Ernst SA men 'protecting them'. Neither man felt safe; both feared being murdered by 'their' SA men when the SA Duo gave the orders. It is believed that some time in October 1933 Goering decided to forge an alliance with the SA Duo's secret foes—the SS Duo of Heinrich Himmler and his deputy, Reinhard Heydrich. Goering handpicked Pilli Korner, already an SS man, to be his liaison between the two Blackguards. In addition, on 9 November 1933 Goering had Gestapo Chief Dr Rudolf Diels join the SS, as a show of good faith to his former opponents for control of the German police.

On 2 December Goering was alarmed when Hitler favoured Röhm by naming him as Minister without Portfolio in the cabinet; this was also Goering's position, partially making the two men equals in government. Indeed, it was not until the very last moment, in June 1934, that it became apparent who Hitler would actually be backing in the coming showdown. There were numerous battles to be fought—Goering *v.* Röhm, right *v.* left, and the Army *v.* the Stormtroopers. The tension would mount for Goering until the first shots were fired.

'Boer General' Goering Establishes Germany's Concentration Camps

As German prisons rapidly filled to the point of overflowing, Goering aped Britain's barbed-wire pens in South Africa in 1899, creating Germany's first domestic concentration camps. Inside, the Reich's foes were confined and reeducated to become what Goering considered to be 'model citizens'. In all, Goering was responsible for establishing four large concentration camps in Prussia, which would hold far more detainees than any other German state by the end of 1933. The camps were: Papenburg, Emsland, in the Reich's northwestern area, bordering on the Netherlands, established in the summer; Brandenburg, on the Havel River, established in August and holding around 1,000 inmates; Lichtenburg, Prettin, on the Elbe River, established in September and holding around 1,675 inmates; and Sonnenburg, established in November and holding around another 1,000. Goering famously ousted the SS from the Emsland camps on 5 November and then handed them over to their rivals, the SA—a reversal of his earlier practices. On the 13th, he instituted what he termed 'protective custody' for detention of all 'professional criminals' who could not be brought to justice immediately due to lack of evidence.

In December, Goering played Santa Claus by freeing 5,000 inmates in his famous 'Christmas Amnesty'—possibly recalling his own pardon from Hindenburg in October 1927. He closed camps at Borgermoor and Neusustrum in April 1934, and also closed Oranienburg that August; meanwhile, the Nazi press extolled his virtues to the German public as the 'guarantor of order'. On 1 October 1946, at his trial at Nuremberg, Goering would be duly convicted of crimes against humanity—at least partially for his 1933 creation of Germany's first concentration camps.

When he reluctantly handed over the Gestapo to Himmler, Goering bequeathed to the RFSS 600 officials at its Berlin headquarters as well as 2,000 other agents

Reich-wide. That December, however, the two men waged a fierce internecine battle over the increasing expansion of the Black Boys' *Konzentrationslager* (KL) empire, with 'Reichsheini' arguing that the system was 'the most effective weapon against the enemies of the state'. Goering was not so sure, and he viewed Himmler's ever-expanding tentacles with growing apprehension.

The Bogus Communist Air Force Scare, 23 June 1933

On 23 June 1933 Goering and Goebbels jointly launched a fake communist air force leaflet drop over Berlin, aiming to scare pacifist Germans into going along with Nazi plans for a reborn German air force. Newspaper headlines blared out: 'Red Plague over Berlin! Foreign Planes of an Unknown Type Escape Unrecognized; Defenseless Germany'. Reporter H. W. Blood-Ryan called Goering for his reaction, and Goering responded:

> I have not one single plane that I could have sent up in defense and pursuit. I am going to do my utmost to build at least a few police planes to be prepared against any future attacks … not … a question of military defense, they are an absolute necessity.

Goering therefore began circumventing the air force restrictions imposed on Germany by the 1919 Treaty of Versailles. Indeed, later in summer 1933 the British government agreed to allow UK aircraft firms to sell the desired aircraft to Goering; Hanfstaengl recalled seeing Goering and Sir John Siddeley discussing British military aircraft blueprints that Siddeley wanted to sell to the Reich. The pair were sitting on the Landhaus Goering balcony on the Obersalzberg.

Few Berliners (if any) could actually recall seeing or reading any of the alleged communist leaflets dropped over Berlin, but the NSDAP ruse succeeded in demonstrating to the population just how open German skies truly were to enemy aerial assault. Politically, Goering used the episode to convince Hitler to let him take control of the current Air Defense League (then operating under Dr Frick's Reich Interior Ministry), thus adding to his already growing aerial bureaucratic empire.

Despite Goering and Goebbels' collaboration on the leaflet project, cracks were appearing in their relationship. On 26 June 1933 the US Consul General in Berlin, George S. Messersmith, sent a letter to US Undersecretary of State William Phillips in Washington:

> … Goering and Goebbels still remain good comrades of Hitler, and are undoubtedly attached to him, but the differences between Goering and Goebbels are becoming more evident.
>
> Goering is more moderate, while Goebbels … is becoming more radical. If it would come to a showdown between the radical and moderate elements, Goering would, however, undoubtedly be likely to be on the radical side, as the one having more chances….

One year later, in June 1934, Messersmith's latter assessment would prove to be entirely wrong.

With few exceptions, the men who are running this government are of a mentality that you and I cannot understand. Some of them are psychopathic cases, and would ordinarily be receiving treatment somewhere.

Others are exalted, and in a frame of mind that knows no reason. The majority are woefully ignorant, and unprepared for the tasks that they have to carry through every day.

Those men in the party and in responsible positions who are really worthwhile—and there are quite a number of these—are powerless, because they have to follow the orders of superiors who are suffering from the abnormal psychology prevailing in the country.

Goering's Palace: His Second Official Residence in Berlin

From August 1932 Goering's official residence in Reich Capital Berlin had been the old Reichstag President's Palace, adjacent to the chamber building itself and connected by the notorious underground tunnel. He did not live there, however, preferring his bachelor apartment on the Kaiserdamm. Despite already holding these two properties, when Goering became Prussian Prime Minister—and Bismarck's successor—he wanted his own townhouse palace, designed by himself and funded by the taxpayer. His wish was granted in the form of the former Prussian State Commerce Building on Leipzigerstrasse; it was situated next door to the Gestapo headquarters, which he relocated to the infamous address of No. 8 Prinz Albrechtstrasse, later the nerve center of Himmler's SS and Heydrich's SD. Goering's man Dr Diels simply took the former Berlin Folklore Museum under the state's right of eminent domain, and thus was born the Gestapo's final home.

After the dual renovations of the Berlin palace's sites—with the townhouse overseen by Hitler's own architect, Albert Speer—Goering also moved his sumptuous new Air Ministry building in next door. Goering had thus established himself architecturally in the nation's center. Until his new Berlin palace opened, Goering used the dreary Reichstag President's Palace for meetings and official receptions, and also worked in the Presidential Office in the Reichstag proper on a day-to-day basis. He was therefore usually at the latter location—but not on the night of the Reichstag Fire, when he instead worked in his office at the Prussian Interior Ministry, on the Unter den Linden thoroughfare, in downtown Berlin's Government Quarter.

Work started on the Berlin palace in June 1933 at the corner of Prinz Albrechtstrasse and the Republican-styled Stressemannstrasse. Goering rechristened the latter street as 'Hermann Goeringstrasse' instead, via Julius Lippert's office, the City Mayor of Berlin. The Berlin palace was completed in January 1934.

Goering and the Secret Black Luftwaffe, 1933–34

When Goering entered Hitler's coalition cabinet on 30 January 1933, one of his posts was as Reich Minister of Civil Air Transport, or Reich Aviation Minister. This was the cover presented for the Nazi ramp-up of that sector of the aircraft industry, which in two years would morph into its real martial identity as the Luftwaffe (Air Weapon). Until then, Goering secretly headed what the Allied intelligence services already knew as the secret 'Black Luftwaffe'—comprised partially of the civilian glider movement and also the national civil passenger airline, Lufthansa.

Goering was aided in promoting flying, air defense, and air warfare readiness by many individuals, groups, and related forces. These actors would play major roles in Nazifying and then expanding the air industry left behind by Gen. Hans von Seeckt and his minions in 1920–27. Even today, authors continue to embrace the Nazi propaganda that asserted Goring and the Nazis created the new Luftwaffe from scratch, but this is false.

In 1933, Goering's initial plan for the Luftwaffe was for it to be a small air force concealed under the guise of civil aviation and amateur flying clubs, so as not to overtly challenge the rules of the Treaty of Versailles immediately. During the three years from fall 1935 to fall 1938, Goering ramped up construction to establish a full-scale Nazi aerial armada. In 1989, David Irving convincingly asserted that Goering was able to do this because he was the one political leader who had the full trust and confidence of the man who counted most—Hitler. Goering's inspired, creative leadership ensured that the first, embryonic, secret air ministry emerged on 11 March 1933.

Dr Hjalmar Schacht

A great deal of money was needed for the project, particularly when Goering's mantra within the air force was reportedly 'money is no object'; he was thus allocated 40 million Reichsmarks in his very first annual aviation budget by Chancellor Hitler. The man who initially controlled the German government and banking financial spigot was Dr Hjalmar Horace Greeley Schacht (22 January 1877–3 June 1970). His indictment at the IMT in October 1945 makes for informative reading:

> Between 1932–45 [Schacht was] a member of the Nazi Party, a member of the Reichstag, Reich Minister of Economics, Reich Minister Without Portfolio, and President of the German Reichsbank.
>
> The defendant Schacht used the foregoing positions in such a manner that he promoted the accession to power of the Nazi conspirators and the consolidation of their control over Germany set forth in Count One.
>
> He promoted the preparations for war set forth in Count One, and he participated in the military and economic plans and preparation of the Nazi conspirators for wars of aggression, and wars in violation of international treaties, agreements, and assurances set forth in Counts One and Two.

Schacht was born in Tingleff, Germany (in modern-day Denmark); his mother was a Danish Baroness, and this is the reason for his Danish first name. His middle names were given in honour of the famous American newspaper man. Schacht received a doctorate in economics in 1899, when Hitler was ten years old and Goering was just seven. On a business trip to the United States in 1905, Schacht met the famed banker J. P. Morgan and President Theodore Roosevelt, also meeting the latter's successor as President in 1933—his cousin, Franklin Roosevelt.

Schacht first became a Reichsbank director in 1916, during the First World War, while Goering was a fighter ace and Cpl Hitler was a trench messenger. In 1923 Schacht was named as the Weimar Republic's Currency Commissioner, charged with helping to stabilize the Mark and reduce inflation. After being named as Reichsbank President for the first time, Schacht negotiated the payment of German post-war reparations with the Allied powers. He resigned the presidency on 7 March 1930, returning under the Nazi government on 17 March 1933. When Carin Goering had still been alive, Schacht and Hitler met at one of her parties at Hermann's Berlin apartment.

In March 1934 Hitler appointed Dr Schacht as Reich Minister of Economics, thereby easing the passage to funding for one of Hitler's key projects—the autobahns. Schacht's famed 'Mefo Bills' helped to fund Germany's rearmament, and in May 1935 Hitler named him as Plenipotentiary for the War Economy. He was also awarded honorary Nazi Party membership and the Golden Party Badge in January 1937. From 1933–34 Schacht got along quite well with both the Reich Chancellor and the Reich Aviation Minister, his colleagues in the cabinet; the funding for the air force thus proceeded apace.

Der Deutsche Luftssports Vergaband *(The German Air Sports League)*

In many ways, the DLV was the predecessor to the Luftwaffe; as its head, Goering established the *Reichsluftschutzbund* (Reich Air Defense League) on 28 April 1933. The Luftwaffe would later adopt several aspects of the DLV's 1933 blue-gray uniforms in 1935, including the basic design of its collar patch rank insignia. The DLV's collar patches featured four colors—white, black, blue, and yellow. According to Brigata Nera, these colors were also replicated by the Luftwaffe on some of its own grades of personnel and branches.

Goering's National Socialist Flying Corps (NSFK), 1932–45

The NSFK was established by Goering via a Führer Decree in January 1932, and was revived in 1937, fifteen years later, when the latter incarnation was brought into line with all other NSDAP paramilitary forces. In 1933 it had replaced the DLV; Friedrich Christiansen, a former merchant seaman, was named as Korpsführer, and he was later succeeded by Albert Keller.

Although the NSFK was made up entirely of men, it nevertheless permitted female participation via the launching and recovery of gliders. Despite being basically a part-time group, the NSFK had a small amount of full-time, paid staff, with an emphasis on ground operation as well as flight. An NSFK school was established at Rossgarten, in the Warthegau. The importance of physical exercise was also stressed—especially skiing, as it enhanced the sense of balance needed by pilots. The NSFK therefore maintained its own ski school in Austria's Zell-am-See resort area. As Reich Minister for Air Travel, Goering was the overall commander of the organization.

Gen. Friedrich Christiansen (1879–1972)

Christiansen was known as 'The Fighter of Zeebrugge' from his First World War glory days; he earned the title by destroying the British submarine C–25. His wartime tally of twenty-one aerial victories included not only airplanes but also flying boats and balloons. Like his contemporaries Goering, Udet, and Lorzer, Christiansen was awarded the Blue Max by the Kaiser. After the war he captained a ship for the Hamburg–America Steamship Lines, but he later returned to the air as the commander of the twelve-engine Dornier Do-X—the globe's largest flying boat. From 1931–32 Christiansen took the craft on a record-breaking aerial cruise.

Goering brought the ace into the Nazi orbit as the head of the new NSFK, and he was responsible for training some of Nazi Germany's first pilots. Later named as a Luftwaffe general, during the war Christiansen also served as the chief of the military government of Nazi-occupied Holland, under Nazi Commissar Artur Seyss-Inquart.

Imprisoned in 1945 and charged with war crimes, Gen. Christiansen was acquitted—Seyss-Inquart, however, was convicted and hanged. After the trial, the general retired; he died in 1972, just eight days short of his ninety-third birthday.

Gen. Alfred Keller (1882–1974)

In 1943, Gen. Christiansen was succeeded as NSFK commander by Luftwaffe Gen. Alfred Keller. He began his military career in 1902, and two years later was commissioned as a Lieutenant of engineers. By 1912 he had joined the Imperial German Flying Service, and during the First World War he greatly distinguished himself for his daring exploits—in 1917, as commander of a bomber unit, he was given the nickname *Bomben Keller* (Bomber Keller). On 30 January 1918 he was also credited with the first aerial attack on Paris, being awarded the *Pour le Mérite* before Goering.

After the war, Keller worked in the German civilian airline industry like Milch; in 1933, Goering named him as a colonel in the Black Luftwaffe, and as commanding officer of the secret 1st Attack Bomber Wing. When Hitler appointed Goering as the first Air Force Field Marshal, Keller was promoted to Lieutenant General and named commanding general of the 4th Flying Corps on the Western Front, following the successful German campaign against Poland in 1939.

Keller was named as Colonel General in 1940 as the commander of Air Fleet 1, but his failures during the first years of the Russian campaign led to his removal in the summer of 1943. Semi-retired, he was transferred to the position of head of the NSFK—its second and final commander. After the war, he recommenced work for a civilian airline.

Goering's Jewish Aerial Assistant, Erhard Milch (1892-1972)

Like Goering, Erhard Milch ended the First World War as a Captain and was promoted on 19 July 1940 to the exalted grade of Luftwaffe Field Marshal. This was despite the fact he was at least partially (and perhaps even fully) Jewish. Milch was born on 30 March 1892, almost a year before his later aerial chieftain. Goering later came to both fear and hate Milch, regarding him as his possible successor as commander of the air force, but he also very much needed his services in the early days of the reborn Luftwaffe. Regarding the anti-Milch Nazi rumormongering about his Jewish heritage, Goering is famously said to have bellowed, 'I say who is a Jew!' On 29 January 1972, Milch's obituary in *The New York Times* stated:

> Milch's father was a Jew. Goering had Milch declared a full Aryan by having Milch's mother produce a statement saying that he was not his father's son at all.

A former director of Weimar Germany's renowned civil aviation airline Lufthansa, in 1933 Milch left this position (at the express request of Hitler and Goering) to prepare for the launching of the new Luftwaffe. The *New York Times* obituary continued:

> Milch, ever grateful, always did Goering's bidding, even appearing in 1946 at the Nuremberg war crimes trials in his defense … [he] started work on the reorganization of the Luftwaffe in 1933, when he was promoted to general and took command of the unborn Air Force … Milch, who started his military career at cadet school in 1910 at the age of 18, served throughout World War I, first as a lieutenant in the artillery, and then as a fighter pilot, coming out with the rank of captain in the aviation service.
>
> After the war, he found work in Germany's budding aviation industry. By 1926, the country's network of lines was united under *Lufthansa*, that received government aid, and Milch became one of the directors.
>
> He attacked the chief problem besetting airlines at the time—safety—and gave *Lufthansa* a solid reputation in this area.

During Goering's time in the Reichstag from 1928–33, Milch was bribing his future boss with 1,000 RM per month (and then a lump sum of 100,000 RM) at a time when taking such money was not considered to be criminal.

Milch turned down Goering's first official job offer in 1933, which was as State Secretary in the Prussian State Ministry (under Goering), and no wonder. It is entirely possible that Milch believed Hitler might appoint him, rather than Goering, to launch the new Luftwaffe, but the opposite occurred. It took Hitler himself to convince Milch to accept Goering's second offer, a State Secretary posting, which cast Milch as Goering's deputy in creating, organizing, and then administering the Luftwaffe. He therefore became Under Secretary for Air within the eventual Reich Air Ministry. However, his acceptance had been conditional—Goering had to assure him that he was no longer a morphine addict, whether this was true or not.

In general, Goering gave Milch an entirely free hand in running the Air Ministry and building the Nazi air fleets, aside from visiting the air force's Rechlin aeronautical experimental station, west of Berlin, where new models were tested. Initially Milch focused more on bombers than other types of planes, seeking a visual deterrent against Nazi Germany's likely aerial opponents. The Goering-Milch team was also successful in getting Defense Minister Gen. Werner von Blomberg to allow them to create the Luftwaffe as a separate, independent, armed force rather than as a branch of the Army or Navy, as was the case in some other countries (such as the USA, whose Air Force only became a distinct organization in 1947).

On 5 May 1933 Goering's former Reich Commissariat for Air was upgraded to a full Reich Ministry by President von Hindenburg, with Goering becoming the new Reich Minister for Aviation. On 6 May, Milch established contracts for the construction of 1,000 new planes in order to help lay the foundation for what the Third Reich needed most of all—an aircraft industry with a trained workforce. In 1933, that force accounted for just 3,500 workers in total; the Junkers firm (which owned the Reich's largest aircraft factories) was making just eighteen Ju-52 transport planes per year at that point. This clearly had to change, and to help it along von Blomberg graciously allowed 182 military and forty-two naval aviation officers to transfer to the fledgling air service. These officers were recruited by Chief of Personnel Col. Hans-Jurgen Stumpff, and all within the first year of operation, 1933–34.

However, it was Milch who joined all these loose ends together; he gathered ground organization, aero laboratories, civilian aviation, flight schools, meteorological services, and more into a coherent whole. In August 1933 he established schools that trained fighter pilots in navigating, combat, naval aviation, engineer flying, and gunnery. Indeed, for the next decade Hitler gave the Goering-Milch team freedom in all things aeronautical, letting them build and run their air force with little recourse to the Führer besides an accelerated building timetable and the preference of bombers over fighters.

To date, Irving has been the only full-scale biographer of the man who would become 'Hitler's Jewish Field Marshal'. According to him, the aerial wizard's 'official' father was the Jew Anton Milch, an apothecary in the Kaiser's new Imperial German Navy who had converted to Christianity. Out of service, Anton Milch established a retail drug business and later became a Navy quartermaster for medical supplies.

However, it is alleged that Erhard Milch's real father was Carl Brauer of Berlin, who died on 23 June 1906 after an affair with Milch's mother, Clara Vetter Milch. Later research revealed that Clara herself may have been a Jew, making the future Nazi Field Marshal at least half (if not fully) Jewish.

Irving noted that Erhard himself told Goering the true story on 14 October 1933— that his father was not Anton Milch, and not a Jew. He claimed that his mother had married Anton in an arranged marriage, but she had vowed never to have children with him because his mother was in an insane asylum; she preferred to conceive by her secret lover, Brauer. To make matters murkier, in 1951 Frischauer asserted that the man listed on Milch's 'new' birth certificate was Baron Hermann von Bier. Reportedly, Erhard had only learned the truth in 1933, and both Anton and Clara had admitted to it. On 1 November 1933, in a secret diary, Erhard noted: 'Goering has spoken with

Hitler, von Blomberg, and Hess about my parentage … Everything in order.' The secret was thus officially kept among these five men.

Nevertheless, Milch was betrayed to Goering as a secret Jew by an SA General who was also in the Luftwaffe—and a Röhm crony to boot. Imperial German Air Service 1st Lt Theodor 'Theo' Croneiss (18 December 1894–7 December 1942) had become a fighter pilot ace during the First World War by accruing the required five aerial victories, and had also been one of the few aces on the Middle Eastern Front. After being awarded both the Iron Cross First Class and the Knight's Cross of the House Order of Hohenzollern in August 1918, Croneiss became a test pilot for Messerschmitt; thus, like Goering and Milch, he became a member of the growing German civil aviation industry. Croneiss also directed a flying club that sponsored Willi Messerschmitt; later, Croneiss would fly one of the latter's first designs (the M-21 aircraft) and win him a prize of 60,000 RM. From 1928–29 he flew Messerschmitt's M-23 model, winning the East Prussia Flying Trophy, and then morphed into a renowned test pilot for the growing firm. He later became a Nazi SA General and a member of the SS, as well as a holder of RFSS Himmler's Sword of Honor; it was in these roles that he denounced Milch to Goering.

Had Ernst Röhm managed to wrest the Reich government away from the Hitler-Goering team, none other than Theo Croneiss was slated to replace Goering as the head of the new German SA Luftwaffe. It therefore seems fortuitous that Croneiss himself was not murdered by Goering during the 1934 Blood Purge. Milch survived the betrayal and went on to greater glory in the Luftwaffe, while Croneiss died on 7 November 1942 as the Allies were invading North Africa.

On 1 April 1936 Goering promoted Milch to Luftwaffe General Officer grade, and on 30 January 1937 he was honored yet again with the Nazi Golden Party Membership Badge. Hitler named him as one of a trio of the first Luftwaffe Field Marshals in 1940. Despite respecting and acknowledging his need for Milch, Goering was also jealous of his over-bright subordinate. He was not entirely unjustified; even before the Second World War, Milch tactlessly bragged to his associates, 'I am the Reich Air Minister.'

Having produced warplanes for Imperial Germany before and during the First World War, famed designer Professor Hugo Junkers (3 February 1859–3 February 1935) wanted to build aircraft only for peaceful means. This was despite a failed financial investment in the secret German air operation at Fili, Russia, which flopped in 1925; further financial disaster followed. Although Milch had been mentored by Junkers earlier in his career, he nonetheless forced the professor out of the German aviation industry after the Nazis took office. Junkers was placed under house arrest on 3 February 1934, with all his visitors monitored by the police; he died in 1935, on his seventy-sixth birthday, still in this predicament. Over the next decade, Milch would continue the fight for control over the Junkers empire with Hugo's widow, Therese. The couple's son, Klaus, finally lost the financial battle.

Wilberg—'The Jewish Goering'

According to the September 1935 Nuremberg Law, Luftwaffe Lt Gen. Helmut Wilberg (1880–1941) was defined as a half-Jew because he had a Jewish mother. However, later that same year Hitler declared him to be a full Aryan because he was so valuable to the Luftwaffe. Indeed, during the First World War Wilberg became the very first German air leader to organize and deploy entire air groups in the ground-attack mode that was so effective in the 1939 *Blitzkrieg*. A glider devotee (like Udet), Wilberg had been one of the very first German pilots, and had even been admitted to the Imperial General Staff in 1910. While Goering was just a fighter pilot in 1917, Wilberg was already the commanding officer of more than 700 aircraft over Flanders. Wilberg and his fellow Jewish air officer Milch were good friends, and the former gave the latter a squadron of his own to command. Wilberg thus outranked Goering and Milch even before the end of the First World War.

During the Seeckt Era of 1920–27, the General chose Wilberg as the Black Luftwaffe's commanding officer, taking the role of the Army's leading air strategist—revered by all in the field of aviation. He sent the first pilots to Lipetsk, Russia, for training. Nevertheless, in 1933 Wilberg was passed over by Hitler in favour of Goering, and by Goering in favour of Milch; he remained in service, and handed over a German air force built on a solid foundation. In 1935, Wilberg drafted the Luftwaffe's initial *Conduct of Air Operations Handbook*, which would be used throughout the Second World War. That year he was also named head of the air force's War College by Goering.

Summer 1933: Snubbed in Sweden

During the summer of 1933 Reich Minister Goering visited Carin's first grave, in the Lovo churchyard in Sweden. He was wearing a civilian suit and a black mourning armband on his left jacket sleeve; he placed a wreath of red roses, formed into the shape of a swastika, on the grave. He was accompanied by Carin's friend, Princess zu Wied, whose husband Hitler had appointed German Ambassador to Sweden on Goering's advice. *The Swedish Daily News* duly publicized his visit, but they criticized his choice of floral arrangements; some anti-Nazi Swedes took the wreath away, replacing it with a note that read: 'Sweden is offended by your use of a grave for propaganda. Let the dead rest in peace'. That night, at Stockholm's Oskar Theater, a student cried out from the audience, 'Down with Goering, the murderer of the workers!' Goering was outraged, and he was also wary of Swedish assassins. He decided to relocate Carin's body to Germany for reburial at Carinhall, the building of which was already underway.

Hindenburg Promotes Goering, 1933

On 31 August 1933 Reich President von Hindenburg promoted Hitler's Air Minister to the rank of Major General in the German Army. Max Domarus, a German reporter who covered the entire Nazi era, later wrote:

To prevent the appointment from attracting too much attention and perhaps prompting opposition in the … *Reichswehr,* Blomberg was simultaneously appointed Colonel General [thus outranking Goering]. Goering's promotion from Captain to General of the Infantry—bypassing five military ranks—was in all probability a unique incident in the annals of German military history. With the exception of later SS generals, Goering was the only *Wehrmacht* General who achieved his rank as a result of a revolutionary step.

The astounding thing was that it was not Hitler, but the [former] Imperial Field Marshal von Hindenburg who made this highly unusual appointment.

Thus Goering once more attained the right to wear a German Army field gray tunic, before switching to Luftwaffe blue in March 1935. It has been suggested that Goering announced his promotion to the press in advance of the actual event, forcing Hindenburg to make the appointment, but Milch later denied this. Milch asserted that he had been sent to then-Defense Minister von Blomberg to discuss a number of future promotions, including those of Goering and himself. Milch reported to von Blomberg that Goering expected to be named as no less than a full General—and not the lowest rank of Major General, as the Defense Minister intended. Milch's date also differs from the one given earlier (31 August 1933), asserting that the promotion was bestowed on 19 October (backdated to 1 October 1931 to give Goering seniority). Goering was reportedly delighted.

It is also alleged that Goering blackmailed Hindenburg into making him an Army General in return for not going public about the Hindenburg family's land dealings in East Prussia, where their family estates (such as Neudeck, the President's home) were situated. Whatever the cause, the Reich President's official notice of Goering's promotion was posted on 30 August 1933, publicly backdated to 10 January 1931. Additionally, Goering was named as General of State Police on 14 September.

The Reichstag Fire Trial: A Public Relations Disaster, 4 November 1933

The Reichstag Fire trial opened at the German Superior Court in Leipzig on 9 September 1933, with eighty-two accredited foreign and forty German press reporters present—including those from the Soviet news agency *Tass* and the Russian communist newspaper *Izvestia* (*Truth*).

The sensational trial lasted for three months, from September to December, and was front-page news across the world. Since the city of Leipzig was not in Prussia, it was outside any legal jurisdiction that Goering had. Reportedly, he wanted the five accused communists—Marinus van der Lubbe, Ernst Torgler, Georgi Dimitrov, Simon Popov, and Vassili Tanev—transferred into one of his own, Prussia-based concentration camps, but he was undermined by his own subordinate, Dr Diels, who also saved the five from being beaten by Karl Ernst's SA men. By November 1933 the proceedings had relocated to Berlin and the Reichstag Building itself; it was there that Goering would appear as a witness for the prosecution.

As lucid as van der Lubbe had appeared during his arrest and his pre-trial interrogations, at the trial itself he appeared to be in a stupor most of the time; it was thought this was induced by his jailers drugging his food. Wearing his striped prisoner's garb, he sat or stood mutely, handcuffed and chained, his head hung low, and his chin resting on his chest. With his nose running and his mouth drooling, the trial's major defendant thus appeared imbecilic most of the time. The rest of the defendants wore civilian clothing, and they all appeared lucid.

One expert testified that in order to account for the blaze, at least 40 lbs of liquid fuel must have been spread by at least two people half an hour before van der Lubbe's arrest—time the accused simply did not have. It was then suggested that perhaps it had been stored in advance in the stenographer's room, below the Speaker's dais. The Nazis asserted that one of the defendants, Communist Party Deputy Ernst Torgler, might very well have stored such materials in the designated rooms of the Communist Party delegation.

Goering was called as an eyewitness on 4 November, and came mainly to refute the public charges made against him in the KPD-inspired *Brown Book of the Reichstag Fire and the Hitler Terror*, published in 1933. In 1947, Hans Bernd Gisevius recalled:

> The Minister ... had a costume made especially for this scene. Never before—and never afterward—did any of his multitudinous photographs show him wearing it, but it was perfectly suited for this particular day. A loud brown hunting jacket, knee breeches, high brown boots—his very appearance was calculated to flout the dignity of the highest German court.

When Goering entered the courtroom to testify, the judges stood to give him the Nazi salute, and all in the courtroom (except for the defendants and the press) returned it as well. Goering was also cheered by the spectators. When Dimitrov screamed out, 'This affair is a police frame-up!' the Reuters news agency reported that Goering was 'literally dancing with rage, shaking his fists wildly'. At one point the two men disputed a point, with Dimitrov asserting, 'My opinion is different.' Goering countered, 'But mine is the one that counts!' Incredibly, the court allowed Goering to make what was essentially a Nazi propaganda speech for fully three hours.

Under German law, the accused could personally cross-examine all witnesses instead of allowing their attorneys to do so. One who chose to do just this proved to be Goering's nemesis, and represented his downfall at the trial. This was the Bulgarian communist Georgi Dimitrov (1882–1949), who, eleven years older than Goering, was neither overawed nor intimidated by his Nazi opponent. He would survive both the trial and the coming war, eventually becoming communist Bulgaria's first Stalinist Premier—the role that Goering held in Prussia in 1933. At the time of the trial, Dimitrov was a leading European Communist Third International (Comintern) revolutionary agitator. Having been arrested along with thousands of others during Goering's police sweeps of communist and socialist leaders, Dimitrov was in Germany at an inopportune moment; however, no one was prepared for how effectively he would cross verbal swords with Goering, least of all the Reich Minister himself.

Dimitrov accused the Reich's 'top cop' of not looking for the real arsonists, meaning the Nazi SA. Goering exploded, 'For me, this was a political crime, and I was convinced that the criminals are to be found in your party!' Shaking a clenched fist at the accused, Goering roared, 'Your party is a party of criminals that must be destroyed!'

Aside from citing the Soviet Union as a communist state with which the Reich traded, Dimitrov taunted Goering with the question, 'Is it not known that communism has millions of supporters in Germany?'

Goering cut him off with a shrill scream. 'It is known that you are behaving insolently, that you have come here to burn the Reichstag … You are a criminal who should be sent to the gallows!' The chief judge backed Goering in his ruling, and Goering yelled, 'Out with you, you scoundrel!'

Dimitrov was duly removed from the court by Goering's police, but he took a parting shot at the enraged, red-faced Goering—'Are you afraid of my questions, Mr Minister-President?'

Now quaking with rage, Goering barked, 'You wait until we get you outside this court, you scoundrel!' This turned out to be one of modern history's emptiest threats, as Hitler had already agreed (in secret negotiations) for Dimitrov to be traded with Moscow for two captive Nazi agents. On 27 January 1934 the trio of communist Bulgarians was released, and on 17 February 1934 they safely reached Moscow by plane. Goering's empty taunt was therefore followed not only by that humiliation, but also by being pilloried by virtually every newspaper in the world for his bullying of the defendant—cartoonists and editorialists had a field day in lampooning the overblown and bombastic Goering. The new Nazi Germany was thus held up to global ridicule in November 1933, at a time when Chancellor Hitler was working hard to establish his regime's legitimacy.

The trial fiasco therefore proved to be a public relations disaster for Goering at a time when he was trying to cement his own still-shaky relationship with the only power in his world who mattered—Adolf Hitler. The flop once again cast doubts that Goering was the 'Iron Man' figure that Hitler needed him to be; the cloud over his head endured until the Blood Purge of June 1934, six months later, that would finally establish him in Hitler's good graces.

As for the sole convicted defendant—the actual arsonist, van der Lubbe—he would not be so lucky. He was beheaded on 10 January 1934, less than a year after his crime. Accounts differ as to the exact method of execution (both the guillotine and a short-handled axe are suggested), but on one thing all reports agree—the men who killed him wore top hats, tails, and white gloves. It took less than a minute in the courtyard of the Leipzig Remand Prison, and with no final statement from the condemned man.

In the final analysis, the German court—while pro-Nazi—went its own way by acquitting all defendants but van der Lubbe. It towed the Nazi line, however, in ruling out any NSDAP role whatsoever in the fire and convicting the former communist van der Lubbe. The German public generally accepted the NDSAP claim that the fire had been a communist signal to incite a national 'Red' campaign of terror; they also accepted Goering's assertion that the communists wanted to destroy government buildings, museums, palaces, and essential plants, and that they would shelter behind women and children as they attacked Hermann's valiant policemen.

Goering's Homes: The Lord of Many Mansions

Goering is recognized historically of a man of many titles, honors, medals and (mostly) uniforms. He was also the lord and master of many mansions, boasting a lifestyle that few reigning princes could match—much less surpass. These splendid abodes included his Reichstag President's Palace, his 'official' Prime Minister of Prussia's residence on the Leipzigerplatz, and a swanky apartment—all three in Berlin.

His favorite property, however, was his private, 100,000-acre estate named after his deceased first wife—the much-ballyhooed country estate of Carinhall, on the Schorfheide, 85 km northeast of the Reich capital.

There was also the Rominten Hunting Lodge in East Prussia (formerly owned by the Kaiser); Landhaus Goering on the Obersalzberg, above the Bavarian Alpine village of Berchtesgaden (near Hitler's own Berghof); Castle Veldenstein, outside Nuremberg in Franconia; and Castle Mauterndorf, in neighboring Austria. At one time or another, all also served as the pre-war and wartime military headquarters for Goering, since the hub of the Luftwaffe was wherever its Commander in Chief happened to be.

The authors Ray and Josephine Cowderry have written extensively on this subject. Josephine Cowderry provided the author with the following recollections after visiting some of the actual sites herself:

> There were different official State residences at different times. The old Prussian Prime Minister's Palace on Leipzigerplatz was the earliest and Goering's least favorite, as it was an old, dark, outdated, early nineteenth century building.
>
> In the early 1930s he had it refurbished, but still found it too dark and old, not 'grand' enough. Then, after the huge *Reichsluftfahrtministerium* (RLM) on Wilhelmsstrasse/ Leipzigerstrasse was finished in 1935, he wanted to refurbish Prussia House behind the RLM, and make that his personal Berlin residence.
>
> However, the planned rebuilding costs were so high that the Berlin and state finance people balked, causing delays. Goering kept insisting and finally prevailed, but by that time the war had started, building was postponed, and in the end, never carried out.
>
> The Prussian War Ministry was torn down during the building of the RLM to create additional space for the huge Air Ministry [which still stands today]; I do not think that there were private apartments for Goering in the RLM.
>
> We visited Veldenstein Castle many times over the years, and there was an interesting marble plate in the south wall that told the history of Goering's ownership of the place and the building of the bomb shelters.
>
> The last time we were there, the plaque had disappeared, and there was no mention of HG anywhere—part of the German effort to obliterate history, I suppose … Goering owned or rented a beach house on the Island of Sylt.

The Goering Beach House in Wenningstedt, Isle of Sylt

This was reportedly the personal property of Hermann's second wife, Emmy, on a large coastal tract. Emmy received the property on 12 July 1937. After the war, the British military used the building as an officer's residence; in 1961, Emmy filed a lawsuit via her attorney, Dr Ziegelhofer, to regain what she saw as her house from the Crown. She was successful, but she sold the property after winning it back; it still stands today.

Master of the German Hunt and the German Forests, 1933–34

Goering's role as a man of the great outdoors is perhaps less well-known than the other aspects of his character. He was a lover of open fields and non-polluted streams, and delighted in hunting—which he did often, even well into the Second World War, and even to the neglect of his other duties. He stalked game in pre-war Poland and Germany from the earliest days of the Third Reich almost until the end of the Second World War in 1945, continuing his pursuit as Nazi Germany collapsed around him. He was an avid outdoorsman all his life, skiing, riding horses, and mountain climbing in addition to hunting—and all despite his problems with weight. In his 1938 biography of Goering, Dr Gritzbach noted:

> In addition to his other offices, a new burden was placed on his shoulders. As Master of the German Forests, he was their trustee and guardian of our noblest monuments of nature, and as Master of the German Hunt, he was the protector of Germany's game.

As the Reich's *Jagerhofmeister* ('Hunt Master'), Goering eagerly designed his own uniform of a puffed-sleeve, white, silk shirt, worn underneath a soft, leather, belted, sleeveless jacket, and a forest-green top jacket with dark lapels, topped off by a jaunty brimmed cap with brush accent. In this role, Hermann merged all of the game and forestry powers of the many federated German provinces into one Reich ministry; this was followed by a series of reforms that were of permanent benefit to Germany.

Hermann's overt love of the great outdoors also manifested itself in NSDAP public policy via irrigation, preservation, and re-forestation programs, with laws enacted to protect wildlife in general—especially endangered species like the elk, bison, wild boar, swan, eagle, and falcon. He also made German game laws stricter, restricting the hunting of these animals to licensed gun owners and introducing quotas. Hunters were required to be accompanied by retrievers so that wounded animals would not suffer or die alone. Goering also passed a law against vivisection, as well as banning poaching, hunting on horseback, the use of wire and claw traps, night lighting, and poison. He asserted, 'He who tortures an animal hurts the feelings of the German people,'—a rare sentimental remark from a violent man. Goering's reputation for introducing the fairest and most humane European game laws still stands today.

The Schorfheide *(Heath), 1933–34*

In 1933 Goering coveted the beautiful Schorfheide Moor in Brandenburg Mark, north of Berlin, which ranged to the Polish frontier. It was a 75-mile-long and 55–60-mile-wide tract of moorland and forests, located between the scenic Lake Wackersee and the Greater Dolln Lake. Stocking the area with wildlife, Goering situated his world-famous country estate, Carinhall, here. The Schorfheide went through four stages of development—ten months from 1933–34, a second stage in 1937, a third in 1940, and a fourth, a doubling in size, from 1941–53. Goering's intention was for it to be donated to the German people on the occasion of his sixtieth birthday, on 1 January 1953—a date he would not live to see. The final stage was announced—complete with blueprints, architectural plans, and maps—at his final birthday celebration on 12 January 1945, located onsite. However, the loss of the war a mere six months later abruptly ended his plans.

Goering had already imported bison and elk from Sweden, Poland, and Canada—an experiment that was not entirely successful. He also established a state park of 100,000 acres, set aside by his Prussian State Council for his own exclusive use. In its center was a Swedish-style hunting lodge that could accommodate group excursions as well, harking back to the time of Kaiser Wilhelm II. Indeed, Goering even appropriated the Kaiser's former Imperial Hunting Lodge in Rominten, East Prussia, as well as one of his smaller examples. Carinhall's initial design was actually inspired by a similar lodge that Goering had seen on the grounds of Rockelstad Castle in Sweden in 1920.

Working together with Berlin government architect Werner March, Goering launched the construction of Carinhall in July 1933, with the initial, small house situated atop a steep hill ridge between the southern shore of the large lake Dollnsee and the smaller Wuckersee. The rustic site was complete with pine trees, reminding him of those he had seen in Sweden and Poland. The beautiful, rolling, wooded Schorfheide also featured oak and beech trees, with juniper bushes providing a dazzling golden-brown visage every fall—plus barberry bushes, broom, and hawthorn to accent it all. The picturesque landscape boasted marshes with rushes and sedge, broken by small lakes ringed with fir and pine trees that were filled with colorful woodpeckers. Gorgeous wild swans dotted the lake surfaces with their cygnets.

Goering established a protected area out of the Schorfheide for deer, bison, elk, and wild horses. His various housing projects overlooking the scene all boasted windows that provided magnificent vistas of the lakes and forests.

Had Hermann Goering done nothing else in his career, today he would be hailed worldwide as one of the globe's premier conservationists, a protector of both fauna and flora—a John Muir-like visionary with a solid record of achievement. His restocking of the Schorfheide and the Rominten Heath were wildly successful; animals were rescued from hunting and poaching to be enjoyed for generations.

The Original Carinhall, 1933–34

From 1933 until 1945 architect Friedrich Hetzelt had aided Goering with the design and construction of Carinhall, even down to its door handles. Hetzelt and his assistant, Tuch, hailed from Goering's Prussian State Department for Architecture; Goering wanted the best people for his project. At the Nuremberg Trials, Dr Gritzbach commented, '...Goering conceived the ground plan and the structure on lines that expressed his own strong and self-willed personality.'

Initially, Carinhall was a small, one-story, rough-hewn, split-log structure with single-gable, thatched roofing sheltering an upper room that was fronted by a balcony. The Great Hall was on the ground floor with a large, open fireplace that Goering loved. Opposite this rather-modest Carinhall was the underground mausoleum that he had built for Carin, which was 'finished' in a mere ten months. It was built on a site that had seen no other edifice, despite some earlier accounts to the contrary. The trees that provided the logs came from the area's surrounding forest, and the thatchwork was done in true Germanic style. Unlike its successors, this version of Carinhall had a simple and unostentatious entrance that was in harmony with the rest of the building. Its stone courtyard opened onto a weighty wooden door, which featured the Prussian eagle and Goering's heraldic coat of arms. Inside this door was an inscription:

> To Minister-President Hermann Goering, who protects the honor of Prussia with a strong hand. We dedicate the land on the Wuckersee for your continuous use. May you find pleasure of nature in Prussia's forest, Berlin, 26 October 1933.

A small foyer led to the entrance to the two-story Great Hall, which measured 10 x 6 meters and featured an open, stone fireplace and exposed wooden beams. This main room connected to a small dining area measuring 5 x 5 meters, and the ground floor was rounded out by a kitchen and two closets.

On the first floor, Goering's personal study overlooked the beautiful Lake Dollnsee; it had a balcony, allowing him to work in the open air, and was furnished with a massive desk and the standard tiled Germanic stove for heating, plus a second open fireplace. The office doubled as a shrine to Carin, with items she had owned found everywhere. A life-sized painting of Goering's dead wife dominated the room, and eternal-flame candles burnt underneath it. Goering's bedroom was adjacent to the study; there were also two guestrooms and a bath, all furnished with large, handmade wood pieces that had been personally selected by Hermann. The walls of the property were decorated with nature scenes and the mounted heads of animals that Goering had dispatched himself.

An accurate and quick shot, Goering generally turned away from game lighter than a roe deer. He never over-hunted—a criticism that had been levelled at the Kaiser and his fellow hunters. In keeping with his own inherent principles of fair play, Goering always ensured that his quarry received a quick death. After his initial appointment as Hunt Master in 1933, Goering added the title of Forest Master in 1934; he was very serious about the duties of both offices. The additional appointment had come in the wake of the Association of German Hunters' invitation for Goering to serve as its official patron. In attaining the post, Goering also persuaded Hitler that the waning German timber industry had problems such as reforestation that could use his devoted attention. The Führer concurred, bestowing the title, funds, and office on his subordinate. A team of zoological scientists started research, and Goering's beloved Schorfheide morphed into a woodland laboratory.

Emmyhall: Reichsjagerhof Rominten

Reichsjagerhof Rominten was situated 5 km southeast of Goldap, East Prussia, an area steeped in the history of the early battles of the First World War, where Imperial Germany was fighting Romanov Russia on the Eastern Front. Konigsberg, nearby in East Prussia, became Russia's Kaliningrad (named after the USSR President Mikhail Kalinin) after the Second World War, on the frontier with communist Poland.

Originally called 'Emmyhall' as a sop to Goering's second wife, Reichsjagerhof Rominten was built as a small house that resembled Carinhall in miniature, and was used as another of Hermann's hunting lodges. With the start of the German invasion of the Soviet Union on 22 June 1941, Goering employed Rominten as his own Eastern Front Luftwaffe headquarters, from which he hurled his 'air weapon' against the numerically superior (even then) communist air force.

Having bought Rominten from the Kaiser's landed Hohenzollerns in 1933, Goering got his money's worth by flying there every ten days or so aboard his personal Junkers Ju-52 government aircraft.

Goering's 'Green Freemasonry'

Hitler referred to Goering and his fellow hunters as 'Green Freemasons'; the Reich Chancellor himself detested hunting, and never took part in it. Irving's diligent 1989 research turned up Goering's personal hunting diaries, which detailed how he met Tsar Boris of Bulgaria, Regent Horthy of Hungary, the kings of Greece and Romania, and Prince Regent Paul of Yugoslavia—all as his special guests.

As a special treat during the war, Goering invited both senior Luftwaffe generals and famed aces such as Galland and Molders to his hunting preserves. It was expected that Goering's guests would praise his game and his hospitality; once, Swedish Prince Gustav Adolf shot a 20-point stag there, but asserted that he planned to do better on his father-in-law's preserve later. In Thomas von Kantzow's diary, he noted that 'things did not go so well between him and Hermann', adding that he would not be 'inviting him back to Carinhall in a hurry'.

When Goering took up his dual role as Hunt Master and Forest Master, he discovered that almost all German parishes and hunting estates had their own hunting laws and even taxes, with wildlife being shot at will. Goering moved immediately; he instructed Reich Chief Forester Ulrich Scherping to establish the German Hunting

Association to protect near-extinct species, regulate, refill the lakes with fish, and care for forested areas. To pay for it all, Goering had Scherping levy taxes on the hunters that were encompassed in draft legislation on 9 May 1933. This new Prussian law became the model for the entire Reich; it was now against the law to kill an eagle, to employ steel traps or artificial lighting, and to hunt with poison. The Prussian State Game Law was enacted on 18 January 1934, and mandated that Goering's new gaming officials had to be animal lovers as well as ardent Nazis.

As Prussian Prime Minister, Goering ensured that no other buildings would encroach on what he viewed as 'his' game preserve and also his official country residence. The only hunters permitted to be in the reservation were the population of the local village, Goering himself, and his guests. Goering's reorganization of the Prussian forests occurred in tandem with the building of Carinhall. In 1951, Emmy stated:

> [Goering's] work had kept him from his beloved mountains, from nature, from hunting—one of his hobbies. The little lodge was just the type of country house that he had missed ever since he had come to stay in Berlin.

Goering would retire to Carinhall for a few days whenever he could, shooting bears or stalking deer. He would put aside his Nazi uniform for a battered hat, flowing trousers, and one of his favorite leather jerkin jackets. Once, when late for dinner with British Ambassador to Germany Sir Eric Phipps, he gave the excuse that he had just returned from shooting; Phipps quipped, 'Animals, I hope.'

When officially unveiling Carinhall on 10 June 1934 (just weeks before the Blood Purge), Goering invited forty members of the Berlin Diplomatic Corps to a gala reception at the property. The Italian ambassador to Berlin from 1932–35, Vittorio Enrico Cerruti, was in attendance with his wife, the Hungarian Jewess Elsabetta Cerruti. In her 1953 memoirs, she recalled how their rude host kept his guests waiting for forty-five minutes until he made his grand arrival:

> Up ran thirty forest guards dressed in medieval hunting costumes, formed a circle, and— lifting their trumpets to their lips—sounded the Siegfried motif. Only then did Goering make his entrance.
>
> His boots, trousers, and sash were of heavy gray leather; his shirt of gray flannel with bright purple stripes on the sleeves. In his hand, he carried a leather cap and his fair hair was intentionally in disorder, as though disheveled by the wind.
>
> Greeting us without a word of apology for his tardiness, he stepped to a microphone to address the people of the Reich. He told them that after gargantuan efforts, he had managed to collect many rare animals on his hunting grounds, thus enriching Germany's ancestral forests.

Another dignitary in attendance was the British ambassador, Sir Eric Phipps. Later, in his dispatch to the British Foreign Office, Sir Eric also recalled Goering's late arrival. He was due to meet his guests at a large clearing in the forest; the guests were amazed to witness Goering skid to a sudden halt before them in his sporty new race car, clad in 'aviator's garments of India rubber, with top boots and a large hunting knife stuck in his belt'. The flamboyant host proceeded to give his visitors a lecture on Germanic flora and fauna with a microphone, detailing how he was engaged in promoting their growth. Various species of imported animals were also displayed.

In his 1941 memoir, US ambassador to Berlin Thomas E. Dodd Jr recalled:

> [Goering] is a big, fat, good-humored man who loves display above everything. While he spoke, three photographers with elaborate outfits took pictures that he was particularly pleased to permit. He next led us about the woods and showed us bisons [*sic.*] and tiny wild horses.

Goering then took his guests to a stockade, where they saw a Canadian bison that was supposed to mate with waiting cows for the guests' edification. Sir Eric Phipps sardonically recalled: 'The unfortunate animal emerged from his box with the utmost reluctance, and after eyeing the cows sadly, tried to return to it.' Elsabetta Cerruti recalled:

> Goering ... addressed the bull himself: 'Ivan the Terrible, I order you to leave the cage.' ... Finally ... two guards entered the cage and prodded him with iron prongs ... We were all having difficulty suppressing our desire to giggle ... The bull approached the pasturing cows, sniffed the air about them, then—scrutinizing us all ... lumbered back into the huge cage. At that, the bonds of restraint broke, and we all roared with laughter.

Miffed at this failure, Goering returned to his sports car and raced off, while his guests were taken by road to the entrance to Carinhall. He rejoined them here, but was now regaled in white trousers and tennis shoes, a flannel shirt, and one of his beloved green leather waistcoat jackets—the hunting dirk still tucked into his belt. Ambassador Dodd was struck by the 'curious harpoon-like instrument' that Goering carried; it was a Scandinavian hunting spear given to him by Count von Rosen, who was due to arrive the next day. Signora Cerruti described what happened next:

> Goering ... regained his high spirits as he prepared to guide us on a tour of his estate. To carry us, there were thirty small hunting turnouts, each drawn by two horses.
>
> When he shouted, 'The Italian Ambassadress is requested to ride with me in the first carriage,' I jumped in with alacrity ... Our two splendid horses trotted at a fine pace, and Goering—who was driving them, seeing my face pale—reassured me that if they were going a bit too fast, it was only because that afternoon marked the first time that they had ever been in a harness. I almost fainted!
>
> Goering had a right to be proud of his enchanting preserve. The following year—he informed me—he intended to hunt wild boar with a sword instead of a gun. This promise duly impressed me, and greatly relieved me as to his future fate.
>
> Our tour over, we once more got into our cars to drive to his hunting lodge, Carinhall ... On our way to the house, he rushed on ahead of the guests, and somehow managed to change his clothes before they arrived ... He was at the gate to greet us, dressed in an

emerald-green costume, a lance in his hand and a silver horn hanging from a silver chain about his neck—Siegfried welcoming the diplomatic corps!

Emmy was acting as hostess, and when Siegfried showed us through the house, he was not in the least embarrassed to point out Emmy's bedroom next to his. This, too, we swallowed with the rest ... Emmy was a nice enough person—though totally uninteresting—and she owed her fortune to the fact that she bore a faint resemblance to Goering's first wife, the glorified Carin ... In all fairness, I must state that as Goering's wife, she always tried to help those who were persecuted, especially if they were ex-colleagues of hers in the theater.

Dodd added:

At 6 p.m., Goering took us about the premises and displayed his vanity at every turn, often causing his guests to glance amusedly at each other. We were led to another lovely lakeshore and shown a tomb, with deep foundations of stone fronting the water, the most elaborate structure of its kind I ever saw.

It is the [future] burial place of Goering's former wife ... Goering boasted of this marvelous tomb of his first wife where he said his remains would one day be laid. For half an hour this went on. Sir Eric and I—weary of the curious display ... went to him to say farewell.

Lady Cerruti saw our move and she arose quickly so as not to allow anybody to trespass upon her right to lead on every possible occasion.

Signora Cerruti had already met Goering in the fall of 1932:

I first saw Goering six weeks after we arrived in Berlin. He was the legitimately elected President of the Reichstag ... the first Nazi to hold an important position ... He lived in the Reichstag building, and asked us to dine there with him on 13 December 1932 ... [it was] given in honour of Gen. [Italo] Balbo ... on a short, semi-official visit ... with whom Goering felt a bond of friendship, since they were both soldiers and aviators ... Goering was a far cry from the person he later became, even though he was already a tower of fat. As he cordially received us, I was surprised how untidy he looked. His disheveled hair fell down upon his moist forehead, which he mopped incessantly with a rumpled handkerchief, and gave a general impression of neglect and discomposure.

There were about thirty guests in all:

Another was plump and jovial Emmy Sonnemann, the future Frau Goering ... When dinner was announced, our host offered me his arm, and with long, unsteady steps, dragged me through a series of empty rooms to an immense dining room.... an ugly room, cold and forbidding... What impressed me was my host's appetite. He swallowed an unbelievable quantity of food with the voracity of a beast of prey ... Gen. Balbo could not speak German, and Goering knew nothing of Italian, so I had to act as interpreter ... On our way home, my husband asked me what I thought ... I told him ... that Goering had a strange look in his eyes, and seemed somehow uncertain in his movements. He agreed ... The next day, he learned that Goering had been in one of his morphine stupors during the entire evening.

Although the more I saw of Goering the less I liked him, I began to understand the reason for his great popularity with his compatriots. He was coarse, his personality expressed force, he was used to—and skilled in—commanding; and above all, he was fat.

All these qualities not only appealed to the Germans, they made them shiver with delight … Such a jovial, fat fellow … The whole nation happily marched this way and that as he commanded … His taste for pomp bordered on the theatrical … With time, Goering underwent a considerable change in appearance, becoming most meticulous in toilette and dress … He is said to have gone to his tailor and ordered fifty-two suits, including several lounging costumes … He felt he had to dress the part—that of a patron of the arts—a great prince of the Renaissance. Often he would wear a gorgeous gown of red velvet lined and trimmed with Russian sable, with cascades of gold Venetian lace at his breast and wrists. I can imagine how sorry he must have been that he could not wear it in public!

In the spring of 1933, Goering had just begun to indulge his insane passion for decorations … Goering was not a wicked man, neither was he a kind one. He liked to play the part of Nero and a charming urchin both. His hidden desires were two, to be the founder of a new Imperial dynasty and to personify Siegfried! … He was devoted to Hitler, and yet at the same time despised him, considering him an obstacle in the path of his own rise to power….

Later Goering would admit that he felt this way about Röhm, whom he made sure was murdered in his jail cell. Goering's justification was succinct—'But he was in my way.' Cerruti continued:

Once he told me, 'The only ruler in Europe who can sleep tranquilly is Hitler, because I am his watchman.' What he needed was to be constantly in the foreground, to be popular, feared, admired, and applauded.

When the Cerrutis ended their tour of duty in Berlin and left for Rome on 13 August 1935, there were no Nazis on the railway platform to see them off—and definitely no Hermann Goering.

Landhaus Goering: Hermann's Alpine Chalet, 1933–45

A decade after Goering lost his mountain abode in Bayrischell in 1923, he built another, atop the Goering Hill on the Obersalzberg, near Hitler's own chalet and overlooking the famous Bavarian Alps village of Berchtesgaden. Goering had reportedly owned a small chalet even prior to 1933; during the construction of his *alpenhaus* from December 1933–May 1934 he wisely limited its size so it was no bigger than that of his neighbor, the Führer.

The chalet featured polished ceilings with light, tinted mosaic facades boasting birds, leaves, butterflies, and flowers; unlike in the mannish Carinhall, perhaps the female influences of Emmy and (later) Edda, their daughter, were coming into play. Other features included plates of marble, brass lanterns, and handcrafted iron. The Goering trio loved living there, even if it was just for a few days in between Hermann's presence being required elsewhere. 'The Two Es' often spent months at a time on the Obersalzberg, enjoying the sunny countryside and fresh mountain air.

The Goering arrivals were simple affairs, and they were only accompanied by their driver and a minimal escort. When Goering was entertaining at the chalet, Emmy stayed put, preferring not to socialize with the unmarried Eva Braun or her fellow Nazi wives, Gerda Bormann and Magarete Speer; indeed, I have seen no pictures of them together.

An outdoor swimming pool with blue interior tiles was added at the front of the house, and in 1941 Goering spent 350,000 RM on labor alone for a renovation—allegedly paid for by the Hermann Goering Special Construction Account. The original house was located above the mountain's Turken Hotel, and in 1933 Hitler had given Goering permission for the initial expansion and reconstruction of this property. In *Hitler, Goering, and the Obersalzberg* (1989), Dr B. Frank stated his belief that Goering had selected the highest, most beautiful spot on the Obersalzberg.

Like Hitler, Goering enjoyed taking walks in the area. One of the local people he encountered while out and about on a winter drive was the modest street cleaner Wegmacher Hansei, aged around sixty. A well-known character, Hansei lived in Berchtesgaden and worked on the mountain roads, doing his best to keep them clean. He was apolitical, and while he was working he took no notice of the passing Nazi bigwigs in their loud and shiny cars. With his rucksack on his back, containing his lunch, Hansei labored unmoved, wielding his trusty broom and shovel. When convoys passed him he stood aside, so as not to be run over, but never saluted nor removed his hat.

One day, Goering's car slid off an icy road and into a ditch, and neither Goering nor his driver could get the car out as they lacked the necessary tools. Hansei had watched the mishap from about 20 meters away, not volunteering to help. Walking towards the irate pair, Hansei heard the driver shout, 'Hurry up and help us dig it out!'

'You lazybones,' Hansei angrily retorted, not recognizing Goering, 'stay at home when you cannot drive in winter!' In the end, however, he did help them move the car. Goering enjoyed the scene immensely, laughing heartily and giving Hansei one of his big cigars in thanks. The next day Hansei was called to Landhaus Goering, where the master of the home presented him further with wine, food, and a box of cigars, plus a 50 RM note placed in his hand by Goering himself. Hansei said, 'I did not know you were Goering. I thought you were one of those lazybones. I hope you will not mind— and thanks.' Goering laughed all over again.

The Reichsforstamt *(Reich Forestry Office), 3 July 1934*

The *Reichsforstamt* was established on the very day of Röhm's murder, the official ending of the Blood Purge killings, after Goering personally requested the halt from his Führer. The Reich Forestry Office administered and managed all public German forests, wood industrial policy, non-public forests, the promotion of forest culture, hunting, and the submission of legislative bills for debate and passage.

Goering held the dual appointments of Reich Forest Master and Reich Hunting Master from 3 July 1934 until 23 April 1945; he was also designated as Reich and Prussian Forestry Master. In addition, as Chief of the Reich Board of Wood and Forests, Goering again held the position and authority of a Reich Minister.

Working under Goering were General Forestry Master/State Secretary Dr (h.c.) Walther von Keudell (3 July 1934–1 November 1937), his deputy, Willi Parchmann, and Ministerial Building Director Barwinnkel. Dr von Keudell was succeeded as General Forestry Master by Friedrich Alpers (1 November 1937–1944), who was in turn succeeded by Dietrich Klagges (February 1944–1945). The RFO post of Standing Deputy was held by von Keudell, Alpers, and Klagges while they were State Secretary. The *abteilung* directors were Eberts, Erb, Parchmann, and Ulrich Scherping.

The State Coach and Parade Flap, 9 September 1933

During the Reichstag Fire trial there was an inter-party fiasco, with Goering attempting to aggrandize himself at the expense of both the SA and the SS. To accentuate his Prussian power base, Prime Minister Goering planned a state coach ride from the Wilhelmstrasse to the State Opera House, with himself as the sole occupant of the coach. The occasion was the opening of his new Prussian State Council.

The highlight of the event was to be a full parade of the Berlin SA and SS, at which he alone would take the salute. Captain Röhm was having none of that, and in the event the idea of the extravagant state coach and accompanying motorcade was abandoned altogether. Instead, only the march past occurred, and it was saluted from a wooden-plank platform by all three new powers in Prussia—Goering, Röhm, and the latter's underling, Himmler. Checkmated, Goering swallowed his pride, joined the other two, and found yet another reason to have Röhm killed.

Reinventing the Beer Hall Putsch, November 1933–39

The Nazi *Blutorden* ('Blood Order') was created by Hitler in 1933, and was given to more than 1,500 party *Alte Kampfer* ('Old Fighters') who took part in the events of 8–9 November 1923. These two days were celebrated as part of the Nazi calendar of historic commemorative events for the next eleven years, until 1944. The annual November celebration consisted of two main events—on the 8th there would be a speech by Hitler or his designate in the Burgerbraukellar (the beer hall in which the 1923 'revolution took place), and on the 9th there would be a march of the Old Fighters through the city, tracing the exact route of the original.

After Hitler became Chancellor in 1933 and until 1939 (when the last march took place), these annual observances grew ever-larger, with hundreds of people involved. Over the years, Army generals and Navy Admiral Erich Raeder (none of whom had been there in 1923) were permitted to attend and even march as well; they wanted to demonstrate the military's solidarity with the nation's new ruling elite, the *bonzen* (big wigs). November 1939 marked the last actual march through Munich, but it was also the occasion for a mysterious bombing that was intended to assassinate the Führer— although historians still have yet to fully determine the validity of that assertion.

The yearly addresses in the Burgerbraukeller continued until 1944; Hitler himself last spoke there in 1942, with RFSS Himmler reading the Führer's speech *in absentia* in 1943 and 1944. In November 1945 both men were dead, and the Allied armies were occupying the divided Reich.

A Dire Prediction, 1933

After Otto Strasser left the NSDAP to form his own, left-wing, Black Front Nazi Party in 1931, he did not see his brother, Gregor, until 1933. This was their last meeting; Otto accurately predicted to his brother, 'Goering will murder me one day in any case, just as he is trying to murder you now. It does not make any difference what I do!'

Chancellor Hitler (center) speaking at the ceremonial opening of the recently elected new Reichstag on 21 March 1933. He is inside the Potsdam Garrison Church, with both Goering (left) and Reich President von Hindenburg (right) seated to his front. To Hitler's right sit the members of his coalition cabinet, with German Army Field Marshal August von Mackensen peering down from the far right of the balcony above. The Reich President also spoke; Goering, who addressed the actual Reichstag later that day at Berlin's Kroll Opera House, did not. (*HHA*)

Hitler (center left) in animated conversation on The Day of Potsdam, 21 March 1933, with the former Imperial Crown Prince Wilhelm (in busby shako at center right), and Goering looking on at far right. Hermann had been proven right in his boast of 'via Hindenburg to power!', and his contacts with the old field marshal as Reichstag President had helped seal the deal. (*HHA*)*Right*

Right: Wearing a brown Party Leader's jacket, Goering gives a backhanded, casual Nazi salute in 1933, his Blue Max also plainly visible at the throat. His only other medal worn is the 1914 First World War Iron Cross on his left jacket pocket. He was already known among the party regulars as '*der Eiserne*' ('The Iron Man'). Nevertheless, the brutal truth was that a known morphine addict had succeeded Bismarck as Prussian Prime Minister, and would later replace von Hindenburg as General Field Marshal. On 18 May 1933 Hitler made Goering one of his *Reichstadthalter* (Imperial) Viceroys, a title harking back to the former Kaiser Reich. (*HHA*)

Below: A 13 May 1934 side view of Goering in Silesia, again in the same uniform, with his cap slung from the hilt of a ceremonial Nazi dagger. A small girl looks on at the rear, as do excited people over the hedge. In 1933, Goering asserted, 'No title and no distinction can make me as happy as the designation bestowed upon me by the German people: "The most faithful paladin of the Führer!"' Hitler himself called Hermann 'The Renaissance Man'. Goering saw the NSDAP swastika—'the sign of the sun'—as the very symbol of purity, honor, and a rising nation. Regarding Goering's debts, Hitler lamented, 'An extraordinary fellow! Why must he live so high?' (*HGA*)

Above: A rear view of Goering addressing an outdoor Nazi rally at Hesselberg (Holy Mountain) in 1933, wearing the same style of uniform as earlier. His audience includes both SA and SS men. The bald head at the left is that of Julius Streicher, NSDAP Gauleiter of Nuremberg and Franconia. Note also the backs of two NSDAP standards. From 1931 onwards Goering routinely spoke to mass audiences of 40,000 or more via microphones and loudspeakers. (*HHA*)

Left: The Prime Minister of Prussia (center bottom) addresses an indoor Nazi rally. In 1933, he roared, 'Education is dangerous! Every educated person is a future enemy!' He was also named Reich Air Minister by Hitler on 28 April 1933. As a presence, he was described as 'short, rowdy, and effective ... A good speaker, and a quiet, convincing one ... His voice had a metallic tone that was well-received in North Germany'. (*HGA*)

Wearing a party leader cap and overcoat, Goering salutes as he arrives at an outdoor party rally. Without any trace of irony, Goering said, 'It is not I who lives, but the Führer who lives in me!' He also sheepishly admitted to Schacht, 'Every time I face the Führer, my heart falls into my trousers!' (*HGA*)

On 21 March 1934, at the dedication of the Reich Autobahn from Berlin to Stettin, Goering speaks behind a lectern emblazoned with a poster with the joint images of the Reich President and Chancellor on it. According to biographer Kurt Singer, who died at age ninety-four on 14 December 2005, Goering's outsized megalomania led him once to trace his lineage back to the Frankish Emperor Charlemagne the Great. (*HGA*)

Above: On 27 August 1933 the Reich's top three leaders appeared at the 1914 Battle of Tannenberg Memorial in East Prussia. From left to right: Col. Oskar von Hindenburg (the President's son and heir), Hitler (holding silk top hat and wearing formal morning coat), Field Marshal von Hindenburg, and Prussian Prime Minister Hermann Goering (in Nazi party leader cap and uniform). The frame Goering holds is possibly the deed of ownership for the Marshal's East Prussian Langenau and Prussian Forest, installed as the tax-free manor *Hindenburg-Neudeck* in return for service in four wars. Goering had personally negotiated with father and son for the appointments of Hitler as Chancellor and himself as General of Infantry, which were in return for the dismissal of a legislative committee that was probing the ethics of the Neudeck land deal. On this day, Goering personally read out the deed of grant to the Hindenburgs at Tannenberg. To help somewhat balance the honor in the public mind, on 30 August 1933 the Reich President promoted Defense Minister Werner von Blomberg to the grade of Colonel General, thus still outranking Hermann within the German defense establishment. Of all the NSDAP leaders, Hindenburg only liked Goering, his fellow officer. (*HHA*)

Previous page, below: A good close-up of Goering wearing the brown cap and suede overcoat of the Nazi Leadership Corps. Although a member, Goering took little interest in party affairs after becoming a member of the formal German government. His Blue Max medal is also visible at his collar. The man behind Goering wears the black uniform of an Apprentice Miner in the NSDAP Coal Miners' Association. (*HGA*)

Reich Minister Goering (left) and an unknown SS man (right), seen in the rear seat of an official car. Goering wears the cap's cord underneath his chin, perhaps due to a windy day. Regarding his drastic governmental firings of all Socialist and KPD rivals, Goering asserted, 'I will make a clean sweep with an iron broom!' From podiums, he roared at the communists, 'I'll put my fist in your necks, with those down there, my Storm Troopers!' (*HGA*)

In 1934, Goering (second from left) arrives with his entourage, wearing a party leader cap and uniform. At the left stands his SA aide, Fritz Gornnert. Note also the Prussian eagle pennant on Goering's official car (on the right), mounted just above the right fender and headlamp. While Reichstag President, he never lived in the Reichstag Presidential Palace, but instead resided in his old Berlin Kurfurstendamm apartment. (*HGA*)

Left: Partners in public, but rivals behind the scenes—Goebbels (left) as Berlin Gauleiter and Reich Minister of Propaganda and Goering (right) as Prussian Prime Minister at an indoor Nazi event. In private, Hermann referred to Goebbels by his diminutive nickname—'Jupp'. On his forty-first birthday on 12 January 1934, Hitler had a street in Berlin named the *Herman Goeringstrasse* in honor of the Prussian Prime Minister. (*HGA*)

Below: Goering's car pulls up in front of his official Berlin Palace, 5 December 1934. He sits up front. Behind him in the mid-car jump seat, is, perhaps, his monocled aide Peter Menthe, and at left rear is one of Goering's two sisters. Goering recalled the exciting days of the 1932 Reichstag election campaign: 'The largest halls were no longer big enough. People stood in the street for hours before the beginning of a meeting!' (*HGA*)

Left: Goering (right) gives a formal speech, with Nazi banners behind and Hitler Youth/HJ drummers down in front, in May 1934 in Munich. One onlooker described him as having 'a surprisingly good ear for vulgar slang and dialectical humor'. (*HGA*)

Right: At another outdoor event, Goering speaks both to a live audience and also to radio listeners via a national radio broadcasting hookup. Note the SA man at the left and the SS man just over Goering's left elbow. They represent the two main Nazi forces in conflict during 1933–34. In rough verbal exchanges with communist hecklers, Goering 'seemed to carry his audience along best', especially when 'he was both hokey and jocular'—a trait perhaps inherited from his mother, Fanny Goering. (*HGA*)

A long-distance shot of the same event, with Goering seen at the lower left. Before him are steel-helmeted SA troops, and the banner behind partially reads: 'The workers and the Leader'. Note the historic statue at center right. Goering's foes within the party considered him to be part of the *Reaktion* of the German military, royals, and big business—and they were right. (*HGA*)

The same event as seen from behind the statue; party SA men make up Goering's audience. Regarding the Time of Struggle, Goering recalled: 'We were often driven and thrown out of the room by overwhelming numbers.' However, they always returned to the fight. He ranted, 'He who tries to destroy the state will himself the State destroy!' (*HGA*)

Above: SA standard bearers at the center make their way down an aisle, flanked on both sides by members of the RAD (Reich Labor Service), their spades held at the salute. The SA man on the left, wearing the metal chest gorget, appears to be the same man with Goering in an earlier photo, taken in Breslau on 12 May 1934, when the SA numbered four million men. (*HGA*)

Right: A formal studio glamour shot by Godwin in 1934 shows Goering in repose, wearing a rain slick. According to the Nazis, their administration was the Third Reich; the first had been Charlemagne's Holy Roman Empire, while the second had been the German Empire created by Bismarck in 1871 and dismantled in 1918. The Nazi Third Empire derived from author Arthur van den Bruck's 1923 book *Das drittes Reich* (*The Third Reich*). In truth, Goering had succeeded Bismarck himself in the role of Prime Minister of Prussia—as a native Bavarian, no less! (*LC*)

Goering, wearing his Reich Aviation Minister's cap and overcoat, standing with his left hand on his hip in a car during a troop review. An SA officer stands behind him in the car. Under his leadership, German aircraft production increased drastically: 368 planes in 1933; 1,968 in 1934; 3,183 in 1935; 5,112 in 1936; 5,606 in 1937; 5,235 in 1938; and 8,295 in 1939. (*HGA*)

Left: A 1934 British cartoon by Bernard Partridge entitled *Loyal Support.* Goering, at the center, helps the aging Reich President give Hitler a Nazi salute. Hitler's right boot rests atop a steel helmet marked 'SA Intrigues'; this piece was published during the period of the alleged Röhm Plot. Privately, Goering fumed, 'That old man [Hindenburg] was fifty years old when I was born!' The right-wing *Reaktion* embraced him as 'Hermann the Bully'. (*LC*)

Right: Goering was embarrassed by the 15 September 1933 'State Coach Flap', being forced to share his reviewing stand near Berlin's famed Under den Linden thoroughfare with others. From left: SS Gen. Kurt Daluge (in steel helmet), SA Staff Chief Ernst Röhm, Goering (saluting as the chief reviewer), and Reichsführer SS Heinrich Himmler. Passing in review at the center is the color guard of the *Landespolizei Gen. Goering*, the Prussian Prime Minister's personal armed unit, who guarded him against all—but especially the SA and SS. Behind Röhm, the squared flag with the eagle is Goering's official standard as Prussian Prime Minister. Fully 100,000 men were involved in the parade. (*HGA*)

A staged photo of the newly minted German Army Gen. Goering piloting his own plane—perhaps for the first time since 1920—in August 1933. Note the leather cap and aviator's goggles, and the general's insignia in gold on red collar tabs. Baron Konstantin von Neurath dreaded Goering; he commented to Sir Horace Rumbold that Hermann was 'the real fascist in the Hitler party!' Another stated that Goering 'in person looks as gross as he is!' (*HHA*)

The scene at Goering's annual Press Ball, this one on 3 February 1934 at Berlin's swanky Adlon Hotel. Wearing a field-gray German Army uniform, Gen. Goering peers into the camera lens while the pretty young woman at the center—perhaps his niece—waves. The man at the far left, wearing a monocle, is Goering aide Peter Menthe. Goering appears to wear facial makeup. For the 1936 event, 'both Goering and Goebbels could be seen gyrating across the floor to the tune of 'Dinah''', although the Nazis supposedly officially frowned on American jazz and swing music. (*HGA*)

Another view of the same event, as Goering (center) shakes hands with one of his sisters, and the same pretty girl appears again at far left. Hindenburg promoted him five ranks, from Captain to General of Infantry, on 30 August 1933, and he wears the requisite uniform here. Eyewitness Max Domarus noted that it was 'an incident quite unique in the annals of German military history'. von Hindenburg initially misunderstood Goering's request, and he was only going to promote him from Captain to Major. (HGA)

At the Press Ball, Goering (left center) shakes hands with an officer of a foreign army—probably an embassy military attaché. Again, Goering appears to be wearing lipstick here. As a General in good standing with the conservative German Army, Goering had a vested interest in protecting its officer corps (and privileges) from the renegade Capt. Röhm, whom Hitler ordered to be killed on 1 July 1934. (HGA)

Above: Gen. Goering (center, right hand in trouser pocket) on another social occasion with a group of officers. At the far left is his aide Paul 'Pilli' Korner, wearing SS black. Third from the left, also in SS black, is Goering aide Dr Erich Gritzbach, and just behind Goering is State Police Gen. Kurt Daluge. Note also the two mounted hunting trophies behind the group, indicating that this may be inside Goering's Berlin Palace on the Leipzigerplatz at either No. 2 or 11a— accounts differ. (*HGA*)

Right: An aerial view of the same group, with Korner at the left, Dr Gritzbach standing behind (with folded hands), Gen. Goering at center (hand in right pocket), and Gen. Daluge at the right center (holding a glass, hand in left pocket). A member of the regular Prussian Civil Service, Dr Gritzbach had originally been an aide to Reich Chancellor Franz von Papen, but quickly came over to Goering when he saw the way things were going; he stayed on for twelve years. (*HGA*)

Above left: Paul 'Pilli' Korner (1893–1957), Goering's aide from 1931 to 1945, enjoys a slim cigar while looking out of a window of his boss's pre-war special train. This was taken during a rail trip near Weimar on 28–30 March 1936, after the reoccupation of the German Rhineland by the Army. (*HGA*)

Above right: Paul Korner (center, wearing belted overcoat) is seen here in the uniform and jaunty cap of the Reich Forestry Service during an official visit to a steel smelting plant at what would later become the Hermann Goering Works. After Korner, from left to right, are Goering aides Fritz Gornnert and Dr Erich Gritzbach, with Goering in Reich FS peaked cap, overcoat, and a cane in his right hand. (*HGA*)

Left: Goering (left) and his aide, Dr Erich Gritzbach (right), pause on land during a 12 July 1939 cruise of Hermann's state yacht, *Carin II*, at the Glindenberg Ship Works near Magdeburg. Goering appears in a typically jaunty cap and a sporting outfit, and leans on yet another cane. (*HGA*)

Left: From 1933 to 1945, Goering's durable and flexible manservant was Robert Kropp, who also took pictures for his boss's personal photograph albums—as seen here, juggling a pair of Leica cameras (one, at the left, with a flash attachment). Known as 'The Uncrowned King of Prussia', Goering would have been astounded when the victorious Allies abolished the State of Prussia altogether after the Second World War. (*HGA*)

Right: Kropp (right) was in daily, constant service to his master, even dressing him. Here, Goering (left) ducks his head to enter a Lufthansa Ju-52 passenger liner in 1934, with Kropp bringing up the rear— literally! His boss was termed 'blunt, jovial, and intense'. (*HHA*)

Another view of Robert Kropp; he is standing outside the Hotel Excelsior in a civilian double-breasted suit jacket, just to the left of the windscreen of the car. Goering is seen wearing a white cap and uniform jacket in the rear seat at left. Notice also the swastika pennant on the car's left front fender. In 1937, Dr Gritzbach noted: 'If Goering has not sufficient time to finish with his morning visitors—or if he desires to continue his talks with them later—they are resumed in the evening. He seldom has his evening meal before 9.30 or 10 p.m.' (*HGA*)

Left: A formal portrait of Goering in his role as commanding officer of the *Landespolizei Regiment Gen. Goering*; it was common in the German armed forces to name a unit after its commander. Note the bright sash worn across his chest and also the ever-present Blue Max at his collar. On 14 March 1933, von Hindenburg authorized the wearing of black-white-and-red cockades on caps, as seen here. (*Bender, Miller, HGA*)

Right: Gen. Goering astride his mount, the lord of all he surveys. (*Bender, Miller, HGA*)

Gen. Goering (centers) renders a traditional hand-to-cap military salute as he reviews Special Purpose Police Group Wecke at Charlottenburg, 1934. To the left, with drawn sword, is the unit's operational commander, Maj. Walter Wecke. Goering earned his reputation as 'the man with the police'. On 1 June 1933 he had his cops seize the Berlin headquarters of the National Party, which was made up of conservative Junker landowners and the captains of industry. (*Bender, Miller, HGA*)

Above: Goering's Green State Police Regiment receives its colors as he looks on at center rear, 29 May 1934. Serving as Goering's Under-Secretary of the Interior for Prussia was Ludwig Grauert. At a speech in Essen, in the Ruhr, on 11 March 1933, Goering declared, 'I repudiate the idea that the police are a defense force for Jewish department stores! We must put an end to the absurdity of every rogue shouting for the police. The police are not there to protect rogues, vagabonds, usurers, and traitors!' (*Bender, Miller, HGA*)

Right: General Walter Weche. On 13 September 1933, Goering's Police Regiment received its first color standard, dedicated by touch with the 1923 Nazi Blood Flag and also that of the famed Imperial Berlin Guard Security Battalion. In his 1934 book *Germany Reborn*, Goering asserted: 'It seemed to me of the first importance to get the weapon of the criminal and political police firmly in my own hands. Here it was that I made the first sweeping changes of personnel! Out of thirty-two police chiefs, I removed twenty-two. New men were brought in, and in every case, these men came from the great reservoir of the Storm Troops.' (*Bender, Miller, LC*)

Two views of the Regimental Band of Goering's State Police troops marching down rain-slicked streets. Behind are men with weapons at carry arms. Emblazoned on the right side of their steel helmets was a white swastika. He replaced their rubber truncheon batons with pistols to fire back at the communists, who had been shooting at them. His first office in the German government was at No. 63 Wilhelmstrasse, as the Prussian Interior Ministry's top cop. (*HGA*)

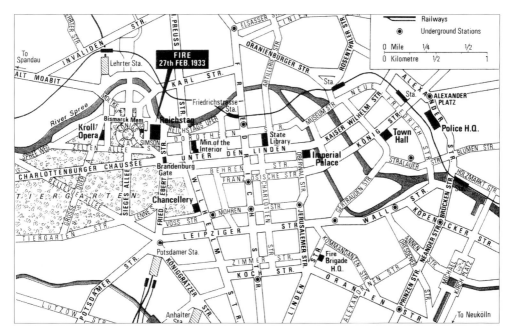

A detailed map of downtown Berlin's central Government Quarter on the night of the Reichstag Fire, 27 February 1933. When he was first elected Reichstag President by a coalition of party votes in 1932, Goering replaced Paul Lobe (14 December 1875–8 March 1967), to whom the Nazis later granted a government pension for his time as the longest-serving Reichstag President (1920–32). They credited the socialists with having done them a favor in 1918—they had gotten rid of the Hohenzollerns and other German royal dynastic families. (*LC*)

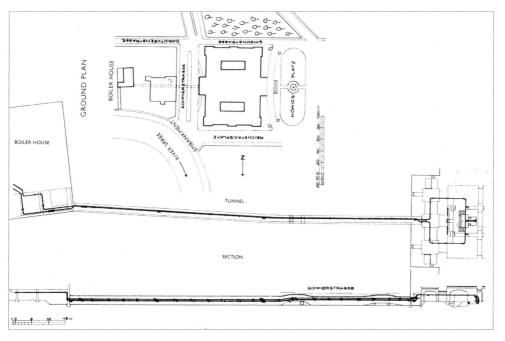

A map of the Reichstag Building (lower right), the official residence of Reichstag President Goering (above), and the Boiler House (left). The tunnel shown in the middle left ran from the Boiler House into the Reichstag Building's chamber, and thus underneath Goering's residence. Goering was accused of sending his SA arsonists to torch the legislative chamber via this tunnel. He denied this charge before the IMT at Nuremberg in 1946, 'in the face of … death'. (*Reichstaghaus in Berlin, Institute for Contemporary History, Munich*)

A photomontage by John Heartfield that reflects what the world thought—Nazi wild-man arsonist Hermann Goering had torched his own Reichstag (seen burning at the left rear) before butchering the rival German socialist and communist parties. The KPD had issued this call to revolt on 6 March 1933: 'Workers, to the barricades! Fresh bullets in your guns! Pull the pins from the grenades!' Goering alleged that the communists planned to poison the Berlin SA during mealtimes, and also to employ human shields against the police. (*LC*)

Were these Goering's accomplices and others in the Reichstag Fire drama? From left to right, coming down the steps of the Berlin Dom Cathedral in 1933, are SA leader Karl Ernst, Berlin Gauleiter Dr Josef Goebbels, unknown SA men, Hohenzollern Prince August Wilhelm ('Auwi') (also in SA kit), and a pair of SS men, followed by a horde of SA and SS men. In 1945, in his typically exaggerated fashion, Goering told US interrogator George Shuster, 'My belt snagged in the door … almost sucking me into the flames!' (*HHA*)

Following page, above: Bulgarian communist leader Georgi Dimitrov (left) plays chess with Karl Haberstock at Altaussee, 1945. During their clash at Leipzig in September 1933, Goering wore a civilian jacket, riding trousers, and black boots. Later, under communist rule, their former courtroom became the Georgi Dimitrov Museum, with recordings of the two men's voices being played for tourists.

After the trial, the trio of acquitted Bulgarians was flown from Konigsberg to Moscow on a Russian plane on 28 January 1934, to spite Goering. Oddly, Dimitrov was not used as a prosecution witness against Goering in March 1946. After the Second World War Dimitrov became Premier of communist Bulgaria, dying in Moscow on 2 July 1949, at the age of sixty-seven. From 1949 to 1990 his mummified corpse was exhibited under glass at Sofia, his capital. In July 1990 the body was removed and cremated by his family. (*US Army Signal Corps photo by Ray D'Addario, Holyoke, MA, USA*)

Replacing the burned former Reichstag Building as that body's official meeting place during 1933–42 was the Berlin Kroll Opera House, under Goering's sway as Prussian State Theater Chief. He considered it an unfair trade, believing the Kroll to be a far more important structure than the 'talk shop' that he and all the elected Nazi deputies hated anyway. The Kroll (seen here in 1920) was destroyed by Allied bombs and then dynamited and bulldozed to the ground on either 27 March 1951 or 1952—accounts differ—never to be rebuilt. Its main entrance was at the lower right here. Accounts also differ as to whether or not Goering's office was burned; it contained an old desk, a huge, heavy armchair, family portraits, and two Gobelin tapestry wall hangings that were willed to Hermann by his late father, Heinrich, in 1913. (*LC*)

The changing façade of the new Nazi Reichstag at the Kroll Opera House, with emphasis on the evolving backdrop behind Reichstag President Goering's Speaker's Chair (rear middle). The Third Reich was born there via NSDAP legislation on 24 March 1933, presided over by Goering. In all three views both Goering and Hitler appear, with the government benches located at the lower left in each frame. The later picture of the façade—with the huge Nazi eagle and swastika—shows the stenographers' well down in front, facing the deputies. During the war, they kept records of Hitler's daily military conferences. In the last of the three pictures—taken on 19 July 1940—Schaub, Himmler, and Martin Bormann can be seen (left to right) sitting down in the audience at the lower right. (*HGA*)

Reichstag President Hermann Goering in command and in his element, presiding over a legislative body that contained only Nazis from March 1933 to April 1942—the last time it met in full session. He loved the *Krolloper*, in which he presided over the first session of the new NSDAP Third Reich on 21 March 1933; it was located at the western end of the large Berlin Konigsplatz. It had been leased after 1900 by the City of Berlin for usage as its New Opera House, but by 1933 it had become better known as the *Krolloper*, as noted by Tony Le Tissier. On 24v March 1933, it was here that Goering passed the Enabling Act, formally establishing one-party rule in the country. He greeted the assembly with the new formal German acknowledgement, the *Hitlergruss* (Hitler salute). Today, the former Konigsplatz is the Platz der Republik, while the site of the former *Krolloper* is but a grassy meadow. (*HGA*)

During his first official state visit to Fascist Rome in April 1933, Goering himself flew his Ju-52 passenger plane part of the way, downing huge snacks and drinks; he became deathly airsick on the return trip across the Alps. On 7 November 1933—back at Rome once more—he secured from Mussolini the recall of Ambassador Enrico Cerruti and his wife home to Italy. (*HGA*)

Left: Erhard Milch (seated) appears to be enjoying the flight. He first bribed Reichstag Deputy Hermann Goering on 17 June 1928, and later asserted, 'I see through him when he starts to brag.' So did Hitler; referring to the Reichstag Presidency, he said, 'He can be glad he has got that … More than once I have been ready to give him the air, but perhaps he would make an excellent air minister?' Instead of elevating the sitting NSDAP Reichstag Vice President Stohr to the Presidency, Hitler nominated Goering—thus handing him the third-ranking Weimar Republic government post. (*HGA*)

Right: Also enjoying the flight to Rome is the unknown officer at the center of this photograph, wearing the Blue Max. Meanwhile, Paul Korner (right, in SS black) downs a swig of liquid from a glass. (*HGA*)

The same unknown Luftwaffe officer prepares to eat a spoonful of caviar on Goering's Ju-52 airplane, April 1933. During Goering's lean time in Berlin, he was known to borrow money from the head waiter at the bar at Rankesh in order to entertain on Hitler's behalf. (*HGA*)

Goering greets the Italian press with Fascist Italy's Air Marshal Italo Balbo (left, with goatee beard) upon landing, with German Ambassador to Rome Ulrich von Hassell wearing a bowler hat at the far left and Balbo's successor as C-in-C *Regia Aeronautica* Chief Gen. Giuseppi del Valle (second from right). Goering would not match his former Italian counterpart Balbo in rank until 1938, five years after this photo was taken. The two airmen got along well. Ironically, Goering was taking over his air force just as Balbo was preparing to leave his for the Governorship of the Italian colony of Libya, in North Africa, where Goering would visit him again in the spring of 1939. (*HGA*)

The official German delegation at The Vatican poses for a press photo. Its leader, Goering, stands sixth from left, chatting with German Vice Chancellor (and former Reich Chancellor) Franz von Papen (1878–1970) in dark suit at the center. Next is Paul Korner (in SS black) and two unidentified others. In between Goering and von Papen stands the tiny Archbishop Giuseppi Roncali, who succeeded the late Pope Pius XII as Pope John XXIII in 1958. Reportedly, in his audience with Pope Pius XI on 12 April 1933, Goering told His Holiness that he was his equal as head of the Protestant Church in Prussia—the old, former title of Kaiser Wilhelm II as *Summus Episcopus*—an assertion that the Pope seemed laughingly to accept at face value. Nazi Germany got its desired concordat with the Vatican, with the Catholic von Papen's help also. (*Eckstein-Halpaus, Dresden, LC, courtesy of Stan Piet, Bel Air, MD, USA*)

Goering gives an unexpected friendly hug to Hitler's personal pilot, Col. Hans Baur (1897–1993), in 1933. In 1933, the religious Goering stated, 'If the Catholic Christian is convinced that the Pope is infallible in all religious and ethical matters, so we National Socialists declare with the same ardent conviction that for us, too, the Führer is absolutely infallible in all political and other matters! It is a blessing for Germany that in Hitler the rare union has taken place between the most acute, logical thinker and truly profound philosopher and the iron man of action, tenacious to the limit ... I follow no leadership but that of Adolf Hitler—and of God!' (HHA)

A picture postcard depicting Prussian Minister President Goering (left) in formal morning attire, with Reich President Paul von Hindenburg (center, in top hat with cane) and Goering's aerial deputy Erhard Milch (on the right, clutching top hat). The occasion is the dedication of the Junkers 0 38 Taufe Lufthansa passenger airliner at Tempelhof Airport in June 1933. The two policemen seen between Goering and Hindenburg are on Goering's orders as Prussia's top cop. Note also the decorative laurel across the plane's open doorway at the top right. (HHA)

Another view of the dedication, with a trio of steel-helmeted military officers rendering a traditional hand salute to von Hindenburg, fourth from left. Goering appears at the center, clutching some papers in his left fist. On 19 February 1934, the Reich President duly authorized the placement of the NSDAP swastika-and-eagle icon above the right breast pocket on German Army caps and uniform jackets. (*HHA*)

The giant D2500 passenger airliner *Field Marshal von Hindenburg* at Tempelhof Aiport, June 1933. The four-engined, forty-two-seater airliner was the pride of Lufthansa, with Goering personally christening it. As of March 1933, von Hindenburg authorized the flying of the NSDAP red-white-and-black swastika flag alongside that of the old Imperial Reich War Flag as the new national colors. (*HHA*)

An evening social event for a gaggle of top Nazis during the 1936 Berlin Summer Olympics. From left to right: Luftwaffe Gen. Friedrich Christiansen; Reich Sports Leader Hans von Tschammer und Osten; Gestapo Chief and SS Gen. Reinhard Heydrich; Lufwaffe Gen. Alfred Keller; and German Regular Police Gen. Kurt Daluge. On 25 April 1933, Goering merged the 250,000-member Steel Helmet veterans' association with the Nazi SA. Hitler made Goering *Reichstadthalter* (Governor) of Prussia, the same post held by von Epp in Bavaria. (*HGA*)

With a Heinkel aircraft serving as the backdrop, German aircraft leaders and other officials pose for a group shot. From left to right: Paul Korner; unknown man; Erhard Milch; Peter Menthe; unidentified man; Goering (white X); and another unknown man. As a morphine addict, Goering's skin changed color, and his body also swelled up. Prior to the 1934 Blood Purge, he was seen as 'the red-faced, enormous general'. (*HHA*)

The head table at a typical aircraft industry dinner. Goering smiles at the center as an also-smiling Milch tells him something at the left, with Bruno Lorzer listening in at center right. At the far right is Goering's Luftwaffe adjutant from 1933–44, Karl Bodenschatz. In 1934 the Lorzer brothers began publishing their serialized First World War combat memoirs in Berlin's *Illustrated Times*, including some of Goering's own aerial exploits. However, an embarrassment came when it was alleged that one of Goering's First World War girlfriends, Helene Duchner, turned out to be a French agent also known as 'Blanche Lalart'. (*HGA*)

Left: The mother of Erhard Milch, Mrs Klara Milch, was reportedly a Jewess. She reportedly had affairs with Carl Brauer and Baron Hermann von Bier. (*Milch, LC*)

Right: Erhard Milch's supposed father, Anton Milch. It was alleged that both of Erhard's parents were Jewish; if this was true, it would mean that the real leader of Germany's air force was a full Jew. (*Milch, LC*)

Left: Luftwaffe Col. Erhard Milch (left) collects coins for the annual Nazi Winter Help relief organization, 1933. Note his donor's saddle shoes, some still worn now. Unwisely, Milch boasted of the German Air Force Ministry, 'The Minister is me!' On 9 February 1933 the Reich cabinet voted to give 1.4 million RM for the black Luftwaffe's first annual budget, and Goering was able to secure a further 1.1 billion RM for 1934. It was all administered and spent by a Jew—Erhard Milch. (*HHA*)

Below: Famed First World War air ace Ernst Udet sits, smiling, at the wheel of his car. The man at the right may be unit adjutant Karl Bodenschatz. (*HGA*)

Udet poses here with his peacetime glider at Berlin's Gatow Airfield. This photograph was taken between the wars, while Udet was a carefree aerial daredevil. The biographer Singer claimed that on 14 June 1928, whilst serving as an elected official, Goering contacted foreign army chiefs about sales in which he would earn a commission. He was walking with a limp at the time, like Dr Goebbels. (*HHA*)

From left to right, Milch, Udet, and four unidentified Nazi officials are seen at a Junkers air show before the war. Milch and Udet were good friends when this snapshot was taken. (*HHA*)

Another view of the same event, with Udet at the far left (X) and a group of admiring youngsters walking along at the right. (*HHA*)

Nemesis. Luftwaffe commander Field Marshal Hermann Goering (left) makes a point to his listening subordinate Ernst Udet (right) on 24 June 1938 at the Berlin *Haus der Flieger* (Airmen's Club) during the International Aeronautical Conference. Note how Goering holds the thin cigar in his left hand. Organizationally, Milch held a job for which he was ill-equipped—technical director of the Luftwaffe. (*HGA*)

Top: Reich Aviation Minister Goering stands with fists on hips at an early Luftwaffe flyby, with adjutant Col. Karl Bodenschatz third from right, briefcase and envelope cradled under his left arm. (*HGA*)

Middle: Bruno Lorzer (center, wearing aiguillette on his right shoulder) listens to one of his SS aides on 1 February 1934, at the International Air Schedule Conference in Berlin's famed *Kaiserhof*. (*HGA*)

Right: Sieg Heil! Lorzer (right) renders a Nazi salute from the front steps of his home, his family members behind him. The man at left is probably Lt Bernd von Brauchitsch, later Air Force adjutant to Goering from 1936–45. (*HHA*)

Lorzer (white X) reviews a formation of his airmen in 1933. Over the course of the rest of his career, he was criticized within the air service for allegedly being nothing more than Goering's crony from the First World War. (*HHA*)

Lorzer speaks at a glider show at a swastika-emblazoned lectern (right) inside an airplane hangar on 12 January 1934, Goering's birthday. Note the color guard at left, standing at attention. (*HHA*)

Previous page, below: A close-up of Bruno Lorzer speaking from the podium at the same event. Goering established an annual flying day every summer since 1933, and also an annual flight around Germany that attracted many keen airmen—including fellow pilot Rudolf Hess. Singer noted that in 1933 all air clubs merged into the Air Club of Germany and the German Air Sport Association; together, they would train Hitler Youth boys to become the future airmen of Germany. (*HHA*)

Left: Goering's much-revered 'Ural Bomber' expert, Gen. Walter Wever (1887–1936). His eventual successor as Luftwaffe Chief of Staff, Hans Jeschonneck, believed (wrongly) that Nazi Germany would never need such a long-range aircraft. Things might have been very different had Gen. Wever lived. (*HHA*)

Right: Gen. Wever (right), effectively the first Chief of Staff of the Luftwaffe, chats with his service chief, Goering (center), who is wearing an overcoat with a fur collar. Note Wever's Luftwaffe dress sword with ornate pommel design. (*HGA*)

Top Nazis on a relaxing sea cruise, 1934. From left to right: Karl Bodenschatz (possibly); an animated Dr Josef Goebbels (in sunglasses); Hitler having a nap in a deckchair (in the background); Rudolf Hess listening (hand to chin); and Reichsbank President and German Economics Minister Dr Hjalmar Schacht (right), appearing to debate Goebbels. From 1933–38, Dr Schacht was the main financial wizard behind the building of the new German air force. (*HHA*)

A study in physical contrasts at the September 1934 Nuremberg Nazi Congress: Deputy Führer Rudolf Hess (left, in Nazi Party Leadership Corps cap) and Goering (right, wearing an SA coffee-can-style cap and togs, Blue Max in place as always). After the war, Hess would joke that Goering 'was about as wide as he was tall'. When he was on drugs, Goering was described as suffering 'a heavy, sodden mood of depression, his eyes becoming distant and glazed'. His wide-set blue eyes were described as 'cold as a snake's'. (*HGA*)

On his forty-first birthday on 12 January 1934, Reich Aviation Minister Goering (left) receives a bouquet of flowers from a Hitler Youth boy as another looks on, smiling. This photograph was taken in the park of Goering's sumptuous Berlin Palace, situated at No. 2 or 11a Leipzigerstrasse. On 10 June 1934, at Carinhall, Goering reminded Mrs Cerruti of the Borgias 'in his concept of a princely existence'. (*HGA*)

6

PURGE, 1934

Goering's birthday in 1934 was his first to fall within the new Nazi calendar of celebratory events; these extravagant occasions continued to occur until 1945, even with USSR tank spearheads bearing down on Carinhall from the east.

On 12 January 1934, when he turned forty-one, Goering was loaded down with presents from all over the Reich—he had even previously specified his desire for certain gifts from certain 'donors'.

Heldengedenktag *(Heroes' Memorial Day), March 1934*

This was the last official public appearance that President von Hindenburg made with Reich Chancellor Hitler and Reich Aviation Minister Goering. The Heroes' Memorial Day occurred on the third Sunday in March every year; prior to 1933, it had been known as the National Day of Mourning, but the Nazis renamed it. It even took place in 1945, as the Allied armies closed in on Berlin—on this occasion, Goering stood in for the absent Hitler.

Like most Nazi commemorative events, the day had a mix of wreath-laying, speeches, and military parades of colorful splendor, with banners waving and bands playing. For the inaugural event (12 March 1933), Hitler proclaimed that the swastika was to be flown nationally—effectively becoming the new standard of the Reich.

The next year, as the showdown with the SA seemed to become more imminent with each passing day, Goering attended the event decked out in his Army General's helmet, uniform, and overcoat, thus visibly siding with the *Reaktion* of the German right against his own party's leftist clique. This sent an important message to the generals—he was one of them.

Goering Loses the Gestapo to the SS Duo, 20 April 1934

On Hitler's birthday—which was not yet celebrated as a national holiday—Goering sadly donned his blue-gray Luftwaffe dress uniform, complete with clanking sabre, for a ceremony at the Prussian Ministry Building. Once there, he officially turned over his prized Gestapo to the SS Duo of Himmler and Heydrich, who were on their way to unifying all of Germany's various police forces under their leadership. In return, Goering gained the SS Duo as valuable allies in the upcoming purge—which was just two months distant. In 1940, Nazi-in-exile Otto Strasser argued that Hitler gave the Gestapo to Himmler as a counterbalance to Goering's reactionary attitude after cozying up to Hindenburg, the Army generals, and the wealthy Ruhr industrialists, whom he felt more in common with than Hitler's SA bully boys.

Goering Confronts Röhm, May 1934

According to Dr Gritzbach, in mid-May 1934, six weeks before the gunshots of the Blood Purge were fired, Goering personally confronted SA Staff Chief Röhm:

> He earnestly begged him to remain steadfast to the Führer and to the German people, but Röhm and his fellow criminals were too deeply enmeshed in their highly-ramified plots, and … downright lying.

Goering had no choice but to advise Hitler that Röhm had to go.

On 14–15 June of that year, Hitler visited Mussolini in Venice for a two-day conference; he was surprised to hear *Il Duce* suggest that the Führer should get rid of Goering, blaming him for the fiasco of the Reichstag Fire and the subsequent trial. In favor of Röhm's 'Second Revolution', Mussolini also reportedly asserted that Goebbels should fall. Meanwhile, back in Germany, President von Hindenburg summoned Goering to tell him that if he and Hitler did not act against Röhm martial law would be declared. The stage was potentially set for a clash with Blomberg and the Army, allied with Goering, on one side, and Hitler, Röhm, and the SA on the other. In 1940, Otto Strasser even went so far as to say that 'Goering had betrayed [Hitler]'.

On 20 June 1934 Goering made a speech to the Prussian State Council that was a thinly veiled attack on Röhm—the man who had called Goering 'the Fat Louse'—and the SA. He tackled the NSDAP left's call for a 'second revolution' head-on:

> It is not our business to decide whether there must be a second revolution! The first revolution was ordered and ended by the Führer … If the Führer wants a second revolution, we shall be ready, in the streets, tomorrow. If he does not want it, we shall be ready to suppress anybody who tries to rebel against the Führer's will.

The Return of Carin Goering, 20 June 1934

Early in 1934, the Stockholm firm Swedish Tenn finished the giant pewter double coffin that Goering had ordered the previous October. It had been designed to one day contain the bodies of Hermann and his first wife.

Goering returned to Lovo Cemetery in Stockholm for the disinterment of his much-loved first wife; it is unclear whether or not he had the approval of the von Fock family, but they did attend the event. Goering's entourage included his aides-de-camp and also Carin's friends, the Prince and Princess zu Weid. Placed in her giant new coffin, Carin's remains were solemnly carried to a German rail coach while a troop of Swedish Nazis dipped their colors in a reverent salute and sang the Lutherian hymn 'A Mighty Fortress is Our God', which had been played at her 1931 funeral. Atop the impressive coffin lay a wreath of white roses with red roses at their center, with a card that had been written by her husband—'To my only Carin'.

The funeral train ran from Tralleborg to Sassnitz, across a Baltic Sea railroad bridge, and then, at a slow pace, into the *Eberswalde* ('Forest'), where it was unloaded onto a cart. It was then escorted by Reich Forestry Rangers along dusty country roads lined with saluting troops and devotees.

At Carinhall families, friends, and dignitaries saluted Hitler's arrival. In a formal address, NSDAP Gauleiter Kube lauded 'Germany's noblest lady'—even though she lived and died a Swede. There then followed the Wagnerian Siegfried Funeral March from the ponderous *Twilight of the Gods*, as helmeted soldiers of the *Landespolizei General Goering* descended into the below-ground, vaulted tomb with the body. Goering and Hitler then descended the steps, alone, to reflect and meditate on the events that had brought all of them there. Ascending the broad steps, Hitler was photographed wiping away a tear. Carin would remain there (in one form or another) into 1950, by which time the other two men had joined her in death—both by suicide.

A Geezer, an Egyptian, a Cripple, and a Tailor's Dummy

At Tempelhof Airfield, outside Berlin proper, on 17 July 1934, SA General Karl Ernst formally accepted (on behalf of the German people) a gift from Goering. It was a large aerial balloon that he had duly christened *Hermann Goering*. The balloon's honoree was not present.

In the run-up to the coming purge, the SA leaders reportedly used codenames to refer to their enemies. Hindenburg was 'an old geezer from Neudeck', Hess was 'the Egyptian bastard' (due to him being born overseas), Goebbels was 'the cripple', and Goering was 'the tailor's dummy'. Himmler was known as 'Black Boy'. Correspondence between the leaders of the SA shows their (perhaps justified) paranoia:

> Hermann is out to skin us alive. He cannot stand the cripple, but will make friends with Black Boy. The Chief [Röhm] is more concerned with skinning Hermann alive. The first thing is to drive a wedge between the bastards. Why not kill them both [Goering and Goebbels]?

In the event, most of those associated with the Reichstag Fire—guilty or innocent—were killed during the purge, including Ernst, Heines, Fiedler, Sander, Röhm, and von Mohrenschild.

On the same day as the *Hermann Goering* balloon was bestowed, Vice Chancellor Franz von Papen, at the University of Marburg, delivered the last-ever speech that was critical of the Nazi government. Ernst and von Papen were marked for death. Almost a week later, on 26 June, Goering gave a speech of his own in Hamburg:

> When one day the cup runneth over, I will strike! We have worked as no one has ever worked before, because we have behind us a people who trusts us. Anyone who gnaws away at this trust is committing a crime against the people, committing treachery, and high treason. He who designs to destroy this trust, destroys Germany. He who sins against this trust has put his own head in the noose!

On Friday 29 June 1934, Goering and Hitler had a final summit before the purge. Here, they finalized plans for the coming action against Röhm, the SA, and other opponents. Afterwards, Goering flew back to Berlin to await Hitler's order to start the purge there; it was expected that this would come the next day. Meanwhile, the Führer himself would lead the purge in Munich and at the SA retreat at Bad Weisee, Bavaria.

Blood Purge, 30 June–3 July 1934

As a left-wing Nazi, Otto Strasser never cared for Hitler or Goering. In characterizing his brother's future murderer, Strasser stated, 'The fat, jolly exterior of this man was a perfect mask for one of the most cruel and unscrupulous characters I have ever met. His was the soul of a butcher.' Goering's own first cousin, Herbert Goering, added that Hermann 'would trample over corpses' to get what he wanted.

Both men were proven right by the Nazi Blood Purge, which shocked the civilized world. It was a rampage of wanton murder, representing the executions of men who had no opportunity to stand trial. While planning the purge, Goering had told his subordinate, Dr Diels, 'I warn you, you cannot sit on both sides of the fence.' You were either with Goering or you would perish.

Dr Diels coolly replied, 'Mr Minister-President, the head of the Secret State Police must sit on all sides of the fence at once!' Unlike Goering, Diels would survive both the Second World War and its immediate aftermath. Martha Dodd, who watched how Diels stood behind Goering and even seemed to coach him during the Reichstag Fire trial, even believed that Hermann actually feared Diels. After all, he had read the police dossier about Goering before his boss had even had the chance, and knew many secrets about him.

The Blood Purge, with the infamous Night of the Long Knives, lasted from 30 June to 3 July 1934; Hitler, in Munich, and Goering, in Berlin, solved most of their party's internal and external personnel problems by simply shooting those who had caused them. The action in Berlin reportedly began on the 30th when Dr Goebbels telephoned from Munich to give the go-ahead, using the code-word '*Kolibri*' ('Hummingbird). Over a decade of animosity then erupted, and those who had made enemies of the Führer and his Iron Man were washed away in a sea of blood.

Victims were found both inside and outside the Nazi regime. The main target was SA Chief of Staff Captain Ernst Röhm, who wanted his two million SA Brownshirts to overwhelm and absorb the official *Reichswehr* and form the Nazi People's Army of the future. He believed that the last war had been lost by its officers—the men represented by Goering—and not the ordinary German soldiers, whom he believed were represented more properly by his SA men. Hitler would eventually agree with Röhm, but not until it was too late; the SA chief was a decade before his time. The 1933–34 standoff was termed as the Brown Tide versus the Gray Rock, recalling the uniform colors of the SA and the Army respectively.

Ironically, by 1944 Hitler and Himmler had utilized a trio of armed forces outside the regular Army—the Waffen-SS of the RFSS, the *Volkssturm* (People's Army), and even Goering's own Luftwaffe field divisions, made up of personnel who were no longer needed to service and support the aircraft that had been blasted out of the skies by the Allies.

For Goering, the death of his two big SA rivals was a necessity; he believed they intended to slay him, so he would kill them first. His FA Brown Sheet telephone transcripts also revealed that they made a slur against Emmy, referring to her as 'Goering's sow'—he could never forgive that, nor that they called him the 'Tailor's Dummy' regarding his well-known penchant for uniforms. In the purge, Goering ensured he was both thorough and ruthless. During his personally led *Landespolizei* raid on the Berlin SA headquarters, he was seen running through the building, pointing and shouting, 'Arrest him! Arrest him! Arrest him!'

The second chief victim was Gregor Strasser, leader of the NSDAP trade union movement. He was also clamoring for a 'second revolution' that would overthrow Goering and the people he represented—the Black Reaction, Junker landowners, big-business steel magnates and industrialists from the Ruhr, and the churches. Again, Hitler basically agreed with Strasser, but Strasser and his younger brother, Otto, were also ten years before their time, as the events of 1944–45 would show. For Goering, Gregor was the man who had stolen the NSDAP Vice Chancellorship from him by convincing Gen. von Schleicher to offer him the position instead. The bold soldier told the fat Nazi, 'You are not fit to hold office!'—an allusion, possibly, to Goering's rampant drug addiction. Both men were threats to Goering, and both therefore died. However, Goering later asserted that his policemen were too late when they arrived at the von Schleicher's home—both husband and wife were found dead, already shot by the SS as their teenage daughter watched.

For the time being, Hitler needed to keep all the various groups that Röhm and Strasser opposed in the fold, so the two men had to go—or else the Army would march on the Nazi regime in Berlin and overthrow it. After all, the Army alone possessed the weapons to do this. Hitler and Goering also understood that the wars they were planning for the near future would demand a disciplined German Army, and therefore not Röhm's unruly mass, which was led by the Strassers' leftist, socialist wing of the party. Hitler himself would replace the murdered Röhm, and Dr Robert Ley (part of the leftist wing) would replace Gregor Strasser after the purge ended on 3 July 1934. Otto Strasser escaped to neighboring Czechoslovakia with his Black Front minions before moving on to France, Canada, and back to the defeated Germany after the Second World War.

Aside from Röhm and Gregor Strasser, the major other victims were members of the Army itself—Hitler's predecessor as Reich Chancellor, Gen. Kurt von Schleicher, and his deputy, Gen. Ferdinand von Bredow. Röhm had been killed in Munich, while Goering handled Strasser and the two generals in Berlin. Ironically, both in 1934 and a decade later the Army plotters considered Goering to be the most conservative Nazi of all—simply put, he should have felt more of an affinity with their class than Hitler's. Von Schleicher may have earned his place on the list of victims to forever obscure the fact that he and Goering might have schemed to put themselves in office and ignore Hitler in December 1932. In this regard, Goering was not taking any chances.

On the afternoon of 3 July 1934, at Dr Goebbels's Propaganda Ministry, Goering held a notorious post-purge press conference. According to an eyewitness from London's *Daily Telegraph*, Goering announced the following in perfect English:

> I know how you boys always like a 'story'. Well, I have got a 'story' for you, all right! General von Schleicher resisted arrest. He is dead … You know me well enough, gentlemen, to realize that I shall crush all resistance remorselessly, whether it comes from left or right. Whoever conspires against the Third Reich will lose his head!
>
> All Germany is in the hands of the Führer. The *Reichswehr* is loyal. As soon as the excitement has subsided, the Führer will address the nation … There must be no exaggeration! You have no need to go out and look for a story—the story is already there for you!

According to Fritz Thyssen in 1941, he asked Goering what crime Schleicher had committed. Goering answered that the General had been 'in treasonable intercourse with the French Ambassador', André François-Poncet.

The fourth target of the purge was the Catholic Church, in the form of the leader of its Catholic Action Society, Dr Erich Klausener. He was also one of Vice Chancellor Franz von Papen's top aides. Many of the NSDAP and SS murderers wanted von Papen shot as well, but Goering protected his former foe by placing him under house arrest for three days, guarded by his own troop of bodyguards.

A fifth group of victims was to be found in what the party regarded as 'the traitors of 1923'—those who had broken their word of honor to Hitler and Goering during the ill-fated Beer Hall Putsch. This included Gustav von Kahr and General von Lossow. Later, Goering would justify the mass killings (of which he was supremely responsible) by stating, 'Their treason was as clear as day! After all, there had been a plot against the Führer's life! The whole point was to act fast, as a deterrent.

In Berlin, the purge had been directed from Goering's personal headquarters in the downtown Government Quarter, the Berlin palace. It was surrounded by the troops and machine guns of his very own *Regiment General Goering*. His chief allies there (and partners in crime) were RFSS Himmler and his deputy, ex-Naval officer Reinhard Heydrich (head of the *Sicherheitsdienst* or Security Service), plus Maj. Gen. Walther von Reichenau, who was acting as the Army's unofficial liaison observer—ready to call in its armed troops, but only if they were needed. In the event, they were not. Goering's aides Paul Korner and Erhard Milch were also reportedly present. After the purge was finished, they all celebrated at two events—a crab feast at Horcher's Restaurant on the evening of 3 July 1934, and then at Carinhall.

An eyewitness to the machinations at Goering's Berlin palace was the Gestapo official (and later IMT prosecution witness) Hans Bernd von Gisevius. He recalled:

> Suddenly, loud shouting reached us from the adjoining room ... Goering's study, and here the execution committee was meeting. Now and then couriers from the Gestapo rushed into and out of this room, slips of white paper in their hands.
>
> Through the door, we could see Goering, Himmler, Heydrich, and little Pilli Korner, undersecretary to Goering in his capacity of Minister-President. We could see them conferring, but naturally, we could not hear what was being said ... Occasionally, however, we could catch a muffled sound: 'Away!' or 'Aha!' or 'Shoot him!' For the most part, we heard nothing but raucous laughter. The whole crew of them seemed to be in the best humor.
>
> Goering radiated cheerful complacency. It was easy to see that he was in his element ... He swaggered about the room—his long hair waving—in a white military tunic and blue-gray military trousers, with high, black boots that reached over his fat knees ... 'There goes Puss-in-Boots,' I thought suddenly. The epithet seemed appropriate—not so much because of the spiteful, catlike attitude of the man—as because there was something puffed-up, counterfeit, and ridiculous about him.
>
> We suddenly heard loud shouting. A police major [possibly Wecke], his face flaming, rushed out of the room, and behind him came Goering's hoarse, booming voice: 'Shoot them! ... Take a whole company ... Shoot them! ... Shoot them at once!' ... The written word cannot reproduce the undisguised blood lust, fury, vicious vengefulness, and—at the same time—the fear, the pure funk, that the scene revealed.

All sorts of wild figures have been tossed around as to the total number of those killed, ranging anywhere from seventy-seven to 2,000. However, as of yet no accurate total has ever emerged. Röhm's successor as Staff Chief of the SA was his former subordinate, Viktor Lutze, who claimed afterwards that Hitler's original list of seven targets grew first to seventeen, and then on to eighty-two. In 2012, the late German author Thomas Friedrich asserted that Goering had been responsible for twenty-four deaths in Berlin. One official report also stated that 1,124 people had been arrested by Goering's State Police. In 1984, Carlson noted that former Reich Chancellor Heinrich Bruning told the author Robert Waite that he had personally seen a death list of 5,000 names—perhaps the highest overall figure yet asserted.

Six years after what he termed 'The German Bloodbath', Otto Strasser wrote:

> 'I enlarged the sphere of action of the purge,' Goering ingeniously confessed on 1 July 1934 ... You mean you multiplied it by ten, if not by a hundred. When the wild beast Goering is let loose, there is little that can stop him ... Goering received no orders to kill his hundreds of victims in Prussia. Under the mask of political assassination, he committed a hundred acts of private vengeance, settling old scores, ridding himself of inconvenient friends.

About his brother's death, Otto recalled:

> He suddenly saw a revolver pointed at him through the grating. The first shot missed, and
> Gregor took refuge in a corner of the cell, but three gunmen … came in, and Gregor—rid-
> dled with bullets—fell to the ground … I had these details from the man who wiped the
> blood from the walls and removed the traces of the shooting. He was able to escape after
> the execution, and he joined me in Prague.

Most of the targets were killed in the courtyard at Munich's Stadelheim Prison by
SS firing squads. The squads were also used outside Berlin, at the same Lictherfelde
barracks where Goering had once studied as an officer cadet. Most accounts stress that
the SS did most of the killing, but in Berlin Goering used a special crack unit of his
green-uniformed State Police for his personal protection, and these officers also took
part. In time, this elite unit would morph into parachute troops and also, later still, into
the men of the Hermann Goering Division and Panzer Corps, who would fight Gen.
George Patton's US Third Army on Sicily in 1943.

In his 1989 biography of Goering, David Irving revealed that secret Luftwaffe troops
also had a role in the purge, at Goering's urging. Indeed, Milch provided fully 600 men
who were at that time undergoing secret training at Juterborg Airfield. These were duly
deployed to Berlin, also guarding the capital's trio of airports. On Hitler's return from
managing the purge in Bavaria, an honor guard of these troops would salute him.

Immediately after the purge, two telegrams were published in the German daily
newspapers that were allegedly sent by Reich President von Hindenburg. In the telegrams, Hindenburg absolved Hitler and Goering of blame in the murders and even
congratulated them—linking his revered name to their deeds. The Army had acquiesced
to the slaying of two of its own officers, a fact that was noted by Hitler and Goering
and that would be used when it was the Army's turn to be purged in 1938.

In a special session of the Reichstag at Berlin's Kroll Opera House, Hitler stated the
official figure of seventy-seven killed in all. Goering sat up and behind the speaker's
lectern, ensconced firmly in the Speaker's Chair. The list Hitler read out also included
fully twelve elected members of the Reichstag. The Führer had high praise for his chief
murderer in Berlin, stating, 'With an iron fist, he beat down the attack on the NSDAP
state before it could develop.'

At Nuremberg Prison after the Second World War, Goering discussed the Blood Purge
with Dr Gilbert:

> Röhm! Do not talk to me about that dirty homosexual pig. That was the real clique of
> perverted bloody revolutionists! They are the ones who first made the party look like a
> pack of hoodlums, with their wild orgies and beating up Jews on the street, and smashing
> windows! … What a gang of perverted bandits that SA was! It was a damned good thing
> I wiped them out, or they would have wiped us out!
>
>   We had to get rid of them to build up the party and the state … I made no bones about
> it. I just told my men to take the bastard out and shoot him!

In his official testimony, given in 1946, Goering testified that the conspirators had planned for the establishment of their own Fourth Reich, and that his SA honor guard was 'to arrest [him] at a given moment'. He also claimed that he had personally confronted Röhm about the rumor in May 1934:

> I knew Röhm very well. I had him brought to me. I put to him openly the things that I had heard.... When the headquarters of the SA leader Ernst in Berlin were searched, we found in the cellars ... more sub-machine guns than the whole Prussian police force had in its possession!

However, was there ever any real Röhm plot to overthrow the Führer? In retrospect it seems unlikely, but Hitler was not taking any chances, for the threat of the Army was very real. Goering also personally felt that his own life would be in danger if Röhm and the SA were to take over, and this was most likely a valid concern. There were a lot of loose talk and threats bandied about by Röhm and his drunken top leaders. These scenarios seemed to include a post-Hitler government with Hohenzollern Prince August Wilhelm (Goering's 'Auwi') as Germany's Reich President, in place of the deposed Hindenburg, von Schleicher as Reich Chancellor once more, Gregor Strasser as Vice Chancellor, replacing Papen, Röhm as Defense Minister for the ousted von Blomberg, and SA generals to replace the regular Army commanders.

For his part in the plot, Goering had the former Richthofen Squadron ace Capt. Gehrt brought before him so that Goering could personally rip off his Blue Max before ordering him to be shot. 'You filthy pig!' Goering screamed. 'I wanted to deal with you myself. Take him away!' Gehrt was killed by a firing squad. Goering also confronted Auwi with an FA sound recording of his last talk with the doomed Karl Ernst. 'You are lucky to have told the truth!' Goering said. 'I am glad that you have decided to go to Switzerland for a few days. Have I not told you that you have the dumbest face in the world? Of course, you want to go to Switzerland!' At last Goering had dropped his mask, belying his lack of support for the restoration of any Hohenzollern to the throne. Auwi had the last laugh, however, as he survived both the purge and the Second World War. He died—peacefully—two years after Goering.

Another of Goering's victims was Dr Fritz Gehrlich, who had once accused him of corruption. The overall success of the purge, in addition to the ruthlessness Goering demonstrated throughout, at last convinced Hitler that Goering was the man he needed at his side. It had been a long road back for Goering over the past eleven years, but his persistence had at last paid off. For the next decade, the Hitler-Goering team was indivisible. Thyssen made an interesting observation about their devils' pact in 1941:

> It was always doubtful whether Göring was party to a secret or not, especially after the Prussian Police Ministry had been taken from him. The present intimate relationship between Hitler and Goering dates only from the great massacre of 30 June 1934, when the National Socialist Party was purged of all members objectionable to the regime ... Goering had so large a part of the responsibility in this massacre that he no longer dared to oppose the regime ... He was much more independent before it ... He has made himself guilty of so

many crimes on account of his personal jealousies that he has come entirely into the grip of the Gestapo, who know too much about him. Ever since then, he has been silent.

Thyssen also believed that Hitler also feared the Gestapo after the purge:

He is almost their prisoner … He is not a daredevil like Goering; he constantly fears for his own security.

In case of possible prosecution over their illegal killings, Goering and the black-coated RFSS, Himmler, combined to erase all traces of their infamy, sending out the following order:

From the Prussian Minister-President and the Chief of the Secret State Police; to all subordinate police stations: All documents concerning the action of the last two days are to be burned, on orders from above. A report on the execution of this order is to be made at once.

However, they were not as thorough as they believed; in 1957, West Germany's new Socialist Party government tried, convicted, and imprisoned as many guilty parties as they could find. Among them was Hitler's SS chief bodyguard, Gen. Josef 'Sepp' Dietrich.

The non-German world was shocked by the purge, uniformly seeing it as a return to barbarism in a civilized, Western nation in the twentieth century. In his diary entry for 8 July 1934, Ambassador Dodd placed the blame squarely on the trio of top Nazis (Hitler, Goering, and Goebbels), writing: 'Never before have I heard or read of three more unfit men in high places'. He considered resigning, but did not.

On 2 July 1934 Goering received this telegram from ailing Reich President von Hindenburg:

I may express to you my thanks and appreciation for your vigorous and successful action in crushing the attempt to commit high treason.

With comradely regards,

von Hindenburg.

The next day, Goering was interviewed by a Swedish newspaper and quoted thus:

The action became necessary not only due to plans for a revolt, [but also because] Röhm's private life as well as that of the other persons who have now been arrested was such that it meant a scandal for the entire SA! They were a moral cancer that had to be cut out.

Germany had not witnessed such a juicy sexual imbroglio since before the First World War, during the reign of the last Kaiser; the public salivated.

The Death of Hindenburg, 2 August 1934

The death of Hindenburg cemented the power of the Hitler-Goering combination more than ever before. Surprisingly, Goering actually hoped and believed that Hitler would take the post of Reich President (head of state), thereby appointing Goering as Reich Chancellor (the actual head of government). Considering another possible political tack, Goering thought it possible that Hitler might declare himself Kaiser Adolf I, restoring Imperial Germany, with Hermann I as his subordinate King of Prussia; the twin offices had been dually held by Kaiser Wilhelm II until his post-First World War abdication.

In the event, Hitler cunningly checkmated Goering's lust for power yet again by simply combining the posts of Reich President and Reich Chancellor into one, and bestowing the new title on himself—Führer and Reich Chancellor. It was a ploy that Hitler would again use with Goering in February 1938.

German Envoy to a State Funeral in Belgrade, October 1934

On 9 October 1934 King Alexander I of Yugoslavia and French Foreign Minister Louis Barthou were assassinated in their car by two Croatian Ustache terrorists, ruining the French plan to create a Balkan containment alliance against the Third Reich. As he had been the Führer's personal envoy to the Balkan states in the spring of 1933, Hitler sent Goering to southeast Europe to represent Nazi Germany at Alexander I's state funeral in Belgrade on 20 October 1934. He arrived by air on the 17th, and on landing gave a press conference during which (according to François-Poncet in 1949) he asserted that 'Germany is not a country willing to tolerate within her boundaries the presence and activity of terrorist elements'. This was a backhanded swipe at Mussolini, whose Fascist Italy had sheltered the Croatian terrorist group Utsache for many years.

On 24 October 1934 Goering privately admitted to François-Poncet that Rosenberg in Germany was indeed in contact with Ustache elements. He also pressed François-Poncet to watch a newsreel of the assassination that the Nazis had acquired, so that the ambassador could study it for ways to improve security—but he declined. Fifteen years later, in his memoirs, Poncet recalled:

> Hitler and his colleagues had a fairly high opinion of France; they believed her a power to be feared. The murder of King Alexander and Barthou was one of the events that contributed to modify their opinion of us, bringing them gradually to consider us a less dangerous adversary than they had first supposed…. A mission—headed by a diplomat—was designated to attend [the funeral] … just as it was about to leave, Hitler wished to raise its prestige, and Goering was appointed to lead it, as special representative of the German Army.
>
> One of the wreaths he laid on the Royal bier bore the inscription, 'To her heroic adversary of yore—the German Army, in heartfelt grief'. To the press, he affirmed that Germany—in her own interests and in those of peace—wished Yugoslavia to be as powerful a state as possible.
>
> In this Slavic land—where France possessed many friends—he openly sought contact with Marshal Petain and took pleasure in appearing in public at his side … The Third Reich

hoped to profit by the decline of the French influence that it believed evident ... Thus, King Alexander's death broke one more link in the chain that had been forged at Versailles, and that Hitler had sworn to smash.

In 1941, Reich Marshal Goering would both bomb Belgrade with his Luftwaffe and reprise his role in again meeting with Marshal Petain—this time in France, as the conqueror meeting the vanquished.

Robert Kropp

Hitler established his own SS Staff Watch, answerable only to him (and not Himmler), while Goering did the same with the *Landespolizei*. When Karl Ernst coyly offered one of his own SA bodyguards as Minister Goering's personal valet, Goering baulked and decided it was high time to have his own man in such a sensitive post—and not a possible future SA assassin.

In April 1933 Robert Kropp thus emerged on the scene, becoming a central figure in Goering's world for the next dozen years. He got the job by answering a classified newspaper advertisement in the *Kreuz Zeitung* (*The Cross Times*); it had been placed by Goering's royal friend Baroness Holdorff. The paper was well-read by German military and naval veterans, and Kropp was indeed a veteran of the former Imperial Navy. Since leaving, Kropp had served as a valet with various industrial magnates from the Ruhr area.

The advertisement had mentioned 'an important gentleman' seeking valet services. The Baroness herself had selected Kropp from the various applicants, sending him to Goering for a personal job interview, and Kropp knew that his prospective employer was Hermann Goering. After keeping Kropp waiting for some hours, Goering called him into his office having already gone over Kropp's résumé, wartime record, and employer references. He was asked if he could drive a car and pilot a motorboat, to which he answered yes to each. In his usual direct way, Goering said, 'You seem just the man! What wages do you want?' Kropp asked for what he believed were the going monthly wages for a first-class valet—140 RM. Goering replied, 'I will give you 80 to start, and if you are satisfactory, you will get a raise. If not—out!' Kropp accepted Goering's offer.

Unmarried, Kropp further agreed to hard work and a flexible schedule that included all times of day and night. Goering was as good as his word, and Kropp's pay was doubled after three months; it was grandfathered back to his first day's service. In addition to that, Kropp appears in photographs in a number of different uniforms—SA, SS, Prussian State Civil Service, and even in Reich Forestry green on occasion.

In 1933 Goering also had Mrs Greta von Kornatzki as his personal secretary. Additionally, he placed Pilli Korner as a State Secretary in the Reich Justice Department, where most of the departmental civil servants stayed on under their new Nazi superiors.

'Unser Hermann'

Despite (or perhaps because of) his ruthlessness, Goering was touted by Hitler as 'the best man' he had, and 'the showpiece of the movement'. He was widely viewed as the Führer's eventual successor and number-two man. As the self-proclaimed 'inheritor of all the chivalry of German knighthood', Goering viewed himself as 'a renaissance man'—even when defeated and on trial during 1945–46.

For a man who lived well above the status of almost all Germans, Goering surprisingly held a real place in the hearts of the people. Like them, he had suffered much after the fall of the empire in 1918, including losing his prestige, his wealth, his work, and even his first wife. All of this resonated with his people. His oversized persona also struck a chord with them, as the nicknamed him both *'Der Dicke'* ('The Fat One') and—even more affectionately—*'Unser Hermann'* ('Our Hermann'). Simply put, he was one of them. He was the only genuinely popular member of the Nazi regime aside from Hitler, who was seen more as a revered figure, loftily removed from the average person. In Goering, the public could see themselves, with all their own faults and virtues. In the guise of the typical jolly, smiling, boisterous, and rosy-cheeked fat man, Goering was able to joke with them publicly about himself—especially about his expanding girth.

As Prime Minister of Prussia, Goering was a patron of art, music, and especially the State Opera—a jurisdiction that was his, rather than that of the overall Reich Minister of Propaganda and Public Enlightenment Dr Josef Goebbels. He liked to read biographies of Genghis Khan, but also enjoyed the detective-genre stories of authors such as Agatha Christie, Dashiell Hammett, and Dorothy Sayers. Together with Hitler and Eva Braun, as a youngster Hermann had loved the American Wild West, derring-do tales of German novelist Karl May, in addition to books on hunting and wild animals.

Goering was an author himself, having dictated (over the course of a few hours) the text of his book *Aufbau Einer Nation* (*The Building of a Nation*), a summary of his political views. The first edition was published by Eher Verlag, the Nazi Party's own publishers, with an English edition later published in the UK and the USA as *Germany Reborn*. Goering boasted that his royalties amounted to one million RM, or £50,000.

As an entertainer, his parties had no equal, and his table was renowned for its fine food and wines from all over Germany, Europe, and the rest of the world—even during wartime. *Der Eiserne*'s (the Iron Man's) well-known favorite Berlin restaurant was Horcher's, which was in business from 1904 to 1943. One reason for Goering's patronage was that it specialized in game dishes, which appealed to him as a hunter. He was known to the restaurant's founder, Gustav Horcher, and his son, Otto; he had visited when he was on leave during the First World War, and again in 1928 when he won election to the Reichstag. During the Imperial era, Crown Prince Wilhelm had been Horcher's most famous patron—a role that was taken over by Goering during the Third Reich. Goering reportedly celebrated the end of the Blood Purge at this restaurant, dining on crab meat with Himmler, Blomberg, Milch, and Korner.

Horcher also catered Goering's food at Carinhall, and this led to wartime Horcher Luftwaffe clubs that included locations at Tallinn, Riga, and Oslo as the war progressed.

Goering ensured that the firm's cooks and waiters were exempted from the German draft, and during the failed Stalingrad airlift of 1942–43, Horcher's wines and champagnes found their way into the besieged city via Luftwaffe transport aircraft. He also tripled the gas-rationing supplies for the trucks of the famed eatery. As all the other famous Berlin restaurants were forced to close, one-by-one, due to wartime austerity, Horcher's was kept open under Goering's personal fiat. In 1943, this would lead to a famous battle between Goering and Goebbels. As the war ground on, the Horcher clientele became ever more dominated by patrons wearing Luftwaffe-blue uniforms, Air Ministry staffers, and aircraft industry bigwigs, and its catering remained all the rage for most Third Reich occasions—even borrowing waiters from Potsdam's New Palace when needed.

Goering owed much of his weight to his eating habits. His maximum weight was said to be 280 lbs on a robust 5-ft-6-in. frame. Oddly, he was only really a sporadic eater, and his big meals only occurred either when entertaining at home or at Horcher's; however, he snacked at all hours of the day and night during his unusual working hours. His voracious energy and drive during the first six years of the Third Reich meant he quaffed down plates of sandwiches with mugs of cold beer, rousing Robert Kropp in the middle of the night to fix them, even specifying exactly which cheese and sausages he wanted. Like his Führer, Goering had a weakness for rich, sweet cakes with lots of whipped cream. Also like Hitler, he stayed up late, watching films in his private screening rooms, until 2–3 a.m., eating and drinking all the while, and got just a few hours of sleep a night. Kropp woke him at 6.30 a.m. for the next day's continued frenetic pace of work and meetings.

Goering's crash diets included vigorous walks in the country on weekends, using the sauna at Carinhall, horseback riding, playing tennis, and taking slimming pills; these methods caused him to lose 10 lbs at a clip, but he always put the weight back on. When playing tennis, he demanded that his opponent hit the ball directly to him so he that he would not have to run after it—rather defeating the purpose. Emmy recalled him falling asleep in an armchair after such excursions, looking 'like an exhausted bear'. He also took part in cross-country skiing—but not downhill, like Eva Braun and the Speers—and swam, and climbed mountains when he had the time. His major outdoor activity remained hunting. Goering later told Dr Gilbert that he had no sense whatsoever of danger during these activities, but it is unclear whether this was true or whether he was just playacting as usual. His weight problem would finally be solved by the US Army in 1945.

Goering's Appearance

Kropp generally found his master already up and shaved in the mornings—he would use a Gillette safety razor—and giving himself a manicure. Kropp believed that this habit was the basis for the later rumors that Goering used makeup. Ready for the new day, Goering would look through all the various newspapers that Kropp brought him as he drank his morning coffee, all the while listening to his favorite phonograph recordings. These included *Fra Diavolo*, *Arabella*, Beethoven's Third Symphony, or the Russian composer Tchaikovsky's Fourth Symphony.

He had to be bullied into letting Kropp cut his hair; indeed, when he surrendered to the Americans in May 1945 he was badly in need of a haircut. Goering was also lazy in dressing himself, with Kropp taking over that duty for the better part of his twelve-year employment with Goering. Tight clothes bothered him, and thus he favoured voluminous, flowing robes and gowns at home, loose-fitting shirts and ample leather jerkin jackets while hunting or touring Carinhall, and uniforms that were taken in and let out day-by-day to keep pace with his ever-fluctuating weight. He wore nightgowns to sleep, but suffered pajamas in captivity at Nuremberg Prison from 1945–46. As he sweated profusely, he changed shirts several times a day, and often all uniform kits as well—just like his first master and hero, Kaiser Wilhem II.

During the first years of Nazi Germany, these uniforms were custom-made for him by the tailor Cap at Stechbarth's, Berlin. He designed many of them himself, with one for each of the offices he held. He never wore any medals that he had not actually been awarded, and he took immense pride in the ones he had; Berliners joked that he had rubber medals for his bathtub and donned an admiral's kit for the opera, but both of these allegations are untrue. He maintained a wardrobe of twenty non-military suits, and delighted in wearing overlong, fur-collared overcoats and capes.

Finances, 1932–34

After his election as Reichstag President on 30 August 1932, Goering's financial status finally got onto a stable footing—remaining thus for the rest of his life. His Presidential salary was 7,200 RM per year, plus an adequate expenses account and rent-free living space in the Reichstag Palace (he never used the latter). His salary as a Reich cabinet minister was another 12,000 RM, and added to that was the 2,000 RM he received as Reich Air Commissioner. His founding of the Prussian State Council in mid-1933 provided another expense account of 12,000 RM.

He also owned *The Essen National News* in the Ruhr, a venture that returned profits, and received royalties for his books, in addition to owning stock gift shares in BMW and Daimler-Benz. He also owned stocks in the Junkers aircraft company, to whom Milch regularly offered government contracts—a definite conflict of interest.

At Goering's forty-first birthday on 12 January 1934, a military band plays in the park as a caped Goering receives birthday wishers at the top of the staircase at the far right, in left profile. Regarding Goering's former fellow cadets at the Lichterfelde Academy, before the First World War and afterwards, Kurt Ludecke recalled: 'From the very beginning, he showed an insatiable hunger for power and applause, and brutality in demanding them ... a braggart and a bully ... Flamboyant the captain certainly is, but to learn what he is like at heart, one has to watch him feeding, a matchless spectacle of gluttony personified.' (*HGA*)

Goering (center) passes in review before the men of his police bodyguard unit, *Landespolizei General Goering*, in what became an annual event. On the left, with a drawn saber, is the unit's commander, Maj. Walter Wecke. In the center is Goering's aide Paul Conrad, wearing a peaked cap. Goering is giving a backhanded Nazi salute. (*HGA*)

From left to right: Kurt Daluge, Paul Conrad, unknown SS man, Goering (wearing an Air Force regulation cape), Paul Korner (in SS black), and others, saluting during Goering's review of the *Landespolizei General Goering*. When he was told, 'But Hitler is an anti-Semite!' Goering countered with, 'I will get him to stop that, you may depend on it!' This phrase became one of his oft-repeated mantras. (*HGA*)

The park of the Berlin Palace during an event for Goering's birthday on 12 January 1939; Goering uses a microphone during his speech. On the right are the top members of his immediate staff. Left to right are: Fritz Gornnert, Peter Menthe, Karl Bodenschatz, Paul Korner, and Dr Erich Gritzbach. All of these men stayed on as Goering's staff from 1933–45, with the exception of Bodenschatz—who was forced to retire after being badly burned and wounded in the 20 July 1944 Army bomb plot against Hitler. (*HGA*)

Left: The very first Nazi Heroes' Memorial Day on 25 February 1934 is commemorated at the Berlin Guard House *Ehrenmal* (Hall of Honor). From left to right: Hitler, von Papen, unknown, Dr Goebbels, von Hindenburg (with his son, Oskar, behind), Dr Hans Heinrich Lammers, unknown, unknown, Goering (in Army overcoat, holding steel pot helmet), unknown, and Defense Minister Gen. Werner von Blomberg. This was the last Memorial Day for the elder von Hindenburg. Goering placed the memorial wreath and later took part in saluting the parade. (*HGA*)

Right: Goering's alleged ancient namesake Arminius in statue form at the *Hermannsdenkmal* (Hermann Memorial) in 1929, built in the Teutoburger Forest by Johann Nacke. This photograph is from the personal albums of Wilhelm II. (*Doorn House Collections, Holland*)

Left: Goering's reported family crest and coat of arms. *Time-Life Books* commented: 'Appropriately, the central motif of his family crest was a mailed fist clutching a silver ring.' (*HGA*)

Right: The mailed fist-and-ring motif of Goering's family crest, in this case used for the 'Hermann Goering Master's School'. One coat of arms resource asserts: 'The surname of Goering is an Ashkenazic Jewish altered form of the name Horn, under Russian influence … The name was adopted by Ashkenazic Jews, referring to the ram's horn, the Hebrew Shofar, that is blown in the synagogue during various ceremonies.' (*HGA*)

Right: A view of the driveway at an entrance to Goering's posh Berlin Palace, with two men of the *Landespolizei Gen. Goering Regiment* on the left, directing traffic, on 8 June 1938. Note the round tower at the far left of the frame, complete with a depiction of the main part of the Goering crest (level with the balcony on the right). The Berlin Palace was the former seat of the Prussian Merchant Marine Ministry; from 1933–34 it was rebuilt (twice) for Goering by Hitler's own architect, Albert Speer. Goering told him, 'Whatever you do, make it look like the Führer's place!' It was here that Goering received the Lindberghs and the Olympians in August 1936. (*HGA*)

Above: A detailed view of the same round tower at the Berlin Palace, showing the crest, in photographs shot on the birthday of Goering's daughter, Edda, on 8 June 1938. (*HGA*)

Right: Goering on the day of his daughter's birth, 8 June 1938, with his full family crest on the wall tapestry behind him, speaking at the consecration of the Hermann Goering Master's School at Kroneburg in the Eifel. In 1937, Dr Gritzbach stated, 'Each evening— and often late into the night—Field Marshal Goering decides upon the people he will receive the following day. When there are no particulars on the list but the name of the visitor and the time limit for the interview, that means that his valet, Robert, must be on the alert.' (*HGA*). *Inset:* Goering's personal bookplate, with his crest and an inscription that reads 'From the library of Minister President General Hermann Goering', also including his signature. Goering firmly believed that 'the white people are chosen for the leadership of this world'. (*LC*)

Left: A rather menacing view of a seated Goering (wearing DNVL uniform), his likeness also above and to the right in the form of a metal plaque. This was taken in the park of his Berlin Palace in 1935. Note also the large ring on his left hand; Goering was to become notoriously fond of jewelry. (*HGA*)

Right: On 13 February 1935 Goering speaks to the workers of Bremen's Wener-Warft, its corporate logo emblazoned on the speaker's dais, where an SS and an SA man also stand. 'Three cheers for our own Führer, Adolf Hitler, Chancellor of the German Reich!' Goering bellowed. (*HGA*)

A party for construction workers celebrating the completion of the framework for Goering's rebuilt Berlin Palace on 8 October 1934, hosted by Goering (fifth from right) and his architect, Dr Albert Speer (second from right). Seen between them, smiling, is the bespectacled Dr Erich Gritzbach. Also smiling, just to the left of Goering, is Fritz Gornnert, another of the Prussian Prime Minister's aides. (*HGA*)

Right: Goering, hands on hips, addresses the construction workers on 8 October 1934, an enlarged mockup of his family crest behind him. (*HGA*)

Below left: Throne-like, high-backed chairs were a regular feature at all of Goering's many palatial residences. One is seen here in 1934 at the ornate Berlin Palace, with a large swastika wall frieze on the wall above and behind the proud owner. Goering took great delight in personally designing his many homes across Germany. (*HGA*)

Below right: Plush stuffed armchairs such as this were also a regular furniture adornment at all Goering homes; this one at the Berlin Palace had a bust of the proprietor above and behind it. (*HGA*)

Left: Religious-themed stained-glass windows were yet another Lutheran Goering home feature, as seen here. Part of it reads 'What is past will not return', according to Mrs Erika Burke of Pearland, Texas, USA. Goering proclaimed, 'I am a hunter by nature.' (*HGA*)

Below: The Berlin Palace's music room, complete with piano and two framed portraits of the late Carin Goering. Note also the furled swastika banner in the corner on the right. In 1937, Dr Gritzbach asserted: 'There must be music! The queen of the arts is not to be overlooked in the artistically arranged house of the Prime Minister. Nor does music disturb him in his work. Robert knows the tastes of his master exactly. With justifiable pride … he knows the right moment to put on a record of *Fra Davolo*, or a scene from *Arabella* or Tchaikovski's Sixth Symphony, or when Beethoven's Third Symphony is most suitable.' (*HGA*)

Top: A cozy fireplace nook in Goering's Berlin Palace that also features a portrait of Carin, this time in an oval frame. Did Goering have an FA file on Hitler? Most likely; the SS certainly did. (*HGA*)

Middle: From 1933–34 construction was underway on Carinhall's initial manifestation. Contrary to one rumor, there was not a previous Imperial hunting lodge structure that was either demolished at or included in the site—although it was alleged that Wilhelm II's *Hubertusstock* was there. Note the logs and thatched-roof architectural motif; it was just a short distance from the structure to the felled forest trees. In *After the Battle*, C. S. West wrote: 'Work on the small hunting lodge began in July 1933 and the two-story, split-log building with its thatched roof was completed in ten months ... The design of the building was inspired by a similar hunting lodge that Goering had seen in the grounds of Rockelstad Castle in Sweden.' (*HGA*)

Right: One of the original 1933 Carinhall entrances, complete with dated stone on the left and deer on the right. The architect was the famous Werner March. He would be replaced by Prussian State architects Tuch and Hetzelt for the 1937 expansion, 'building his own Sweden' in the 1933—34 first version. (*HGA*)

Left: Typical A-frame balcony construction at the 1933 structure—as seen on 7 July 1934—featuring Goering's beloved open-air balcony office above the seating area. Note the ultramodern outdoor lamp as well. German authors assert that this structure was modeled on a Swedish blockhouse-motif architectural design. (*HGA*)

Right: The balcony's frontage festooned with flowers. The proud owner stands with his aides at the center, enjoying the rustic view. From his tribune in the Reichstag, President Goering asserted triumphantly, 'Weimar is overcome! We have gone back to Potsdam, that stands for duty, work, discipline, and cleanliness.' (*HGA*)

A wide-angle view of one side of the original 1933–34 Carinhall, a far cry from what it evolved into later. The driveway is on the right and the chimney on the left. The name '*Schorfheide*' ('Scrape Heath') derived from the 'scraping' of acorns from its forests of oak trees, which were then used to feed pigs before potatoes replaced them as fodder. (*HGA*)

Below and in front of the structure were boathouses such as this one, near the 'Waldhof' ('Forest Court'). (HGA)

Ornate statues in the grounds of Carinhall. With the advance of the Red Army in 1945, several of these statues were simply dumped in the lakes nearby so they could be retrieved later; some were still being found in the late 1990s. (HGA)

Left: A view through a picture window from inside the house, out onto Dollnsee, its shoreline ringed with forestry. Note also the flagstone patio. (*Helmuth Kurth, HGA*)

Below: An interior view of the original Great Hall or Reception Room of the 1933–34 Carinhall. Note the inset swastika above the stone fireplace, and the antlers festooning the walls. C. S. West described it as 'the main hall of the first building where the heavy Gothic furniture and hunting trophies reflected the personality of its owner'. (*HGA*)

Two views of a grouping of chairs next to the fireplace at Goering's *Rominter* hunting lodge, a building formerly owned by the Hohenzollern dynasty of Kaiser Wilhelm II. (*HGA*)

Another fireside alcove—note the heavy wooden overhead rafter beams. (*HGA*)

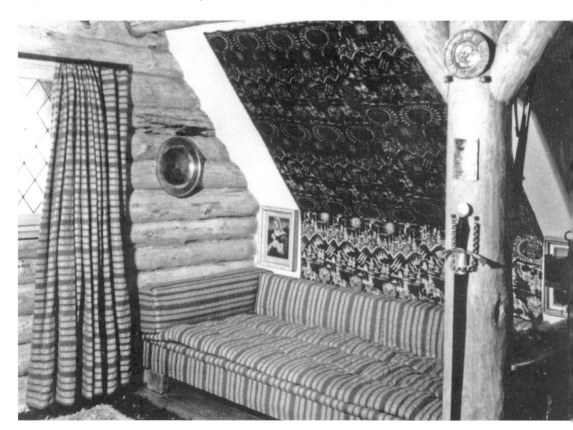

A rustic sofa-bed alcove complete with an iconic portrait of the Virgin Mary and Child (on the left). There is a Viking-like hunting sword adornment on the right. Goering was a religious man, and he enjoyed singing hymns and carols with Carin and her family in Sweden in 1920. (*HGA*)

A traditional Germanic kiln heating stove (left) and pewter dishware adorn this sideboard. (*Binder, HGA*)

Rustic dining area. (*HGA*)

Log staircase. (*HGA*)

A closer, more detailed view of the same stairway. Note the carvings. (*HGA*)

A stained-glass window showing Adam, Eve, and the apple from the serpent. (*HGA*)

A stained-glass window showing a lover (left) making a sexual advance. (*HGA*)

According to Signora Cerruti, Goering arrived for the dedication of Carinhall on 10 June 1934 at the wheel of a sports car, as seen here. The identity of the passenger is unknown, but we can tell it is raining by the raindrops on the windscreen and on Goering's jaunty forestry cap. He is smoking one of his favorite slim cigars. (*Helmuth Kurth, HGA*)

Goering leading his guests at Carinhall on 10 June 1934. As 'Lord of the Schorfheide', he renders a casual, backhanded Nazi salute to his forest rangers, who respond with the more formal, stiff, outstretched version. Note the 'India rubber aviator suit' jerkin and boots he wears; in his left hand he carries the 'harpoon-like instrument' mentioned by American Ambassador William E. Dodd Jr. This instrument was a Scandinavian hunting spear given to him as a present by his Swedish brother-in-law, Count Eric von Rosen—formerly an explorer in the Far North and Africa. The two men on the right are Reich Forestry Service officers. (*Helmuth Kurth, HGA*)

Above and overleaf: At the start of the 10 June 1934 Carinhall dedication, Goering delivered a short speech to his minions. (*HGA*)

Two prominent foreign diplomats who attended the Carinhall dedication were American Ambassador William E. Dodd Jnr (left) and British Ambassador Sir Eric Phipps (right, 1875–1945). The latter is wearing a traditional gold-brocaded diplomatic jacket. After the Blood Purge, Dodd never again received Goering the American Embassy—he considered him to be a murderer. Phipps became the British Ambassador to France from 1937 to 1939, while Dodd retired after he left Berlin. (*Helmuth Kurth, HGA*)

The dedication was followed by a tour, via horse-drawn cart, of much of the Schorfheide area on which Carinhall was located. Goering led the way, with his requested passenger of honor, the Hungarian Jewess and former opera singer Elisabetta Cerruti, sitting next to him. She was the wife of the Hungarian Ambassador. (*HGA*)

Above: Wearing a traditional Bavarian *lederhosen* outfit, Goering salutes drawn-up Hungarian Levante Youth at Carinhall on 16 July 1934. He gives his usual Nazi salute while they stand at attention to receive it. (*HGA*)

Right: Two color guards side by side—on the left is a Hungarian Levante Youth with a flag and commander, and on the right is a Hitler Youth standard bearer and officer. This photograph was taken on 16 July 1934 at Carinhall. Goering asserted, 'Youth came to us because the future is with us!' (*HGA*)

Below left: Carin Goering died of tuberculosis on 17 October 1931, aged forty-two; she was buried on Drottingholm Island, outside Stockholm, in Sweden. Here, members of her family assemble at her original gravesite in the Lovo Churchyard Cemetery, where she had been buried on what would have been her forty-third birthday, 21 October 1931. Note the traditional wooden cross on the right; this photograph dates from 19 June 1934. (*HGA*)

Below right: A close-up of the same site, with the cross on the left and the flat tombstone on the lower right of the frame. Carin's return to Germany was modeled after that of the famous Prussian Queen Louise in 1810; as one source boasted, it was 'the way queens used to be buried!' Carin's crypt was nestled on Rarangsee Island. (*HGA*)

Above: Carin's 1931 coffin is disinterred for the first time by Swedish graveyard workers on 19 June 1934; it is being transported to Nazi Germany. (*HGA*)

Previous page, below: A view of the giant pewter casket in which Carin's coffin was placed before transit to the Third Reich, complete with floral Christian cross (right) and several wreaths (lower left). (*HGA*)

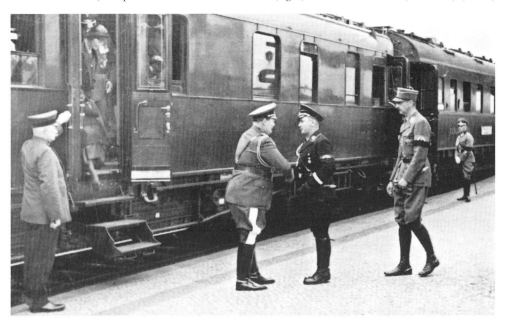

Goering (center left, shaking hands with welcoming SS man) arrives by train for the ceremonial transit of Carin's remains to Germany, 19 June 1934. The tall man on the right, wearing a black mourning band over his swastika armband, is Prince August 'Auwi' Wilhelm of Prussia, and to the far right is Paul Conrad, a top Goering aide. One of Carin's sisters is on the left, disembarking from the train. Oddly, the train conductor at the far left is giving a Nazi salute with his left arm. (*HGA*)

The various mourners gather at the side of the train on 19 June 1934. From left to right: Paul Korner (in SS black), unidentified group, one of Carin's nieces (facing the camera), two of Carin's other female relatives with Goering between them, Countess Fanny, and Goering's brother-in-law, Swedish Count Eric von Rosen (with cane). (*HGA*)

Left: On 20 June 1934, in front of the Eberswalde railway station, a somber party awaits the arrival of Carin's body. It was travelling there by train from the port of Sassnitz, having arrived there from Sweden on the 19th. From left to right are: Karl Bodenschatz, Prince 'Auwi', Carin's sisters, and Goering. At Sassnitz it was received by Carin's son (Thomas von Kantzow) and Goering. (*HGA*)

Above: Goering (left center) clasps his hands together, biting his lip, waiting for Carin's body to return from Sweden to Germany on 19 June 1934. Second-right is Count von Rosen, while the man in the dark overcoat, to the left of Goering, is probably Count Richard von Wilamowitz-Mollendorff. The taller, dark-haired, younger man in the center is Carin's grown son, Count Thomas von Kantzow. The women on the right are three of Carin's four sisters. Carin and Hermann never had any children together. (*HGA*)

Left: One of Carin's sisters, deep in thought, in transit to the reburial—she is Mary, Countess von Rosen. (*HGA*)

Paul Conrad (left) welcomes Countess and Count Rosen by the side of the train, 19 June 1934. (*HGA*)

The casket arrives in Germany by sea, 19 June 1934, amid German and Swedish bunting and flags. (*HGA*)

A steel-helmeted band and Honor Guard of the *Landespolizei Gen. Goering* is drawn up to welcome Carin's casket to the Third Reich, complete with a Jingling Johnny Bell Tree musical instrument at the front. Note the small white swastikas affixed on the helmet sides. (*HGA*)

The black-shrouded sarcophagus containing Carin's remains is brought forth from the Eberswalde Station by a steel-helmeted State Police Honor Guard of pallbearers, as the mourners give a Nazi salute on the left. (*HGA*)

A panoramic scene sweeping the town square at Eberswalde on 20 June 1934. On the left are the Honor Guard and the band, and on the right are mourners and the coffin. The cars of the official motorcade are at top center. (*HGA*)

The casket mounted atop a truck is now draped with a swastika banner, the pall bearers standing to attention at its left. The motorcade's motorcycle-escort outriders stand to attention at the far right, with the mourners at center left. The cars are ready for the motorcade to depart from Eberswalde (top left). (*HGA*)

Left: The truck bearing Carin Goering's swastika-covered casket is about to leave the German railway town of Eberswalde on 20 June 1934, with an escort of NSKK/Nazi Motor Corps motorcyclists seen below right. (*HGA*)

Above: The motorcade is now en route from Eberswalde to Carinhall, on the Schorfheide, on 20 June 1934. The casket vehicle is fourth from the rear, going forward. (*HGA*)

The casket is taken to its destination at Carinhall, named after Carin nearly three years after her demise. Her sister Fanny recalled: 'School children were gazing with astonished eyes at Hermann Goering, at last able to bring his dead wife home. The vehicles slowly made their way through long lines of people to get to the Schorfheide. In all the villages, the church bells were ringing, with such a strong current of warmth pouring out to meet the participants that this journey would never be forgotten.' Here, Nazi BDM (League of German Maidens) give the Hitler salute on both sides of the bridge being crossed. (*HGA*)

Right: Awaiting the hearse at Carinhall, Chief Mourner Goering (right) greets the arriving Dr Josef Goebbels and his wife, Magda (left). The other two men are unidentified. (*HGA*)

Middle: Goering (right) greets the arriving Deputy Führer Rudolf Hess (wearing SS black). On the left (also in SS black) stands a bespectacled man who may be Party Treasurer Franz Xaver Schwarz. The tall man with gray hair, second from left, is Reichsbank President and Reich Economics Minister Dr Hjalmar Schacht. (*HGA*)

Below: German Reich Interior Minister Dr Wilhelm Frick (1877–1946), second from right, arrives. It is just ten days before the Nazi Blood Purge, which he objected to on legal grounds but nonetheless acquiesced to. At far right is Luftwaffe Col. Karl Bodenschatz. (*HGA*)

Hitler arrives. From left to right are: SS Gen. Josef 'Sepp' Dietrich, commander of the Führer's escort-guard detachment; Führer chief adjutant SA Gen. Wilhelm Bruckner; Hitler (saluting); SS Führer ADC Julius Schaub; Reich Governor of Bavaria Franz Ritter von Epp (1869–1947); an unknown SA man, saluting; and Goering. (*HGA*)

Left to right: unknown young woman, one of Carin's sisters (most likely her younger sister, Lily); Hitler, shaking hands with Goebbels, with an unknown man between them; and possibly Baron Wichert or Richard von Wilamowitz-Mollendorff. (*HGA*)

Following page, above: Hitler shakes hands with his Reich Interior Minister, Dr Wilhelm Frick. One of Carin's sisters stands between them—most likely Fanny, Baroness von Wilamowitz-Mollendorff, who would later become her sister's biographer. (*HGA*)

German Foreign Minister Baron Konstantin von Neurath stands at the far right, holding a silk top hat. From right to left, the others are: Hitler; Goering; unknown woman; Count von Rosen, in uniform with epaulettes; two of Carin's sisters, with Count Thomas von Kantzow standing behind; and Paul Korner and Dr Erich Gritzbach, both in SS black. At the far left is a Jingling Johnny Bell Tree with a swastika. (*HGA*)

The stone face marking the steps leading down into Carin's new crypt at Carinhall. The raised inscription underneath the edelweiss flower at the center and the pair of swastikas reads: 'Carin Göring (Fock) 1888–1931'. Note that her first name is spelled with a 'C' rather than the 'K' used by many of Goering's past biographers. C. S. West wrote: 'An underground tomb was excavated on the high ground overlooking the smaller of the two lakes, the Wuckersee.' (*HGA*)

The Führer and his paladin stride forth to the stone steps leading down into the underground crypt, with Hitler's wreath being carried behind them by members of Goering's Reich Forestry Service. Flanking the pathway are men of the Reich Labor Service (RAD), wearing black mourning bands over their swastikas. Carin's sister, Fanny, noted, 'On all sides were black obelisks with sacrificial flames burning with a group of musicians playing.' (*HGA*)

An overall view of the pastoral scene at the new gravesite with Hitler and Goering at the center, backed by a steel-helmeted formation of Goering's Green State Policemen on the banks of the Wuckersee Lake. According to C. S. West, there were 'eight red boulders like prehistoric menhirs, some individually inscribed … set up surrounding the clearing'. At least one was emblazoned with Carin's own ancestral coat of arms—a crest of shields. (*HGA*)

Above left: A floral wreath tribute from her grieving father: 'To Carin from Pappa'. Carin's sister Fanny recalled: 'Lovely as in a fairy story is this peaceful spot in the German forest, and one felt that spirits from ancient times were watching from above.' (*HGA*)

Above right: From Adolf Hitler. Fanny noted: 'Through the window there was a glimpse of edelweiss growing by the lake. (*HGA*)

Left: From Carin's widowed husband: 'In constant love and loyalty and sincerest gratitude. Hermann.' (*HGA*)

Left: From the Swedish colony in Berlin. Fanny concluded: 'Above the earth lay the same gravestone that had once been at Lovo, and Swedish soil surrounded it. Beyond were the loveliest flowers. When Carin's sarcophagus was brought into the open place, muffled drums sounded a tattoo.' (*HGA*)

Middle: Members of Carin's extended families take a break from the solemnity. From left to right: Carin's sisters, Count von Wilamowitz-Mollendorff, Count Thomas von Kantzow, a niece, and Countess Mary von Rosen (in a hat). (*HGA*)

Below: Having arrived at the Schorfheide, the pewter coffin was transferred from the flatbed truck to a horse-drawn carriage led by steel-helmeted State Policemen. It was taken to the underground crypt for placement, remaining there for the next sixteen years. (*HGA*)

Removed from the carriage, the heavy pewter coffin—welded together by artisans from the firm of Svensk and Tenn—is borne by both State Policemen (front) and airmen (rear) past the saluting (right to left) Hitler, Goering, Dr Goebbels, one of Carin's sisters, and Count von Rosen (in uniform). Wagnerian funeral music was played. (*HGA*)

The view shared by Hitler (left) and Goering (right) of the scene overlooking Lake Wuckersee. The pewter sarcophagus is about to be taken down into the underground stone crypt, flanked by four red stone menhir columns to the left and right. The columns stood in silent sentry duty for the next eleven years, before the arrival of the Soviets in April 1945. (*HGA*)

Above: The same scene, minus all the trappings (save the menhir monuments). From across the lake, Goering could see this idyllic spot from his windows. 'To my own Carin', Hermann wrote. (*HGA*)

Left: Below ground, from outside the memorial crypt, looking inward. Flowers are at the foot of the pewter coffin. In 1990, the two heavy, bronze doors to the crypt—one partially seen on the left—were sold to collectors by the Hermann Historica House of Munich for 25,000 DM. The small blue window at the rear could be tilted open to let in light, and also to provide a view of the beautiful lake. (*HGA*)

Right: The wide pewter coffin was built big enough for Hermann's own remains to join Carin's one day— Emmy was apparently to be buried elsewhere. Here, the name Carin Goring appears below the ancestral crest of Hermann (left) and Carin herself (right). One eyewitness noted, 'To the sound of hunting horns and trumpets, the coffin was deposited in the vault.' (*HGA*)

Below: Having descended together down into the sacred crypt alone, Hitler and Goering are seen here emerging, with the Nazi Führer brushing away a tear. This was ten days before the two men murdered many of their domestic political foes. (*HGA*)

Left: On a later (and less solemn) visit, Hitler uses one of the red stone menhirs as a reading platform. On the left is Goering's alleged family crest, with his last name below it in old Germanic script. Goering himself stands at right profile, between his Führer and the stone. (*HGA*)

Below left: Swedish Countess Mary von Fock von Rosen (right) stands at one of the red stone menhirs bearing the von Fock family crest. The girl on the left is most likely her daughter, and thus the late Carin's niece. The Princely zu Wieds attended the first two of Carin's three burials in 1931 and '34. (*HGA*)

Below right: A reverent Hitler makes another descent into Carin's crypt, with two menhirs forming a backdrop. Like Hermann and Emmy, Adolf was also an actor. (*HGA*)

Goering peers pensively at one of the menhirs bearing his family crest. He is wearing his favorite leather jerkin jacket and a sheathed hunting dagger. (*HGA*)

Goering also makes another descent into the crypt, this time bearing flowers. The various wreaths around the shrine suggest that the occasion might be the anniversary of Carin's death. Again, an unknown woman watches from behind, along with an unidentified man. (*HGA*)

Berlin SA leader Karl Ernst (center, 1904–34) taking part in a forced route training march in 1933. A former bellhop at the capital's Eden Hotel, Ernst knew far too much and his ambitions were too great for the comfort of Hermann Goering. Next to Röhm himself, Ernst was top of Goering's list of victims. He was shot on 30 June 1934. (*HHA*)

An uneasy lineup of top Nazis in 1933. From left to right: two unknown men; Karl Ernst, looking downwards; an unidentified SA man; Goering, looking to his right; an unknown SS man; pensive Berlin cop Kurt Daluge (in SS cap and overcoat); unidentified SA man; Prince August Wilhelm von Hohenzollern, reading a paper; and other unknown men. When Hindenburg died, one monarchist plan was to have 'Auwi' named as Reich Regent for the restored Hohenzollerns—but Hitler had other ideas. (*HHA*)

During an outdoor May 1934 speech at Munich, Goering is guarded by an SA man on his left and steel-helmeted SA men down in front. He was convinced that these SA 'guards' were present, in fact, to arrest him at Röhm's whim—but he and Hitler struck first. Indeed, on one recorded FA transcript, Goering read about himself: 'The fat pig has to be done away with!' Reportedly, Hitler himself presided over the swearing in of the Staff Guards units of both Goering and Röhm—indicating that he, too, might have played a political game until the moment of the final decision to murder the SA leadership. (*HGA*)

The man who ratted out Röhm's treasonous intentions to Hitler was reportedly Röhm's subordinate SA leader (and later successor as SA Staff Chief) Viktor Lutze (1890–1943). He is seen here with Goering in 1934. At the far left are NSKK Korpsführer Adolf Huhnlein (1881–1942) and German Defense Minister Col. General Werner von Blomberg (just behind Goering, who is wearing his Luftwaffe uniform). (*HHA*)

Left: The famous photo of Goering (right) 'handing over' his Gestapo Secret State Police to its new chief—SS Reichsführer Heinrich Himmler (1900–45)—on Hitler's birthday, 20 April 1934. The unit was actually run by Himmler's deputy, Reinhard Heydrich, 'under' Goering. This lasted until the unification of all German police by the SS Duo in June 1936, when Goering lost all control over his former creation. Note the leather riding crop that Goering is using as a prop in his left hand, overlapping his ornate Air Force sword pommel. (*HGA*)

Right: The other big loser on that day was prior Gestapo administrator Rudolf Diels (1900–57), seen here on the left shaking hands with Goering, his former chief. Himmler stands between them. As the head of the former State Political Police (prior to Goering's appointment as Prussia's top cop), Diels was actually in charge of his new boss's police file—something that Goering never forgot and always feared. Indeed, for two weeks in September 1933 Goering replaced Diels with Altona Police President Paul Hinker; however, for some reason he was forced to recall Diels from Czechoslovakia, representing a humiliating back-off for Hermann. Prior to the Blood Purge, Diels was described as 'a frightened rabbit', fearing that he too would be murdered. Goering ended up protecting his former protégé until the end of the Second World War, sending him off to become a provincial police president in Cologne. (*HGA*)

Another of Goering's protégés from 1933–34 was German Orpo (Regular Police) chief Gen. Kurt Daluge (1897–1947), seen here exiting a swanky Mercedes-Benz Type 320 Cabriolet sports car. Daluge was a university student at Berlin in the summer of 1921, thus preceding both Dr Goebbels (1926) and Goering ('28) in the Reich capital. Goering promoted Daluge to Ministerial Director in the Prussian Interior Ministry on 11 May 1933, and later to Police Commander. At the age of thirty-six, Daluge thus became Europe's youngest general officer since Napoleon Bonaparte. He was named as commanding officer of the Orpo by Goering on 9 May 1934. The Orpo was not used for the purge on 30 June 1934. Although Daluge was initially opposed to the SS Duo of Himmler and Heydrich coming to Berlin, he wisely accepted their leadership after 20 April 1934. He even succeeded the murdered Heydrich as Reich Protector in Prague in 1942. (*HHA*)

German Defense Minister Col. Gen. Werner von Blomberg (1878–1946) was pressing Hitler for the suppression of the unruly SA in 1934. He is seen here (second from left) on a ship, with a leather-capped Hitler (at the center) and Goering (on the right) looking through binoculars. The Army saw Goering as its man, but politically it is not unlikely that Goering gave thought to what might happen to him if Röhm's SA prevailed over the Army and Hitler. Might Goering have made peace with his former SA men? In politics, anything is always possible. (*HGA*)

Another photo of a waterborne outing. From left to right are: Goering, Hitler, Adm. Dr Erich Raeder (the Navy C-in-C), and the Army's Col. Gen. von Blomberg (this time wearing glasses). Hitler later opined, 'I have a reactionary Army, a Christian Navy, and a Nazi Air Force!' Goering reportedly got seasick on the naval vessel *Deutschland*, leading a naval cadet to joke that he was 'The Reich fish feeder'. Goering was not amused. (*HGA*)

Hermann Goering in summer Air Force dress—a white cap and uniform, with saber—during his visit to Emmerich on 3 June 1934. All the NSDAP men behind him are unidentified. (*HGA*)

Left: Goering renders an informal, casual, backhanded Nazi salute in Cologne during his trip on 27–28 June 1934. At the center, in SS black, stands his trusty aide Dr Erich Gritzbach, wearing glasses. A reported one million Germans heard Goering speak both in and outside of the Köln Exposition Hall on the 27th. (*HGA*)

Previous page, below right: Nazi Gauleiter of Nuremberg and Franconia Julius Streicher (center), suppressing a laugh at something humorous that Goering is saying, left, while Dr Gritzbach stares into the camera lens. This photograph was taken in Dinkelsbuhl on 24 June 1934. Note the woman in the open window at the upper right. Goering attended a children's party there, and on the 26th he visited Emmy's beach house on the Isle of Sylt, on the Baltic Sea. (*HGA*)

A tense-looking Goering atop a reviewing stand emblazoned with a puny-looking Nazi eagle! On the left may be State Policeman Walther Weche. The photograph was taken on the trip to Cologne on 27–28 June 1934. Had the SA duly risen and won against Hitler, the alleged plan was for the Fourth Reich Nazi government to look like this: 'Auwi' as Reich President; von Schleicher as Reich Chancellor; Gregor Strasser as Vice Chancellor; and Röhm as Defense Minister, with the SA replacing the 100,000-man regular German Army. (*HGA*)

Host Goering (fifth from left) welcomes his guests, the King and Queen of Siam (center right), at Carinhall on 7 July 1934, as Dr Erich Gritzbach (in SS black) looks on at the right. Goering wears his favorite leather hunting kit and holds one of his treasured long, slim Austrian cigars in his right hand. (*HGA*)

Left: On 1 July 1934, Goering persuaded Hitler to halt the killings; in March 1946, he asserted that they had gotten out of hand. Here he is on 3 July 1934, behind the wheel of one of his many cars, biting his lip, his hair askew under his cap. At that day's Reich cabinet meeting, it was officially noted that forty-three people had been shot, and Goering's Reich Game Law was also passed. (*HGA*)

Below left: Hunter Hermann with his latest severed bull elk's head trophy with antlers—the photograph was taken in Jasnitz, Germany, 2 October 1934. In 1937, Dr Gritzbach noted: 'The roar of the red deer in the rutting season gives him an extraordinary thrill … He does not hesitate to go deer hunting at 4 a.m., were it only for the pleasure of the stag's roar, and when he hears it, Hermann Goering's heart beats more quickly, as does that of every true German hunter.' (*HGA*)

Below right: A smiling Goering (left) beams happily, with a dead elk at his feet and a brace of Reich Forestry servicemen to his right, at Nemenien on 11 September 1934. At Stockholm's Oskar Theater in 1933, Goering had been accosted by Swedish theology student Dahlberg, who shouted, 'Worker's murderer!' at him. On the other hand, on the same trip Goering was also officially received by the King of Sweden. (*HGA*)

Expert bowman Goering prepares to loose his arrow. The man on the left is unidentified. There does not appear to be any evidence that Goering ever hunted with this weapon, however. In his postwar memoirs *Stuka Pilot*, Hans Ulrich Rudel recalled visiting Goering's Castle Veldenstein, near Nuremberg, in 1944, observing his chief's target shooting: 'He pays no attention to me until he has shot off all his arrows. I am amazed that not one of them misses its mark!' (*HGA*)

Left: Falconer Hermann surveys a hooded hawk on his leather glove on 4 November 1935 at Reich Hunting Box Braunschweig. This was for the first State Hunt of the Hermann Goering Foundation. Note Goering's jaunty hunter's cap with feather. (*HGA*)

Right: The sign reads 'Reich Hunt Master Hermann Goering we have to thank for the new Hunting Law of the German Wild, 1934'. (*Helmuth Kurth, HGA*)

Above: Reich Forestry Service Falconry Order bandsmen such as these played at the dedication of Carinhall on 10 June 1934, according to several eyewitness accounts. Note their jaunty caps and hunting daggers. These bandsmen are seen in September 1937, during Mussolini's visit to Goering. The uniforms were green, with darker forest-green lapels and cap bands. (*HGA*)

Left: A contemporary German political cartoon asserts 'Vivisection forbidden', depicting Goering returning the Nazi salute of various forest and other animals that he is helping to save via his humane new Reich Game Law. The cartoon appeared in the satirical German journal *Simplissimus* in 1934. (*LC*)

Conservationist Goering (center) feeding a tame deer. The woman on the left may be one of his two sisters. (*Helmuth Kurth, HGA*)

Left: A wooden buffalo sign at the entrance to Goering's famed bison preserve at Carinhall. (*HGA*)

Right: One of Goering's many famous hunting guests was fellow Nazi Reichstag Deputy Franz Ritter von Epp, seen here with shotgun and shell bandoleer on 4 November 1935 at Reich Hunt Box Braunschweig. (*HGA*)

Another of Goering's hunting guests was RFSS Himmler (left), also seen here on 4 November 1935 at Reich Hunt Box Braunschweig. In May 1937, visiting Briton Lord Halifax described Hunter Hermann thusly: 'Brown britches and boots all in one, with green leather jerkin ... and red dagger.' (*HGA*)

Left: One of my favorite posed portraits of Hermann Goering, looking somewhat like a cross between a Chicago gangster of the late 1920s and a Wagnerian folk opera star. He is complete with thin cigar dangling from his lips. Note the theatrical hunting spear, knee-high boots, leather jerkin with belt and dagger, jacket, and jaunty cap. This was when Goering was at his most expansive—the flamboyant showman that he always was at heart. The jacket and cap were green, with the jacket lapels and hatband a darker forest-green. The leather jerkin here was brown, and the boots were black. The photo dates from 12 September 1938. (*Helmuth Kurth, HGA*)

Right: Happy Nazis, outdoors on Hitler's Obersalzberg mountain in Bavaria, on 15 January 1935. From left to right: Hitler; Goering; Reich Press Chief Dr Otto Dietrich; Reich Photo Reporter Prof. Heinrich Hoffman; his second wife, Erna Hoffman; and (possibly) Julius Streicher. Goering was the first of the Nazi *bonzen* (bigwigs) to have a summer home on Hitler's restricted Obersalzberg. (*HGA*)

Hermann's own *Haus Goering*—it was located 300 feet higher than Hitler's Berghof, but smaller by far in both size and scale. Delgano was the chosen architect. Here we see the traditional tree placed atop the structure—a wooden-frame, brick building—as in 1933. According to Mrs Erika Burke of Pearland, Texas, 'The construction ridge pole went up when the roof structure was completed, and it used to be a tree—like a Christmas tree—not a pole with a sign on it.' (*HGA*)

The same building is almost complete, with construction still going on at the far left. According to Dr Gritzbach, Goering was almost killed in an avalanche during a pre-First World War climb. (*HGA*)

The same building seen from another angle, and in winter snow. Note the small patio entranceway at the front left. In 1989, Dr Frank stated: 'Bormann's house—as was to be expected—looked down to the Berghof; Göring's house, however, looked up, to the Kehlstein.' It was there that Bormann had built Hitler another eyrie for his fiftieth birthday on 20 April 1939—it was popularly known as The Eagle's Nest. (*HGA*)

Goering plays his accordion; in May 1945, in the custody of the American Army's 36th Infantry Division (Texas), he would play the accordion at their request. His skis, bindings, and poles are stacked along the left-hand wall. (*HGA*)

An interior shot of the office inside *Haus Goering*. His desk and chair are at the right, complete with family portraits of his loved ones. Goering ensured that he did not surpass the grandeur of Hitler's own mountain home, the Berghof. He had owned the original lodge before 1933, and afterwards had it remodeled. (*HGA*)

Another *Haus Goering* interior view, this one of the living room, with the fireplace on the left. Note the carpets, wall tapestries, and ornate door hinges. C. S. West noted: 'Light, tinted, polished ceilings with mosaics inlaid with flowers, leaves, butterflies, and birds were his taste.' (*HGA*)

Left: Haus Goering's owner in silhouette against one of the French windows. The diary entry of his stepson, Thomas von Kantzow, for 23 December 1934 noted Goering's boast that his future Reich Air Ministry Building in Berlin would be a site 'where airplanes can land and take off from the roof!' However, this never happened. (*HGA*)

Right: Goering asserted: 'I know two sorts of men only—those who are with us, and those who are against us!' By 1931, a friend of Goering stated: 'Goering had changed. His voice was louder ... as if to drown out his thoughts, his manners rougher, his movements jerkier. When I discussed him with the men who were closest to him ... perhaps it was true that he had taken refuge again in the syringe.' (*HGA*)

In the girl's shadow is Reich Labor Leader Dr Robert Ley, beaming, and between him and Goering is a smiling Paul Korner (wearing a bow tie), while just over Goerin's left shoulder is Fritz Gornnert. (*HGA*)

Left: Goering, wearing a mourning band for his dead wife, Carin, welcomes two young boys (possibly his nephews) on 20 June 1934 at Carinhall. Goering had planned to donate Carinhall to the German people as a national museum on his 60th birthday in 1953 had he lived. In 1945, however, the Red Army decided otherwise. (*HGA*)

Right: Unser (Our) *Hermann* (right) chats with a young fan at what might be a horse show arena. Note his Air Force dress sword. Even after the Blood Purge, Goebbels was bold enough to decry Goering's mania for medals (though not directly by name) during a speech praising Hitler at a Berlin stadium. (*HHA*)

Goering in a tuxedo (second from left) at one of his annual Opera Balls for the media. Also present is the same unknown young woman (right) we have seen in previous pictures. (*HGA*)

Marksman Goering (left, wearing protective goggles) tries his luck at an outdoor Oktoberfest carnival midway on 18 September 1934. On trial for his life in 1946, Goering asserted of the German people, 'I don't care what they say now! I know what they said before!' After the Purge, von Hindenburg sent Goering a published official telegram of thanks on 2 July 1934. (*HGA*)

Right: On 5 December 1934 Goering (center) visits Germany's famed Ufa movie studio at Neu-Babelsberg, outside Berlin, with Emmy behind him and one of her nieces in tow. *Barcarale und Zigeuneerbaron* was being filmed. (*HGA*)

Below: Hermann (center) squints through one of the Ufa Studio cameras as Emmy smiles behind him, her niece at center right, on 5 December 1934. Goering always loved to have his family members with him. (*HGA*)

Left: A rather well-known shot of one of the annual Winter Help Relief donation events. Left to right are: Col. Bodenschatz; Goering; Himmler (with donation can); and Hitler. In 1998, Richie noted: 'The *Winterhilfe* was called a "voluntary charity", but by the mid-1930s had become a method of social control. The *Winterhilfe* ground into high gear each year with an *Eintopf*, or one pot meal: families were asked to forgo their normal fare once a month and donate money to the cause.' (*HGA*)

Right: Goering himself happily donates some pocket change to Winter Help Relief for the cameras, wearing his brown Party Leadership Corps jacket with swastika armband, on 5 December 1936. In 1998, Richie noted: 'Goering would bring out bulging purses of gems after dinner at Carinhall.' Standing at the corner of the Unter den Linden and the Wilhelmstrasse in Berlin, Goering would call out to passersby, 'A few pennies, please!' He loved it all, as did the Berliners. They called him 'good old Hermann' for the relief of hunger, unemployment, and winter fuel shortages. (*HGA*)

A beaming Goering as annual Christmas party host, 24 December 1934. He is flanked by an excited young girl on the left and the German version of Santa Claus on the right. Soon, Hermann Goering streets sprouted up all over the new Nazi Germany. (*HGA*)

Another favorite annual Goering event was the Christmas party at Clou, which he hosted for 500 needy children. Here, he points out some of the features of a toy airplane to some of the excited children on 24 December 1934. Paul Korner (right center) looks on. (*HGA*)

Goering caught in mid-munch at his breakfast table aboard his motor yacht, *Carin*, in July 1935. His eating habits and gluttony were notorious. Meanwhile, a plaque was placed to honor his birthplace at Rosenheim, Bavaria, in southern Germany. (*HGA*)

Goering's ever-present and wildly fluctuating weight problem as revealed in these two comparative views. In the second photo Hermann looks bloated, and Emmy looks concerned. (*HGA*)

Left: One exercise remedy was sledding, as seen here at *Haus Goering* on the Obersalzberg, in Bavaria, Southern Germany. Goering retained his love for the great outdoors until the very end of his life, enjoying both hiking and rock climbing. At the time of his surrender in May 1945, he weighed 280 pounds. Undressing for an examination, he said, sheepishly, 'I am very fat.' (*HGA*)

Right: Another exercise was his ever-popular mountain climbing; here he is in lederhosen, complete with headband and Count von Rosen's gift harpoon, on the Roth in 1937. (*HGA*)

Left: There was also tennis, as long as his opponent hit the ball to where he was standing so that he would not have to run after it! Here Goering serves, at Berchtesgaden, on 15 July 1936. (*HGA*)

Right: Then there was horseback riding, with Hermann seen here aloft. Prior to his later weight gains, equestrian Goering enjoyed having his mounts jump fences. (*HGA*)

Left: He also enjoyed swimming with a friend in the outdoor pool at Carinhall. (*HGA*)

Right: A bust depicting Goering in aviator's leather cap and wearing his Blue Max medal during the First World War. Goering visited the Rechlin Luftwaffe Test Station for the first time on 29 March 1933. Hans-Jurgen Stumpff recruited 182 German Army officers and forty-two Navy officers to staff the secret Air Force during 1933–34. In December 1934, Goering told Milch that he would become Goering's successor if anything happened to him. (*HHA*)

Goering (center, back to lens) takes in a painting of the late Baron Manfred von Richthofen's famed red Fokker fighter tri-plane in combat, with Robert Kropp holding up the left end. At the far left is Bodenschatz, while third from right is Erhard Milch, smiling. (*HGA*)

Left: Hitler's pilot, Hans Baur, has written about how he helped bring Goering up to speed as a pilot in 1933 after a hiatus away from flying since 1920. One aspect that was entirely new to him was night flying. Here he poses for a publicity photo at the controls of an aircraft, wearing Luftwaffe summer whites. (*HGA*)

Right: A serious Goering poses for another publicity still, wearing an Air Force cap and overcoat. Having it with the rear-collar flap up was against regulations! (*HGA*)

Left: A formal portrait of Goering as Reich Aviation Minister in 1933, wearing his Blue Max with ribbon at the neck, Nazi Airman Wings, 1914 Iron Cross, Imperial German Pilot-Observer Badge (left) and Wound Badge (right) on his left breast pocket. (*HGA*)

Right: A period picture postcard entitled 'Reich Chancellor Adolf Hitler and Minister President Goering'. Note the original tiny Luftwaffe eagle and swastika on Goering's left sleeve, changed and enlarged in 1935. Goering's birthday celebrations of 12 January 1934 marked the first of twelve such events during the history of the NSDAP regime, up to and including 1945. (*Sven Hedin Foundation, National Museum of Ethnography, Stockholm, Sweden*)

Goering as the impassioned Nazi orator in full cry. Indeed, starting in 1928, Goering earned 800 RM per month as an official NSDAP speaker. After Hitler's post-Purge explanatory address before the Reichstag on 13 July 1934, Goering addressed him directly before the deputies, stating, 'You have succeeded!' During the same speech, Hitler asserted that had the Beer Hall Putsch been successful in 1923, he would have appointed an Army officer to head the military, 'and not Capt. Goering, who was then the commander of [his] SA'. (*HGA*)

Reich Air Minister Goering (center) is greeted by a German Army officer (right) at a railway stop, 1934. He saw the Führer's appointment of him as Prussian Prime Minister on 10 April 1933 as a full reconciliation after the botched Beer Hall Revolt a decade before. (*HGA*)

Left: Another Goering arrival (left) with yet another Army officer. Note also that Goering's air wings have been switched from over his left pocket to his right in this view. Reportedly, Goering played no role in the murder of Austrian Chancellor Engelbert Dolfuss nor the attempted Austrian Nazi coup on 25 July 1934; his own part in the Viennese conflict was three-and-a-half years away. (*HHA*)

Right: Prussian Prime Minister Goering (left) is greeted by an unknown SA man, with future Reich Justice Minister Hans Frank (as of 19 December 1934) seen between them, on 1 November 1934. This was during his arrival at a Great Hall to speak before the Academy of German Right. (*HGA*)

Right: Air Minister Goering (right) seems in fine fettle in this 1933 airport snapshot. According to official Reich finance records, his budgeted Luftwaffe annual expenditure during 1933-39 was as follows: 0 RM in 1933–4; 642 million RM for 1934–35; 1,036 million RM for 1935–36; 2,225 million RM for 1936–37; 3,258 million RM for 1937–38; and 6,026 million RM for 1938–39. (*HHA*)

Middle: Reich Air Minister Goering (fifth from right) poses happily with a group of young airmen bearing a trophy, 1934. At his notorious Blood Purge Propaganda Ministry press conference at Berlin on 1 July 1934, Goering was said 'to have arrived in one of his full dress uniforms and strutted up to the platform with slow, mincing steps'. He then denied that he had ordered for von Papen to be arrested. On 30 June, Hitler had fired Röhm as SA Staff Chief and replaced him the same day with Viktor Lutze. (*HHA*)

Below: A smiling Goering (left) salutes a lineup of some of his older airmen, 1934. On 2 December 1934 Goering made his last speech concerning the Blood Purge at the Rheinhausen Steel Works: 'He who dares to interfere with the trust vested in the Führer—he who attempts to undermine that which is faithful in the people—is a traitor! He who agitates against the Führer is agitating against the people!' (*HGA*)

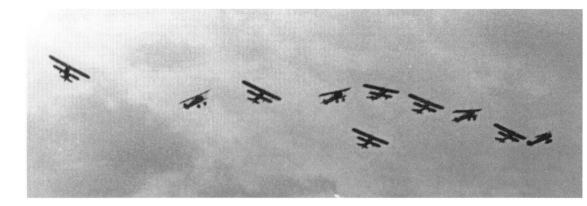

Above: Either consciously or unconsciously, Goering's first new planes aped those of Fascist Italy in that both were already obsolete, First World War-style biplanes, as seen here in 1935. The Luftwaffe soon switched to monoplane fighters, while the still-outmoded *Regia Aeronautica* was deploying biplanes even during the 1940 Battle of Britain! Hitler sent Goering to see Mussolini yet again on 7 November 1933, whom he called 'a gifted statesman'. (*HGA*)

Left: Some observers felt that the early, formative years of the Luftwaffe—1933–35—were the happiest of Goering's life, as evidenced by this 1934 scene of him saluting with a broad smile. When Hitler returned to Berlin at 10 p.m. on 30 June 1934, he noticed an unknown honor guard awaiting him at Tempelhof Airdrome—two companies of black Luftwaffe troops posted by Milch. Goering and Himmler showed their Führer a death list of eighty-three murders they allegedly committed in the capital alone. (*HGA*)

Below: The commander-in-chief of the secret 'black' Luftwaffe—Hermann Goering (fourth from left) is seen here at the annual fall military maneuvers at Mecklenburg, Germany, in September 1935. (*HGA*)

Goering (center, wearing Luftwaffe dress sword and overcoat) pauses to chat with young Hitler Youth trumpeters, swastika flags adorning their instruments, at Neuwied on 3 November 1935. (*HGA*)

As Hitler's roving goodwill ambassador, Goering (center, in white cap and overcoat) embarks on yet another aspect of his many-faceted career, this time as a Nazi diplomat landing at Bulgaria's capital, Sofia, in the spring of 1933. In 1937, Dr Gritzbach recalled that sixty men stood to attention at Athens as Goering arrived at the Olympic Festival, preparing for the 1936 Berlin Games. At Naples, Goering stood on a balcony with Italian Savoyard Heir Crown Prince Humberto, receiving the cheers of the population. In this picture, behind him is his official Junkers Ju-52 aircraft, D-2527, which is painted in scarlet like the late Red Baron's tri-plane. Just over Goering's left shoulder is Paul Korner (wearing a bow tie). That same spring, Goering flew on to Greece, Hungary, and Yugoslavia, receiving warm welcomes at all. He had at last arrived after a decade of strife. (*HGA*)

Above: Goering (left) arrives at Belgrade airport with German Education Minister Bernhard Rust (center, wearing light-brown raincoat and coffee-can-style cap), with Erhard Milch between them in left profile. (*HGA*)

Left: On 17 October 1934, the Third Reich's official mourner, Hermann Goering, deplanes at Belgrade to attend the state funeral of the assassinated King Alexander I. Greeting him with a Nazi salute at bottom right is Paul Korner. (*HGA*)

Newsreel cameras record the arrival at Belgrade of the German delegation, 17 October 1934. (*HGA*)

The members of the German delegation pause for a press photograph on the rain-slicked Belgrade runway, 17 October 1934. From left to right: unknown German Naval officer; Air Force Chief Goering; and German Army Gen. Johannes von Blaskowitz. Because he protested German atrocities in Poland in 1939, Blaskowitz was not awarded a Field Marshal's baton in 1940. Like Goering, he also committed suicide at Nuremberg in 1946—or was murdered by being pushed to his death. On the far right, Robert Kropp is seen interacting with an unknown German sailor. For this trip, Goering used a Lufthansa passenger Ju-52, as denoted by the iconic bird logo seen here on the tail fin. (*HGA*)

A somber Goering (left) gives a press conference to local news reporters at Belgrade, 17 October 1934. In May 1934, Goering made the following official trips representing Hitler and Nazi Germany: 16 May 1934, start of Balkan trip at Belgrade, Yugoslavia; 17 May 1934, at Salonika, Greece; 18 May 1934, continuation to *Greichenland* (Greece); and 25 May 1934, Budapest, Hungary. (*HGA*)

Goering deplanes during another airport arrival on his trip to Yugoslavia on 17–20 October 1934. This time he is wearing a black mourning armband on his left overcoat sleeve. (*HGA*)

A lineup of the foreign and other official mourners at the late King Alexander I's state funeral in Belgrade. Fourth from the left, in a dark cap and uniform, may be the Chief of Staff of the French Air Force, Gen. Joseph Vuillemin. Next is Marshal of France Philippe Petain, wearing a light-blue French Army dress uniform. Next along are German delegate Gen. Hermann Goering, an unknown British Army officer, and the new Prince Regent of Yugoslavia, Paul (wearing a distinctive Serbian Army cap). Pétain and Goering would meet twice again, in 1935 and 1941. Goering gave the older man high praise in his later speeches and writings. (*HGA*)

Another view of the 1934 Belgrade State Funeral events, with Generals Johannes von Blaskowitz and Goering seen between the bars of the fence (fifth and sixth from left). Goering's trip into Belgrade in an open car drew wild applause, since the King had been shot in such a vehicle at Marseilles the week before. (*HGA*)

A marching lineup of the various official national delegations to the state funeral of King Alexander I of Yugoslavia in Belgrade, October 1934. Goering is third from the left, wearing a sash over his German Army overcoat, while Maréchal Pétain is in the long, light-blue French Army overcoat, seventh from the left. In 1937, Dr Gritzbach noted: 'He lowered his sword when he saw weeping Serbs as the 1st Yugoslavian regiment marched past, and people chanted, "*Heil Goering!*"' *HGA*)

On 11 December 1934 Goering's place within the top strata of leadership of the Nazi Third Reich was secure, especially with the German military establishment. Seen here are, from left to right: Bodenchatz; Col. Gen. von Blomberg; Imperial Army Field Marshal August von Mackensen (1847–1945); unknown man wearing spats; Goering; and Nazi party philosopher Balt Alfred Rosenberg. This picture was taken during the 'Battle Against Communism' conference reception for foreign diplomats and journalists at Berlin's famed Aldon Hotel. (*HGA*)

Used in both the American magazines LIFE in September 1939 and again on the cover of TIME on 1 April 1940, this is Goering wearing his beloved leather jerkin belted with hunting dagger as he liked to be seen: Reich Forest Master and Master of the Hunt. (Hugo Jaeger.)

EPILOGUE

As we take our leave of Goering at the close of 1934, we can appreciate how eventful this period of his life had been. He began in 1919 as the former last commander of the world-famous Richthofen Squadron, using this experience to go on to make a living in post-war Scandinavia—marrying a Swedish countess—and to secure the command of the Nazi SA from Hitler. However, compared to the later heads of the SA, Goering held the leadership for the shortest time, and it is significant that Hitler never again trusted Goering with it.

Nevertheless, Goering had shown during the Beer Hall Putsch that he was willing to operate outside the law on Hitler's behalf—even taking near-fatal bullet wounds for him on that Black Friday. Of the main former Imperial Army officers in the party—Goering, Hess, Röhm, and the Strasser brothers—Hess and Goering always sided with Hitler against the others, as well as against the party's left wing (which included Goebbels). Hitler keenly recognized this, and he appreciated that he had the unwavering support of Goering in particular. Goering brought valuable funds to Hitler through contacts such as Fritz Thyssen and Dr Hjalmar Schacht, at a time (1927–33) when money was what counted most. He also enlisted the help of people whom Hitler simply could not reach—the Hohenzollern royals like the former Crown Prince, Wilhelm, and his younger brother, the Nazi Prince 'Auwi', who were standing in for their absent father, Kaiser Wilhelm II.

These connections, combined with Goering's election to Reichstag President in 1932, opened up the most important door of all, giving access to Reich President von Hindenburg—the only man who had the authority to appoint a Reich Chancellor. Without Goering, it is difficult to imagine Hitler ascending to this position with such ease.

As one of only three NSDAP members in Hitler's 1933 coalition cabinet, Goering's wartime experience proved invaluable to the new and inexperienced Reich Chancellor. As Prime Minister of Prussia, Goering presided over the largest single government entity within the overall federal German Republic (later the Third Reich). His FA Brown Sheet tapped telephone records provided the final nudge for Hitler to engage in murderous action against Röhm and von Schleicher. Goering might just have easily sided with the Army and their plot to kill the Führer, but he instead reasserted his loyalty with enthusiastic participation in the Blood Purge. He was rewarded with dip- lomatic missions to Rome, Budapest, Sofia, Warsaw, and the Vatican, where he helped to negotiate the concordat between Berlin and the Holy See with Cardinal Eugenio Pacelli—the future Pope Pius XII. *Unser Hermann* had once more proven his worth, despite his many detractors.

With his marriage to Emmy Sonnemann and his patronage of the Prussian State Theatre, Goering inserted himself into another sphere of German society—that of the stage and screen. Hitler soon joined him. From 1933–34 he was also busy with gov- ernmental business, establishing new state entities—the reborn Air Force and the twin bodies for hunting and forestry. The latter added tax revenue to the state coffers. After the First World War, Goering had taunted War Minister Gen. Hans-Georg Reinhardt that a new Germany would one day rise from the ashes of defeat—he was right.

Despite his major accomplishments over this period, the reemergence of a personal problem would jeopardize Goering's flourishing career. As early as January 1931, Goebbels wrote in his diary: 'G. has given way to the vice of morphine again.' Goering would struggle with morphine and other drugs right up until the spring of 1945—an increasingly tumultuous time for both the country and Hermann himself.

BIBLIOGRAPHY

Books by Hermann Goering

Aufbau einer Nation (*Building of a Nation*), 1934
Der Geist des neuen Staates (*The Spirit of the New State*), 1934
Germany Reborn, 1934, (London: Elkin Matthews & Marrot, Ltd.)
Reden und Aufsatze (*Talks and Essays*), ed. Dr Erich Gritzbach, 1938
Goering's Atlas
The Political Testament of Hermann Goering: A Selection of Important Speeches & Articles by Field Marshal Hermann Goering, arranged & translated by H.W. Blood-Ryan, 1939 (London: John Long Ltd)

Biographical Material on Hermann Goering

Bewley, C., *Hermann Goering and the Third Reich: A Biography Based on Family & Official Records*, 1962, (Toronto: The Devon-Adair Co.)
Black, M., *Hermann Goering: A Very Brief History*, 2013, (Kindle Edition)
Blood-Ryan, H. W., *Goering: The Iron Man of Germany*, 1938, (London: John Long Ltd)
Butler, E., and Young, G., *Marshal Without Glory: The Troubled Life of Hermann Goering*, 1951, (London: Hodder & Stoughton)
El-Hai, J., The Nazi and the Psychiatrist: Hermann Goering, Dr Douglas M. Kelley, and a Fatal Meeting at the End of WWII, 2013, (New York: Public Affairs)
Fortner, N. W., *Hermann Goering's 1935 Photo Album: A Contradiction of Humanity*, 2015, (San Bernardino, CA)
Fraenkel, H., and Manvell, R., *Goering: A Biography*, 1962, (New York: Simon & Schuster)
Frischauer, W., *The Rise and Fall of Hermann Goering*, 1951, (Boston: Houghton-Mifflin Co.)
Gritzbach, Dr E., *Hermann Goering: The Man and his Work*, 1980, (Decatur, GA: Historical Review Press)

Irving, D., *Goering: A Biography*, 1989, (New York: William Morrow & Co., Inc.)

Kersaudy, F., *Hermann Göring*

Knopp, G., Goering: A Career, 2006, (Gutersloh)

Kube, A., Pour le Mérite and Swastika: Hermann Goering in the Third Reich, 1987, (Munich: Oldenbourg Verlag)

Lee, A., *Goering: Air Leader*, 1972, (New York: Hippocrene Books, Inc.)

Mosley, L., *The Reich Marshal: A Biography of Hermann Goering*, 1974, (Garden City, NY: Doubleday & Co.)

Overy, R. J., *Goering: Hitler's Iron Knight*, 2012, (London and New York: I. B. Tauris)

Overy, R. J., *Goering: The Iron Man*, 1984, (London and New York: Routledge & Kegan Paul)

Paul, W., *Hermann Goering: Hitler Paladin or Puppet?*, 1998, (London: Arms & Armour Press)

Singer, K., *Goering: Germany's Most Dangerous Man*, 1954, (London: Hutchinson & Co.)

Sommerfeldt, M., *Hermann Goering: Ein Leibbild* (*Hermann Goering: An Illustrated Life*), 1933, (Berlin: Mitter & Son)

Swearingen, B. E., The Mystery of Hermann Goering's Suicide, 1985, (New York: Harcourt, Brace Jovanovich)

The Third Reich: Hermann Goering, 2012, (Kindle Edition: Parkway Publishing)

Wunderlich, D., *Goering and Goebbels: A Double Biography*, 2002, (Regensburg, Germany: Puster)

Wyllie, J., The Warlord and the Renegade: The Story of Hermann and Albert Goering, 2006, (Phoenix Mill, UK: Sutton Publishing)

Other Goering Texts

Andrew, S., and Williamson, G., The Hermann Goering Division, 2003, (New York: Osprey Publishing Co.)

Angolia, J. R., and Littlejohn, D., NSKK/NSFK: Uniforms, Organization & History, 1994, (San Diego, CA: R. James Bender Publishing Co.)

Baur, H., I Was Hitler's Pilot: The Memoirs of Hans Baur, 2013 (S. Yorks., UK: Frontline Books)

Bender, R. J., and Peterson, G. A., Hermann Goering: From Regiment to Fallschirmpanzerkorps, 1975, (San Diego, CA: R. James Bender Publishing Co.)

Button, V., and Neumarker, U., Goering Area: Hunting and Politics in the Rominter Heath, 2012, (Berlin)

Carter-Hett, B., Burning the Reichstag: An Investigation into the Third Reich's Enduring Mystery, 2014, (New York: Oxford University Press)

Cerruti, E., Ambassador's Wife, 1953, (New York: The Macmillan Co.)

Cole, H. G., Exposing the Third Reich: Col. Truman Smith in Hitler's Germany, 2013, (Lexington, KY: The University Press of Kentucky)

Dodd Jr, T. E., Ambassador Dodd's Diary 1933–38, 1941, (New York: Harcourt, Brace & Co.)

Dodd, M., Through Embassy Eyes, 1941, (New York: Harcourt, Brace & Co.)

Dornberg, J., Munich 1923: The Story of Hitler's First Grab for Power, 1982, (New York: Harper & Row)

Friedrich, T., Hitler's Berlin: Abused City, 2012, (New Haven, CT: Yale University Press)

Gallo, M., The Night of the Long Knives: Hitler's Purge of the SA, 1972, (New York: Harper & Row)

Gisevius, H. B., To the Bitter End, 1947, (Boston: Houghton Mifflin Co.)

Goering, E., My Life with Goering, 1972, (London: David Bruce & Watson)

Goldensohn, Dr L., The Nuremberg Interviews, 2004, (New York: Alfred A. Knopf)

Gordon Jr, H. J., Hitler and the Beer Hall Putsch, 1972, (Princeton, NJ: Princeton University Press)

Grafin, F. (Countess von Wilamowitz-Mollendorff), Carin Goering, 1935, (Berlin: Verlag von Martin Warner)

Hamilton, C., Leaders and Personalities of the Third Reich: Their Biographies, Portraits, and Autographs, Vol. 2, 1996, (San Jose, CA, USA: R. James Bender Publishing)

Hanfstangl, E., Unheard Witness, 1957, (Philadelphia, PA: J. B. Lippincott Co.)

Hanser, R., Putsch! How Hitler Made Revolution, 1970, (New York: Peter H. Wyden, Inc.)

Heiden, K., Der Führer: Hitler's Rise to Power, 1944, (Boston: Houghton Mifflin Co.)

Hitler: Memoirs of a Confidant, ed. Turner Jr, H. A., 1985, (New Haven, CT: Yale University Press)

Hitler's Table Talk 1941–44, 2000, (New York: Enigma Books)

Irving, D., The Rise and Fall of the Luftwaffe: The Life of Field Marshal Erhard Milch, 1973, (Boston: Little, Brown & Co.)

Kurowski, F., The History of the Fallschirmpanzerkorps Hermann Goering: Soldiers of the Reich Marshal, 1995, (Winnipeg, Manitoba, Canada: J. J. Fedorowicz Publishing, Inc.)

Lange, E., Der Reichsmarschall in Kriege: Ein Bericht in Wort und Bild, 1950, (Stuttgart: Curt E. Schawb)

Le Tissier, T., 'The Third Reich Then and Now', After the Battle, 2005 (UK)

Lemmons, R., Hitler's Rival: Ernst Thalmann in Myth and History, 2013, (Lexington, KY: The University Press of Kentucky)

Longerich, P., Goebbels: A Biography, 2015, (New York: Random House)

Ludecke, K., I Knew Hitler, 1937, (New York: Charles Scribner's Sons)

Maracin, P. R., The Night of the Long Knives: 48 Hours That Changed the World, 2004, (Guilford, CT: The Lyons Press)

McNab, C., Hitler's Masterplan 1933-45, (London: Amber Books Ltd)

Miller, M. D., Leaders of the SS & German Police Volume 1: Reichsführer SS–SS Gruppenführer (Georg Ahrens to Karl Gutenberger), 2006, (San Diego, CA: R. James Bender Publishing Co.)

Pritchard, R. J., The Reichstag Fire: Ashes of Democracy, 1972, (New York: Ballentine Books)

Rigg, B. M., Hitler's Jewish Soldiers, 2002, (Lawrence, KS: University Press of Kansas)

Rigg, B. M., Lives of Hitler's Jewish Soldiers, 2009, (Lawrence, KS: University Press of Kansas)

Schacht, Dr H., Account Settled, 1949, (London: George Weidenfeld & Nicolson Ltd)

Speer, A., Inside the Third Reich, 1970, (New York: The Macmillan Co.)

Strasser, O., Hitler and I, 1940, (Boston: Houghton Mifflin Co.)

Sven Hedin's German Diary, 1951, (Dublin: Euphorion Books)

The Diary of Georgi Dimitrov, 1933–49, 2003, (New Haven, CT: Yale University Press)

Thyssen, F., I Paid Hitler, 1941, (New York: Farrar & Rinehart)

Tobias, F., The Reichstag Fire, 1964, (New York: G. P. Putnam's Sons)

Wachsmann, N., KL: A History of the Nazi Concentration Camps, 2015, (New York: Farrar, Strauss and Giroux)

Articles

Carlson, LTC V. R. (Ret.), 'The Night of the Long Knives', *Military Review*, 1984, (Ft Leavenworth, KS, USA)

Gilbert, G. M., 'Hermann Goering, Amiable Psychopath', The Journal of Abnormal and Social Psychology, Vol. 43, No. 2, pp. 211-229, April 1948

MacDonough, G., 'Otto Horcher, Caterer to the Third Reich', *Gastronomica*, winter 2007, pp. 31-38

Palumbo, M., 'Goering's Italian Exile 1924–25', *The Journal of Modern History,* Vol. 50, On Demand Supplement, pp. D1035-D1051, March 1978

Talyor, B., 'The World of Hermann Goering', *WWII History*, July 2002, (Leesburg, VA)

Taylor, B., 'Health in History: Hermann Goering and Josef Goebbels: Their Medical Case Files', *The Maryland State Medical Journal*, Medical & Chirurgical Faculty of the State of Maryland, pp. 35-47, November 1976

Taylor, B., 'Hermann Goering: The Kaiser's Observer', *Aces & Aircraft of the Great War,* 1994, (Canoga Park, CA: Challenge Publications)

Taylor, B., 'Part Five: Goering, Vain Reich Marshal', *The Suburban Times East*, Baltimore County, MD, 19 December 1974

Tayor, B., 'Hermann Goering: From Fighter Pilot to Flying Circus' Last Commander, 1915–18', *Aces & Aircraft of the Great War*, 1994, (Canoga Park, CA: Challenge Publications)

West, C. S., 'Carinhall Revisited', *After the Battle*, No. 71, 1991, (UK)

Other Resources

Andreas Harz at BMW Group, Munich

Dem Deutschen Volke (To the German People)—The Reichstag in German History, Press and Information Center of the German Bundestag, (Bonn: Verlag Le Pere)

Marlana Cook, Curator of Art at the West Point Museum, for Hermann Goering Wedding Album 1935 (22 April 2015)

National Archives & Records Administration I (Washington, D.C.) and II (College Park, MD)

The Bundesarchiv Museum, Berlin and Bonn, Germany

The Hermann Goering Collection at the US Army 101st Airborne Museum, Ft Bragg, KY, USA

The library at The German Historical Institute, 1607 New Hampshire Avenue, NW, Washington, D.C. 20009

The Library of Congress, Washington, D.C.

The Military Attaché at the Embassy of the Federal Republic of Germany, 4645 Reservoir Road NW, Washington, D.C. 20007

A scene that captures Goering's panache and drive as he (third from right) renders his version of the casual, backhanded Nazi salute on 1 May 1934, the National Holiday of the German People, as Berlin policemen restrain a cheering crowd. The occasion was formerly known as the communists' May Day. At this stage, Goering was Prussia's 'top cop', and these were his men—including the man at the far right, wearing the peaked cap. (*Hermann Goering Albums (HGA), Library of Congress, Washington, D.C., USA*)

'*Ministerpraisident H. Goring, General d. Inf.*', a popular 1933 picture postcard portrait of Goering. He is wearing his *Pour le Merite*, that was awarded to him in 1918, at his throat; the portrait was issued after Reich President Paul von Hindenburg promoted Goering from Captain to General. (*Heinrich Hoffmann Albums (HHA), US National Archives, College Park, MD, USA*)"